# Tog
on
Interface

Bruce Tognazzini

Addison-Wesley Publishing Company, Inc.

Reading, Massachusetts   Menlo Park, California
New York   Don Mills, Ontario   Wokingham, England
Amsterdam   Bonn   Sydney   Singapore   Tokyo
Madrid   San Juan   Paris   Seoul   Milan
Mexico City   Taipei

Cover concept by Bruce Tognazzini
Cover photograph by Bruce Cook
Cover design by Jean Seal
Text design by David Kelley Design
Set in 10-point Century Schoolbook by ST Associates

5 6 7 8 9 10-MA-99989796
Fifth printing, May 1996

To Thaddeus Muradian, who taught me how to write,
and to Barbara Miller, who taught me why.

Contents

Preface

In the early days, developers wishing to break into the marvelous new world of the Macintosh were forced to make pilgrimages to Cupertino to sit at the feet of the masters (an unpleasant prospect at best) in the hope of being able to capture the essential flame of the Macintosh philosophy, to carry it forth to their own companies, gently cupping the flickering light until they could make it burst forth into their own first Macintosh application. (Tog's official title at Apple is Human Interface Evangelist. Can you tell?—*Apple Direct* Editor)

But after the Macintosh shipped, the developer community began to swell to ever larger numbers and began to fan out across North America and around the world. We published the *Apple Human Interface Guidelines* to help people write Macintosh-standard software, but I soon began seeing programs that followed all the specifics of Apple guidelines, but were clearly not "Macintosh." These programs were coming from developers who had had no direct contact with the Macintosh team. Something intangible but vital seemed to be lost when people only had the guidelines, when they didn't have direct contact with the Macintosh team.

The Macintosh interface was more than a cluster of specific guidelines; it was built upon principles, a rich set of rules which were embodied in a culture passed down from one person to another. There was no written history of the principles that drove the Macintosh. In fact, there was not even an oral history; none of us could even put into words what this interface was about. The principles were so ingrained in the culture they were taken as natural laws. After all, one need not write down gravity: People are bound to catch on when they find themselves unable to fly. The principles were felt, rather than spoken of, and understanding them required immersion in the Macintosh culture.

It became clear to me, as the success of the Macintosh grew, that what had worked in the early days to promulgate the culture would work no longer. I launched a research project, headed up by Kristina

Hooper, to identify and codify the principles upon which the interface is built, and we set out to capture the elusive spirit of the Macintosh.

Those first principles helped provide a foundation, but there was still something missing, and aberrant applications continued to appear. It was then that I decided to begin writing this book. I wanted to be responsive to the real needs of real designers, so I moved from research into the Apple Evangelism Group, where I can interact every day with new developers and new projects. But even that wasn't enough. I wanted the book itself to be interactive. Human-to-human interactive. So I started a monthly question-and-answer column in *Apple Direct*, a magazine with a circulation of some 8000 people, all of them involved in the design of Macintosh software.

Now, three years later, the book is done. It is drawn from the *Apple Direct* columns, with the addition of excerpts from some of my papers, plus a great deal of correspondence and other writing never before published. The issues discussed are real and relevant, having arisen from letters sent to me at Apple and from visits I was making to developers around the United States and around the world.

The column, and thus the book, was written against the backdrop of System 7, whose development was underway at the time. The secrecy surrounding the project made it impossible for me to be as candid about our plans for System 7 as I might have liked. As you read through the book, you will find me periodically discussing changes that "may be made someday in the far distant future," changes that, in fact, were already underway.

The column was also a device for gathering "public opinion" from Apple's developer community, and many of the changes in System 7 that eventually occurred were the result of or strongly influenced by letters, published and not published, sent in to the column.

I have tried, in assembling the book, to change as little of what was originally written as possible. In this, I was influenced by the book, *The Good Old Stuff*, by John D. MacDonald. In the late 1970s, Mr. MacDonald set about assembling a collection of some of his early stories written from 1947 to 1952. In an effort to contemporize the tales, he updated radio shows to television shows, 1947 prices to 1970s prices, and World War II soldiers to Vietnam soldiers. By the time I read the book, in around 1985, the stories were again dated, but they also often made no sense: The cultures of the mid '40s and the Vietnam era were drastically different. The writhing embarrassments that his characters experienced for their behaviors such as (gasp) kissing in public in the World War II era did not ring true set against the the wide-open culture of the late '60s.

I have retained all my writhing embarrassments, just as they were originally. I have tried to limit changes only to statements of fact that are no longer valid. For example, when the column, "Command Keys vs. the Mouse" (see Chapter 6) was originally written, Command-P stood for Plain Text. Now it stands for Print.

My thanks to all the Macintosh developers who responded to my pleas for letters with great ideas, difficult questions, undeserved praise, and richly deserved brickbats.[1] You have kept me informed, involved, and honest. You have also provided much of the interesting writing in the book. (Some have said most.—*Apple Direct* Editor)

I also want to thank Martha Steffen, for making the book happen from Apple's side, and Joanne Clapp Fullagar, Diane Freed, Jean Seal, Cris Gutierrez, Ted Laux, Abby Cooper, Ann Lane, Keith Wollman, and Steve Stansel for making it happen from Addison-Wesley's side. Thanks to my fellow evangelists and to the many Apple engineers and independent developers who have listened to my crazy ideas over the years and incorporated them into a lot of major hardware designs and software packages, enabling me to find out whether the ideas actually worked. Thanks to all those who have helped me and supported my work at Apple over the years, from Jef Raskin and Steve Jobs in the beginning, to Eric Zarakov and Lisa Raleigh at the end. Thanks to William Page, John Glathe, John Ruark, Barbara Reilly, Bill W., Dr. Bob, and a lot of other special friends. And finally, thanks to my wife, Julie, and my two wonderful stepchildren, Joshua and Rebecca, who lived with a shadowy figure hunched over his word processor for so many months and offered nothing but encouragement and support.

In writing the column and assembling this book, I have made every effort to look past the crises of the moment to get at the fundamentals beneath. Those are what this book is about. We did something special when we created the Macintosh, and much of it is being lost today. My fervent hope is that people, sorting through my blather, can hear the spirit of the Macintosh come through.

---

[1] This is the part of the book where you are supposed to be very, very humble. Bear with me. I'm not used to it.

Introduction

Problems are arising in visible user interface applications today, problems for the first time making it difficult for people to understand and use them.

I have purposely used the term, "visible interface," rather than "graphical interface," because there is a difference: A visible interface is a complete environment in which users can work comfortably, always aware of where they are, where they are going, and what objects are available to them along the way. To be labeled a graphical interface, an interface need only make use of objects that have a distinct graphical representation. Many aspects of the graphical interface may remain invisible.

A library, with its visibly-structured and labeled collections, oaken card catalogs, librarians, and lots of light, has a visible interface.

The library's interface is also a graphical one, in that it is populated with objects having unique graphical representations, such as books, "Shhhhh" signs, librarians, and fire extinguishers. These objects can be easily differentiated by their unique appearances (although the woman who ran the library in my elementary school did bear an uncanny resemblance to a fire extinguisher).

In contrast to the library experience, imagine yourself driving late one moonless night on unfamiliar country roads. You see plenty of graphic objects in the form of signs warning you of deer in the area, alerting you to falling rock, telling you you can shed pounds and inches by drinking lots of light beer. Inevitably, you will run across a familiar, eight-sided red icon informing you that you must stop, even though there is not a soul within 500 miles. (If you fail to stop, of course, you will see a bright red flashing light signifying there was one person within 500 miles.) There are many graphical objects in the interface of that dark country road, but the actual navigation is invisible, and you may very well become lost.

The Tunnel of Love, with its day-glow monsters (graphically represented objects) lining a pitch-black tunnel might, at first glance, also seem to be a graphical user interface, even though users of the Tunnel of Love never have any idea where they are and where they are going. (Of course, given a friendly travelling companion, they don't really care.) But the Tunnel of Love is not really a graphical user interface at all; it is an interface for displaying graphics. The monsters are not your friends.

There is no intrinsic connection between graphics as the subject matter of an application—even when those graphics appear as distinct objects—and graphics as a driving element of the interface itself. If the Tunnel of Love's many iconic signs, such as the familiar red stop sign that displays the warning: "Stop! Bottomless pit straight ahead!" actually were both truthful and helpful, the Tunnel of Love would be magically transformed into a graphical user interface, but so much of the rest of the interface would continue to be shrouded in darkness, it could hardly be termed a visible interface.

Interfaces resembling the Tunnel of Love are based on a metaphor called the black cave metaphor. These interfaces are left over from an earlier era, an era in which graphics played no part at all.

From the Black Cave to the Light of Day

When I first became involved with computers back in 1958, the interface typically consisted of flashing lights, punched cards, and TeleType printers. These computers sported a purely abstract, command-line interface. Users were expected to understand the structure of an application filled with a myriad of menus like so many rooms connected with twisty little passages, all with absolutely no visual cues. These applications were as much a black cave as the Tunnel of Love, and people often became lost and confused.

Eventually the original TeleType printer was replaced with a computer monitor, but the interface designers dutifully reproduced the actions of the historic printer in the green light of the new screens, faithfully duplicating every limitation of the mechanical device in the process. (I remember the first time someone wrote a routine for the original Apple II that would allow it to scroll down as well as up. People gasped in amazement, as though the lack of a downward scroll was an inherent property of computers, rather than the faithful reproduction of the behavior of a thirty-year-old printer.) The structure of the programs was still hidden in the black cave, and people continued to be lost and confused.

Then came the visible user interface, with its rich use of graphics, consistent behavior, visually apparent structure, and clear communication. It rose from a culture that started at Stanford Research

Institute and spread throughout Silicon Valley, a culture dedicated to the single task of bringing the power of the computer to people everywhere, instead of concentrating it among a select priesthood. This primordial graphical user interface (GUI[1]) culture eventually produced the first visible, graphical interfaces, built on metaphors based in the real world, interfaces such as Xerox Star, Lisa, and Macintosh. Non-computer professionals for the first time gained a sense of competence and control over the computer. They knew where they were and what they were doing at all times. People were no longer lost and confused.

Recently, some applications and entire computer interface systems based on graphical user interfaces have begun to lose the visibility of their underlying structures. These semi-visible graphical user interfaces are found in systems that are filled with lots of pretty windows and all sorts of check boxes and buttons, but have left key functionality hidden and invisible.

Such lack of visibility is particularly bewildering to users of a graphical user interface because it seems as though everything really is visible—after all, there is all that graphical stuff on the screen. If one continually collides with the walls of a black cave, one accepts that one cannot see well in pitch darkness. But should the same thing happen in a clean, well-lit library, one can only dwell on the possibility of a brain tumor, or worse.

The emergence of the semi-invisible graphical user interface can be traced to at least two factors: First, as mentioned before, the principles of visible interface design have been so late in being written down. But another important factor lies within programmers, who still do so much of the design work: Programmers can use any kind of interface. They have exceptional minds that embrace, enjoy, even thrive on abstract, invisible interfaces. They assume that everyone else has a wonderful memory and enjoys manipulating abstract symbols. (While many people may have good memories, I think the current dearth of Algebra Fun Clubs And Family Centers in our communities speaks volumes about our collective delight in manipulating abstract symbols.)

The number of programmers designing applications to run under various graphical user interfaces has increased exponentially in the last few years, much faster than the original culture with its "natural laws" could spread. Programmers, having not shared in this understanding of users, and infused by a love of the abstract, have been slowly drifting back toward the invisible interface.

But people want to operate in a self-consistent, stable, visually apparent virtual reality, populated with visually apparent objects

---

[1] I have never understood why anyone would let an engineer name something. In computers, we are faced with "gooey" interfaces and "scuzzy" disk drives.

which, when manipulated, will behave in predictable ways. They need to be able to see the structure of the world in which they are operating and they need to explore without fear of becoming lost or causing irreversible damage. The Macintosh interface is one example of such an interface. It offers a visual/behavioral "language" that is simple, clear, and consistent. Users interact with the system in a way that closely mimics the way they interact with the real world.

"Yeah, sure," some will say, "people are always grabbing a live mouse and rubbing it on their desk top. Makes a fine eraser."

True, many of us do avoid rubbing real mice on our desk tops after some initial experimentation (much to the relief of the mice), but the computer mouse soon ceases to be that "bar of soap" on the desk and becomes the glowing pointer on the screen, enabling your hand to dash through the virtual world of the desktop.

On the original electronic computers, there was no metaphor between the user and the raw reality of vacuum tubes and wires. In today's visible interfaces, that raw reality has been replaced with a softer, virtual reality—an illusion spun of nothing more than light and logic.

PART I

The Early Letters

I have a strong sense that there is a Macintosh developer's community. Over the years we've all talked to each other. We have a lot of mutual goals. We want to make our software as good as it can be. Even if I'm competing directly with someone, I would still want to see them make their software be "Macish" and have a very good Macintosh user interface. That way, all products for the Macintosh are superior. This enhances the Macintosh computer itself, and to the extent that there are more sales of Macintoshes, we all benefit.

—CHARLIE JACKSON, FOUNDER,
SILICON BEACH SOFTWARE[1]

[1] From appearance in *World Builder, Macintosh User-Centered Design* (Tognazzini, 1989b).

CHAPTER 1

Closing the Window of Vulnerability

Have you ever wondered how you start an advice to the design-lorn column? I mean, what do you do for those first few issues when no one knows you're there, so no one has sent in any letters? I solved the problem, rather neatly, by making up my own letters.

❏ ***Dear Tog:*** Every time I release a new version of my software, I lose a percentage of my customers to the competition. Tell me, Tog, what can I do, human-interface-wise, to help close this window of vulnerability?
—JOHN SCRIBBLEMONGER, *Milpitas, CA.*[1]

◼ John, when a software team finally gets that final release off to production, they celebrate. But when users hear it's coming, they often as not let out a loud groan of anticipated agony.

We know that once a user has become comfortable with a piece of software, a competitor must break down enormous inertia to pull that user away. He or she has learned the software, has become comfortable with its features, resigned to its limitations, and probably has more than a few disks full of its resulting documents.

Along comes release 2.0. Suddenly, the competition prepares to move in for the kill.

---

[1] John Scribblemonger came to life in February, 1978, when Scot Kamins, noted author of various and sundry books on HyperCard, and I were assembling the first issue of *Apple Orchard*, the house organ of the San Francisco Apple Core users group we were in the process of founding. We needed a name for the editor of the newsletter and, wishing to make the Apple Core appear populated by more than two members, we invented the name, John Scribblemonger, assuming no one would suspect. Since then we have gone on to invent an entire family of Scribblemongers and sprinkle them liberally in our writings.

Here are steps you can take in your human interface design to minimize user flight.

➤ **GUIDELINE**   *Eliminate user's need to perform housekeeping operations.*

Most important! Do not force users to type in 500,000 old file names from memory. For some strange reason, the first second-release piece of Macintosh software, upon opening a pre-existing document, insisted on changing its name to "Untitled." Practically every developer has followed that ill-conceived precedent ever since. This "Untitled" business is absolutely counter to (a) what users want, and (b) what the Apple Human Interface Guidelines say: "Users... shouldn't have to remember anything the computer already knows."

Users should be offered, as a default name, the current file name. Just as with any opened document, if the user wants a different name, he or she can Save As under a different name. Such new names are still more likely to be a variation of the original name than a variation of the name "Untitled."

➤ **GUIDELINE**   *Make changes clearly visible.*

Eschew obfuscation! Users are far more confused by a myriad of subtle behavioral changes than one or two big, visually apparent ones. Users expect to learn new things when they receive an update. Don't try to hide your changes so the users keep tripping over them for months.

➤ **GUIDELINE**   *Plan ahead.*

Don't jump around. You should already have the foundation in place for the next major release before making the current one. It is far better to hit users with a steep learning hurdle once, with a promise of smooth sailing further on, than to hit them over and over again with each year's hot new design. Users struck with repeated learning burdens, particularly when they perceive them to be interface "bug fixes," are likely to leave for the promise of greener and more sedate pastures.

➤ **GUIDELINE**   *Limit changes in your interpretation of the user's behavior.*

The user doesn't mind so much when the "computer" behaves differently. He or she will become very upset when his or her own behavior is suddenly reinterpreted.

➤ **GUIDELINE**   *Test new designs on old users.*

New designs tend to "drift": By the time you've been working on the new product six months or so, you'll no longer know just how different the new version feels. Every few weeks, you should run a couple of experienced users through the new program and find out where they are colliding with old learning, old behaviors. Then think through each conflicting change: Is it really so beneficial that it's worth torturing your installed base? Testing need not be time-consuming or expensive. Avoiding testing always is.

➡ COLUMN 1: MARCH, 1989

Write Soon!!!

❑ **Dear Tog:** My goodness! What a marvelously succinct response! I had no idea you were so knowledgeable! It is comforting to know that you didn't get your sagacity (at least on *this* subject) from the back of a cereal box. But how is this column of yours going to work?

—THROCKMORTON SCRIBBLEMONGER, *Milpitas, CA.*

■ Well, Throck, as a man of letters (and there are 14 in your last name alone), I'm sure you must realize the challenge I face: As the one and only Human Interface Evangelist, I can either spend one minute per year with each of you, or talk with all of you through this column, where we can really get something accomplished.

The format is simple: You write me questions, suggestions, and general hate mail. I answer letters that are (a) interesting, (b) not too tough, and (c) say nothing bad about the columnist. (You folks can lean on the Clan Scribblemonger as hard as you want.) If no letters meet those requirements (and they won't for a while—this magazine operates on a 72-month lead time), I'll be forced to start making up phoney questions myself. After all, I'm an evangelist, not a journalist.

Figure 1–1 shows how the process looks.

I'm sure you immediately picked up on the real significance of this process: I am your link, as terrifyingly tenuous as that might sound, with the human interface arm of Apple's mighty Research and Development organization. I will be maintaining a high level of communication with R & D to see that all your concerns are aired on a company-wide basis.

You may also notice that while I have chosen an auditory metaphor for my developer–evangelist communications links, I actually eschew the telephone in favor of AppleLink and the U.S. mails. (Yes, I do use "eschew" in my daily conversations—it helps keep the masses at a respectful distance, perhaps out of an ill-founded belief that I'm sneezing.)

What some may find surprising—nay, shocking—at first, is that I have no intention of responding to any incoming mail except through the organ you now hold in your hand. I had two choices: either answer all the mail or write a decent column. (There has been some suggestion on the part of my detractors that I can do neither. I deny the allegation, and I defy the allegators!)

Finally, Dear Throck, you may have been as surprised as I to discover the high proportion of Apple's developers who wear funny hats.

Please, all of you, write soon and often. Whether you have a design problem, a solution that you think will be of general interest, or you just want to flame about something that is bothering you, let me know.[2]

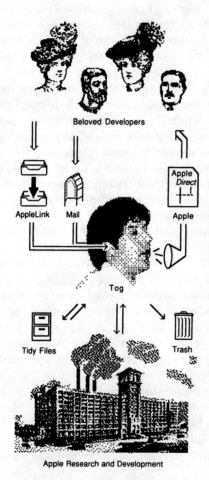

Beloved Developers

AppleLink Mail Apple

Tog

Tidy Files Trash

Apple Research and Development

Figure 1–1. *The Information Process*

---

[2] And write they did, on every subject imaginable, some even having to do with computers.

CHAPTER 2

The Creeping Learning Curve

➥ *COLUMN 2: APRIL, 1989*

The first column has still not hit the street. Time to invent a new letter-writer.

❏ **Dear Tog:** Last month, you talked about the Window of Vulnerability which opens when a new version of an application is released. You mentioned we might want to open up existing documents with their existing names, rather than "Untitled." What else can we do, human interface-wise, to hold onto our customers?

—MAISY DAE LATHROP, *Newton, MA*

■ We can avoid The Creeping Learning Curve.

Every change made to the software, even those "trivial" little changes assimilated day by day by the design team, will be re-experienced, all at once, by each user upon first running the new revision.

Those burdened with an Ivy League education will recognize this as the same problem first noted by Earnst Heinrich Haeckel in the last century. As his concise yet incomprehensible coinage put it, "Ontogeny recapitulates phylogeny." Earnst was attempting to communicate, in his own light-hearted way, that a new individual joining an existing culture must learn everything that culture has learned. And if that culture is five thousand years old, the new person must learn all five thousand years of stuff in perhaps less than twenty years! (And we wondered why second grade was so tough.)

As shown in Figure 2–1, software works the same way: If your team spends six months preparing Rev. 2, adding just one itty-bitty new feature per day, your users are going to be hit with six months worth of changes—all 180 of them—in the first 6 minutes!

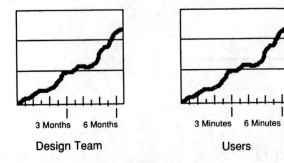

Figure 2–1. *Comparison of Learning Curves*

Meanwhile, the design team thinks everything is cool. The gentleness of the Creeping Learning Curve is seductive: The members of the development team so gradually lose sight of the old software they don't even realize it has happened.

What can you do? Do user-testing. Test real people who are still using your original version. And don't retest with the same people. One round of tests and they will have begun to learn your new tricks.

Does that mean we should stifle innovation in favor of keeping the learning burden low? No. Handled the right way, one can strike an excellent balance between the need to maintain a low (re)learning burden and the desire to improve power and productivity.

In our finest moments at Apple, we go through a careful design, test, and review cycle, based on the following guidelines:

➤ **GUIDELINE** *In the earliest stage, design the new software to be the best it can be with little concern for the existing system.*

➤ **GUIDELINE** *Toward the end of the design period, test the new software to find out where current users will become tripped up.*

➤ **GUIDELINE** *Objectively weigh every new feature against any resultant increase in the learning burden. Then:*
  • *include the feature anyway*
  • *throw it out because it is disruptive and not clearly more productive, or*
  • *modify it to get the same effect without torturing current users.*

➤ **GUIDELINE** *Redesign and test again.*

We always wait until we are well along in the product design cycle before doing extensive reviewing so we don't stifle innovation. What might seem a disruptive change along the way can often further evolve into a particularly elegant innovation that may have little or no effect on current users.

An example of how a product can pass through a transitional phase and "return to its roots" can be seen in the evolution of the Macintosh environment, from Finder to Switcher to MultiFinder (known as simply "Finder" again under System 7. Switcher was a very different model from the Finder; existing users had to form new and somewhat confusing mental models to be able to understand it.

MultiFinder required no new models to use. In fact, it made visible what had been an invisible navigational model in the original Finder. It was far more powerful than Switcher, and yet, as a model, didn't require the user to learn anything new.

CHAPTER 3

Making Your First Macintosh Application a Success

➡ *COLUMN 3: MAY, 1989*

This column turned out to be one of the most fun to write, even though the problem I was discussing was deadly serious: the difficult transition from writing standard, programmer-in-control software to visible-interface software with the user in control. I had watched programmer after programmer founder for months trying desperately to somehow impose the lessons learned from traditional languages and systems onto the Macintosh, but always failing. I wanted to talk about the real experience of successful transition, as I had felt it myself, so I invented Wilhelmina Wilson, a young developer from my wife's home town.

❏ *Dear Tog:* I've just finished my first Macintosh software design, and it wasn't fun, but I learned a few things along the way that should make the next one really easy.

There seemed to be three major transitions I had to pass through en route to learning to "speak" Macintosh. These had nothing to do with learning the operating system, or how the toolbox works, or anything technical at all. They had to do with changing, on a fundamental level, the way I think about people and about computers.

The User In Control   The first transition I went through, and perhaps the most painful, was accepting the fact that, on the Macintosh, the user is in control. I didn't even recognize there was a problem for the first couple of weeks, because I thought I had always put the user in control.

I have always had the most profound respect for users. Upon occasions, it has bordered on love. The kind of deep, abiding love a parent would have for a particularly backward child. And therein lay the problem: I was overprotecting my users. I kept them from straying from the safe, sure path I had plotted through my application. I figured out the best, most efficient way to accomplish a task and made sure I offered no alternatives. I wanted to keep them from hurting their own productivity. I didn't expect them to already know anything about the computer, so I made every step as small, simple, and straightforward as possible. I made sure the manual explained everything about not only my application, but the system. After all, they might not have read their computer manuals.

In general, I drove the users stark, raving mad. Every time they tried to make a move, I was one step ahead of them, protecting them from any possible hurt. The 500th time they used the program, they had to take the same laborious, if easily understood, path they took the first time. I didn't want to frighten them with options and alternatives.

Consider how you'd feel if every day when you came into work, Mom was there to make sure your nails were clean and your seat wasn't too high and you didn't have too much coffee. Mea culpa. This is what I did to my users.

In my new designs, my users are truly in control. I assume they have an IQ that lies above room-temperature. I assume they know how to use a Macintosh. I assume they can make their own decisions on how they want to work. I have become their communications partner instead of their parent.

What a relief!

User-Centered Design   The second transition was a snap after the first one. My applications had always looked something like with the user shown in Figure 3–1 wandering around my carefully laid out maze, while I, as parent, gazed down fondly, offering help, as appropriate.

On Macintosh, I finally got it through my head that the user doesn't move at all! Our job is to surround him or her with everything he or she might want to do. I think of it as a sort of daisy, (shown in Figure 3–2) with the user in the middle, able to get to each command instantly and fluidly.

I can't tell you the horror of the six weeks I spent trying desperately to figure out how to fit the event-loop concept into my flow-chart view of computer applications. It was like beating my head against a brick wall. When I finally abandoned the flow chart entirely, everything suddenly made sense. And my head didn't hurt anymore.

Speaking Macintosh Like a Native   The final transition came when I had immersed myself in Macintosh long enough to be able to "think" in Macintosh. The best analogy for this is the process of learning a foreign language. For the longest time, you translate the language word-for-

Figure 3–1. *Traditional Navigation Interface*

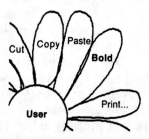

Figure 3–2. *Macintosh User-Centered Interface*

word, learning the grammar along the way, slowly reaching the point where native speakers don't laugh behind their hand at your pitiful efforts. Finally, a magic moment occurs, often during the night or early in the morning, when you first actually think in the new language. From then on, it's easy.

Failing to go through this process can be disastrous. As a man of letters, I'm sure you are familiar with that great work of literature, *The New Guide of the Conversation in Portuguese and English* (Carolino), first published more than 100 years ago. The Portuguese author seemingly launched into his project just a little prematurely:

DIALOGO 36. *Côm ô dentista*	DIALOG 36. *With a dentist.*
Doêm-me ôs dêntes.	I have a teetht-ache.
Têm Vm. úma deffluxão ôu úm dênte pôdre ?	Is it a fluxion, or have you a bad tooth?
Pênso quê é úm dênte pôdre;. Quér Vm. examinárme â bôca ?	I think that is a bad tooth; please you examine my mouth?
Vm. têm úm dênte pôdre; quér quê lh'ô tíre ?	You have a bad tooth; will you pull out this tooth ?
Não mê pósse decidír â îsso; porquê â dôr é grânde.	I can't to decide me it, that make me many great deal pain.
O sêu dênte estâ dê tôdo cariádo; ê, sê ô dêixa estragará ôs ôutros.	Your tooth is absolutely roted; If you leave it; shall spoil the others.

This, as you know, is one of the more lucid passages from the book. It was strictly downhill from there. And what held true for Pedro Carolino, the author of the piece, was equally true for me: My first designs were literal translations of MS-DOS, with only a few changes to the visual appearance. The words might have been Macintosh, but the grammar was strictly IBM. When I look at those first designs now, I realize what weird stuff it was, but at the time it seemed just fine.

I finally set aside my design project and just used the computer. I ran and used applications in several major areas, two word processors, a spreadsheet, a painting program, and a drawing application. I avoided all contact with other computers. Macintosh became my life. When I emerged, a few weeks later, I had absorbed the language, grammar, and "music" of Macintosh. I could "think" Macintosh. I intuitively knew how to handle situations that used to baffle me. Even the Apple Human Interface Guidelines began to make sense!

These transitions—accepting that the user is in control, coming to understand user-centered design, and absorbing the music of Macintosh—seem to have made me into a competent Macintosh designer. Does every successful designer who comes to the Macintosh from another environment undergo a similar shift in perspective?

—WILHELMINA WILSON, *Pensacola, FL*

■ Yes.

CHAPTER 4

*The Lowdown
on Layers
and the Finder*

➼ *COLUMN 4: JUNE, 1989*

❑ ***Dear Tog:*** Glad to see you'll be writing monthly; I've enjoyed your stuff in the past.

Not sure if *Apple Direct* is really the forum for this, but don't the Finder's application "layers" violate the Mac interface? Yes, they keep many applications from breaking, but can you predict what happens when you click on an inactive window? Chances are, it'll come to the front, but will other windows come to the front also? Is there a user-interface tradeoff about layers that's worth the loss of predictability, or is this an implementation issue?

—DAVID DUNHAM, *Pensée*

■ Hurray! A real letter from an actual person! Yes, folks, the column has finally been coming out for enough years to get ahead of the lead time.

The glib answer to your question would be easy: The Finder is a primary standard for the Apple Desktop Interface. If something is part of the Finder, it is part of the interface. Of course, I would never stoop to such an answer, particularly since I would rather die than defend this silly business of throwing disks in the trash in order to eject them. (I can't tell you the horror I have felt when I have accidentally thrown a document in the trash, trying to eject it.)

The Apple Desktop Interface is built around an application-centered model: In order to draw, you must open a document *within* an application. This is roughly equivalent to having to squeeze your house inside a hammer in order to be able to put a nail in the wall. This is the fundamental premise upon which the current interface is based. As long as it remains so, (and that will be a long time, indeed),[1] documents will cluster around their applications like chicks around a mother hen. It is my expert opinion (I've always wanted to say that!) that the system image must reflect this immutable reality, and part of that reflection is having the documents float to the surface at once.

In a perfect world, each window could act independently; after all, just the fact that two documents are open in the same word processor doesn't mean they are related to each other. Rather, they might be related to other documents in other open applications. For example, you might be (1) writing a letter in response to an AppleLink and (2) assembling a report for which you've created a drawing and a chart. If anything, you should be able to group documents according to *your* context, rather than the computer's. Clicking on the report might bring up its associated drawing and chart, instead of an unrelated letter that just happened to be created using the same tool as the report. But that is not the way documents-within-tools works.

The layers are not a function of the Finder. They have existed from Day One in the metaphor that has always driven the Apple Desktop Interface. Until we change the metaphor, we must reflect the layers in the visual design and behavior of the system.

Actually, the clustering of documents you speak of in the new Finder was much worse in the old Finder. There, you couldn't even have documents on the screen that hadn't been created in the same tool. In fact, I think what we now call MultiFinder[2] is one of the most brilliant concepts ever to land on the Macintosh. (I say that with a heavy heart, since it was not one of my brilliant concepts.)

It seems now that MultiFinder, whatever its faults, was the most obvious way to extend the power of the original Macintosh so that the user could skip from application to application without having to constantly quit and re-open everything. But it took several years before anyone actually came up with it. I'm sure, David, that you remember Switcher, but for the youngsters in the audience, Switcher arrayed all applications around a loop, as in Figure 4–1.

---

[1] A handful of Apple's human interface types had been arguing for including a document-centered architecture in System 7. At the time of writing this column, that idea had been rejected as far too ambitious given our schedule.

[2] At the time of this column, Finder users could select from two different Finder modes: Finder mode would close the Finder upon an application launch, so that a single application was the only thing running in the computer. MultiFinder mode (now the only mode, starting with System 7) would enable the Finder and multiple applications to remain open at the same time.

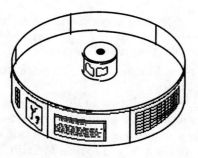

Figure 4–1. *Simplified Model of Switcher Interface*

By clicking on one of two arrows displayed in the menu bar, users could cause the wheel to turn, sliding the next application across their field of view. By pressing a miniscule rectangle between the two arrows, the user could plunge downward into the loop, thereby reaching the Finder that lay in the center.

Switcher seemed to be a wonderful solution at the time. Users could maintain a clear mental model of where each application was (with the exception of the Finder which kind of moved around on you) and could move among them fluidly. Its major drawback seemed to be that it required the user to develop in his or her mind a new and completely separate "wheel" model, in addition to the Finder's "desktop" model. And, of course, windows from separate applications continued to be walled off from one another.

Enter MultiFinder. One day, a couple of those computer genius types wandered into Apple with the forerunner of MultiFinder in their foxy pockets. They started up MacWrite, then peeled back the active window (using the size box) to reveal Finder running underneath. We were flat-out blown away. (Of course, by the next day, we all were claiming that was the way we would have done it in the first place, if we'd really thought about it. That's the problem with really great intuitive leaps.)

The original prototype we saw didn't work particularly well. It took a lot of hard work and expert engineering at Apple to actually bring a product to market, but we had seen the light.

The reason I've brought up this ancient history is that it demonstrates the importance of really considering the impact that features added to the second or third release of a product will have on the metaphor and the system image.

➤ **GUIDELINE**   *If a feature is good enough to be included in a new release, it is good enough to be fully integrated, not left to grow out of the side of the old metaphor like a goiter.*

You've all seen what I mean. There are more than a few goiters running around out there.

It's unfortunate we have layers in the metaphor, but as long as they're part of the metaphor, they must be reflected in the system image. And when you create a second or third release, work for that intuitive leap that will enable you to do a MultiFinder, rather than a Switcher. Maybe you'll be luckier or more brilliant than we.

CHAPTER 5

Make the Most of Modes

➡ COLUMN 5: JULY, 1989

I had been disturbed for some time by the arrival of modal dialog boxes that looked and acted similar to, but different from, modeless dialogs. With the arrival of the following letter, I was galvanized into action; within several weeks, the human interface community had decided upon a new movable modal dialog box with a unique appearance. I had shown it at Apple's annual Worldwide Developer Conference, and interested developers had joined in finalizing the design.

❑ **Dear Tog:** I read your article in *Apple Direct* this month and I decided to write to you about a human interface problem I'd like you to think about.

I believe the idea of a modeless dialog box is underspecified in the Human Interface Guidelines. They look pretty much alike in the applications that use them, but they often don't act alike.

Our approach in PowerPoint has been the following: A modeless dialog is a control center where commands may be given that affect the selection in the frontmost document window. The frontmost document window, therefore, always displays its selection when a modeless dialog is the active window.

When a modeless dialog is active, the menus operate normally (although many commands are dimmed) and another window may be activated simply by clicking on it. The dialog box has a close box to remove it from the screen.

I don't believe this is necessarily the only model one might follow, but it bothers me to have dialogs that look the same but work differently. As examples:

- Some dialogs look modeless, but they are really modal. They appear modeless only to allow you to move them on the screen.

- Some dialogs allow you to use menus while they are active, but don't allow you to switch to a different window without closing the dialog.

- Some dialogs have a close box, but also OK and Cancel buttons.

I think it would be helpful if you defined a few different models and then suggested the appearance that a dialog should take on if it is using that model. The torn-off menu window is a great example of this. Everyone knows exactly how one of these is supposed to act.

Thanks for listening.

—DENNIS AUSTIN, *Microsoft*

■ Well, Dennis, I've decided to answer your letter even though you failed to include a stamped, selflessly addressed piece of cheap flattery, such as, "I read your article in *Apple Direct* this month and I decided to write to you because you are probably the finest designer I have ever come across."

In direct response to your letter and a similar one from Elaine Height at Symantec, the human interface team at Apple has formulated the following addition to the Apple Human Interface Guidelines.

Dialog boxes have historically come in two flavors: modal and modeless. Modal dialogs bring the entire world to a crashing halt while some vital question of the moment can be answered, such as whether you want this particular footnote to be like every other one you've done in the last five years, or whether you want this one in the San Francisco font. Modeless dialogs, on the other hand, can be left open and answered or manipulated at any time, enabling the user to flit from task to task without being forced to complete any of them. In other words, modal dialog boxes represent tyranny, while modeless dialogs promote chaos.

In the past, modal dialogs have been unmovable, based on the rationale that since you are not going to be doing anything else until this question has been answered, there is no reason to allow you to move the dialog around. This has the unfortunate effect of preventing those of us with no long-term memory from referring back to the material the modal dialog is asking us about. So we have to cancel the dialog, look at the material again, then reopen the dialog. Of course, we have by that time forgotten the material again.

Recently, developers have adopted a third kind of dialog, in addition to the current Unmovable Modal and Movable Modeless. (I have yet to see anyone attempt the fourth possibility, the unmovable modeless. I pray no one will.) The current problem with movable modal dialogs is that they look substantially the same as modeless dialogs. The only difference is the presence (usually) of OK and Cancel buttons. This differentiation is not enough.

About Objects   Before diving into the new movable modal dialog definition, let us first pause to define objects within the Apple Human Interface.

The interface is made up of a number of **elements**. Visual elements, auditory elements, kinesthetic elements, behavioral elements. These elements are then combined to form **objects**. A given object may be as small as the ellipsis object (. . .) or as large as an application object, such as PowerPoint. An element is a word; an object is a sentence. For example, the **ellipsis object**, used in menus, and so forth, to trigger dialog boxes, consists of several different elements:

- Visual—The ellipsis object always looks like this: . . .

- Kinesthetic—The ellipsis object is always selected by dragging to or pressing on it, then releasing the mouse button.

- Behavioral—The ellipsis object always triggers a dialog box.

Similarly, the drop-shadowed square button, known as the **closed pop-up menu** object, consists of

- Visual—Displays a square drop shadow around current selection, possibly preceded by category.

- Kinesthetic—The pop-up menu object is always selected by pressing on it, then releasing the mouse button.

- Behavioral—The ellipsis object always triggers the **open pop-up menu** object.

Objects, once defined, can be used freely in new contexts, but never substantially redefined. If it becomes necessary to redefine kinesthetic or behavioral elements of an object, the visual appearance of the object must also be changed, thereby creating a new object.

Back to Dialogs   The object that denotes a movable window in the Macintosh is the **Drag Region**, shown in Figure 5–1.

Figure 5–1.   *Drag Region*

The object that denotes a modal dialog is the double-stripe border, shown in Figure 5–2.

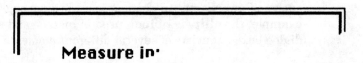

Figure 5–2.   *Double-stripe Border*

The new, Official Movable Modeless Dialog Box object-combines these two objects. Nolan Larsen of WordPerfect thought our first "final" version, as shown at the 1989 Developer's Conference, was dumb, so he offered us his own. Figure 5–3 is Nolan's new and improved version (which we could've thought of if we wanted.)

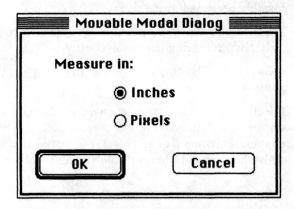

Figure 5–3.   *The Official Movable Modeless Dialog Box*

Another problem with dialogs concerns those that are semi-modal. Usually these have been presented to the user as modal dialogs with exceptions: Everything to be done is to be done within the dialog except you can use the Edit menu. Or everything is to be done within the dialog except you can use the rulers. At the same time, a modal dialog does not gray out the menus, and so on. They all appear active. The user has been left to formulate the following rule:

"In a modal dialog, everything you can use is within the dialog except that anything outside the dialog may also be usable, so you should try to select everything on every display and see what happens."

In one fell swoop, developers removed every indication of what is active and what is not, then set the user free to explore. Unfair.

With System 7, we will change all that: From within a modal dialog, the user will be able to get at any and all menus relevant to that dialog. The rest of the menus will be grayed out. Just as a user might expect.

Even though we have opened the way to enabling access to other parts of the program, modal dialogs should remain reasonably self-contained. If the user needs to set rulers, consider designing a box with the rulers in it, as shown in Figure 5–4 (wording approximate).

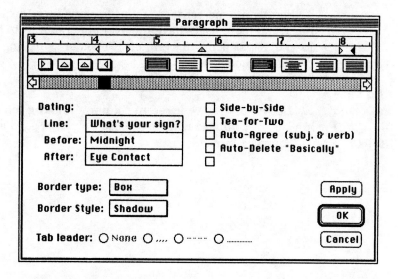

Figure 5–4. *Self-contained Dialog Box*

Our original reason for not allowing access to the menu bar was to strengthen the modality. This is seemingly in contradiction with the Macintosh philosophy of modelessness, but not so: We suggest avoiding modes, but once the user is in a mode, it should act like one. Otherwise the user may fail to recognize whether a mode is in force or not. That makes people very confused. Developers have demanded we open up the menu bar for good reason—because today's applications are just too complicated for us to require every option be held within the dialog box—but that does not mean that we should abandon all efforts to maintain a cohesive center of attention.

As for your particular definition of modeless dialogs, Dennis, I think that's fine. At the same time, others may want a given dialog, such as Preferences, to act on the entire application, rather than a single window or single selection. The scope of the dialog's actions should be clear to the users.

A couple of additional thoughts: People are getting really sloppy about circling the default button in modal dialogs.

➤ *GUIDELINE* *If you have a button in a dialog box that is activated by pressing the Return key, it must be circled. If you don't have a default button, don't circle any button.*
(You may have to trick the system into not supplying a default button by not using the button the system assumes to be the default.)

Finally, the percentage of people using large displays is going up. More and more users have the available real estate to leave frequently used dialogs open and available. Consider switching over existing modal dialogs to modeless.

And One Reader's Encouraging Response. . .

❑ *Dear Tog:* Re: your recent column, "Making the Most of Modes," I am clearly confused whereas before I was befogged and confused.
Thanks a bunch,

—LEO D. BORES, M.D., *Scottsdale, Arizona*

CHAPTER 6

Command Keys
vs. the Mouse

➡ COLUMN 6: AUGUST, 1989

A few months before this column was written, my editor, tiring of reading my made-up letters from the clan Scribblemonger, had put out the following clarion call for letters to Tog: "We've started a "Let's Help Tog Stop Pontificating" movement here at Apple, so send in your donations in the form of real questions or suggestions now!" Aaron Rosenbaum was quick to reply:

❏ **Dear Tog:**

Subject: Stop pontificating already!

Okay, here's a question to examine. It's pretty basic but fairly important.

I'm worried that the command key is breaking down as a valid method to communicate instructions. There is very little consistency between programs these days and I really have too many functions to address with a small set of commands. So here goes:

1. The basic life-or-death question of command keys: is Command-P Print . . . or Plain?

2. How do you feel about three-key command sequences (for example, Shift-Command-C)? They have often been restricted to "system" functions as opposed to editing functions. Is this my imagination or a good rule?

3. How about user-configurable command keys (a la Quark Style sheets)?

4. With one level of undo, Command-Z undid, Command-Z again re-did. With multiple levels of undo could you propose a key for re-do?

I would like the current list of suggested command keys to be expanded. Command-K is used as a delete function in some programs, yet it initiates something in others (AppleLink).

A separate but related issue would be a tutorial on ordering items on the menu bar and within menus. I used to order functions in workable groups, but found the Programs easier to use if the functions were grouped with the most-used towards the top. How do you feel about this?

—AARON ROSENBAUM

■ Frankly Aaron, I mainly feel saddened that you, a pillar of the software community, would have the audacity to accuse me, a Cupertino-renowned evangelist, of pontificating. But I will lay all that aside (particularly since I am sadly lacking in a defense), and answer your question.

We've done a cool $50 million of R & D on the Apple Human Interface. We discovered, among other things, two pertinent facts:

- Test subjects consistently report that keyboarding is faster than mousing.
- The stopwatch consistently proves mousing is faster than keyboarding.

This contradiction between user-experience and reality apparently forms the basis for many user/developers' belief that the keyboard is faster.

People new to the mouse find the process of reaching for it every time they want to do anything other than type to be incredibly time-wasting. And therein lies the very advantage of the mouse: It is boring to find it because the two-second search does not require high-level cognitive engagement.

It takes two seconds to decide upon which special-function key to press. Deciding among abstract symbols is a high-level cognitive function. Not only is this decision not boring, the user actually experiences amnesia! *Real* amnesia! The time-slice spent making the decision simply ceases to exist.

While the keyboard users in this case feel as though they have gained two seconds over the mouse users, the opposite is really the case. Because while the keyboard users have been engaged in a process so fascinating that they have experienced amnesia, the mouse users have been so disengaged that they have been able to continue thinking about the task they are trying to accomplish. They have not had to set their task aside to think about or remember abstract symbols.

Hence, users achieve a significant productivity increase with the mouse in spite of their subjective experience.

Not that any of the above True Facts[1] will stop the religious wars. And, in fact, I find myself on the opposite side in at least one instance, namely editing. By using Command-X, -C, and -V, the user can select with one hand and act with the other. Two-handed input. Two-handed input results in solid productivity gains (Buxton, 1986).

Command-Key Illusion   Since users do experience the illusion that keyboarding is faster, there is market pressure to supply them with "shortcuts" even when using "shortcuts" will actually slow them down. What I generally recommend is supplying as many "shortcuts" as demanded by the market—the real market, not the programmer in the cubicle next to you. But only if these "shortcuts" are not to the detriment of the user of the Macintosh visual interface. This leads to two important guidelines.

➤ *GUIDELINE*   *The keyboard interface must not dictate the design of the visual interface.*

➤ *GUIDELINE*   *The work to design and build the keyboard interface should not sap resources that are needed for the creation of the visual interface.*

In other words, don't violate the primary interface for the benefit of so-called "power-users," who may well end up achieving lower productivity by using the keyboard interface anyway. This is a major problem right now.

(Thank heavens I gave up pontificating!)

And now on to your specific questions:

1. P stands for . . . .

(At the time this column was written, at Apple, P stood for Plain, the command that would make bold, italic, or otherwise styled text into unstyled text. Unfortunately, everywhere else in the civilized world—like in all our developer's software—P stood for Print. I wrote in this column, in no uncertain terms, that P still stood for Plain. I also began a dialog inside Apple the led to changing it. I was helped in that effort by letters from the readers demanding a change. The result? P now stands for Print.)

---

[1] True Fact: A product of conventional wisdom. Something we know today to be absolutely, positively, universally, and forever correct, but tomorrow may discover was never true at all. (By the day after tomorrow, we will recall we knew it was wrong all along, but we didn't want to say anything for fear of embarrassing everyone else.)

2. Multiple-key commands (for example, Option-Command-Shift-9) started out only applied to system functions, but they have certainly proliferated beyond that. At this point, there are no rules beyond common sense for how many keys can be used: The more keys required, the slower the action and the fewer the people who will have the dexterity to use them. Again, because the so-called power user is rocking away at high speed on the keyboard is no evidence that he or she is being more productive; it only means he or she is having to work really hard to accomplish the task.

3. User-specified command keys are the best solution to the current problems, leading to the following guideline:

➤ **GUIDELINE** *All command keys should be user-specifiable. The developer can and should supply an initial set, but the user should be able to overrule those choices.*

In the early (pre-release) days of Lisa, we had command keys instead of pull-down menus. One of the primary reasons we abandoned command keys was the difficulty of coming up with fixed definitions that could be easily transported from application to application. Users were constantly confused.

I remember one mainframe company in the sixties that came up with the following command-key guidelines:

- Use the first letter of the command word.
- If the first letter is already used, use the last letter.
- If the last letter is already used, use the second letter.
- If the second letter is already used, use the second-to-the-last letter.
- And so forth.

A real power-user paradise!

Users are better able to remember disconnected data when they are the source for that data. They can remember shortcut keys far better if they assigned them. This fact was the basis for our decision to enable users, not applications, to control the programming of F1 through F15 on the USS Saratoga—I mean, extended—keyboard. (USS Saratoga was our code name during development of the extended keyboard because of its eerie resemblance to the popular aircraft carrier. Not so much the shape as the size.)

Specifiable command keys also give the handicapped—who cannot use the mouse—access to applications without burdening the rest of us with cluttered menus and the siren song of improved productivity where none exists.

4. "With one level of undo, Command-Z undid, Command-Z again re-did. With multiple levels of undo could you propose a key for re-do?"

How about Command-Shift-Option-Control-Help-triple click? Oh, it's been used?

On September 19, *MacWeek* will be hosting InterfaceDesign (ID '89), a conference in San Francisco on the Macintosh interface. This will be a working conference where you developers can tell us what you want. We expect to incorporate many of your suggestions into the Guidelines. Let us know what key you think should be used for re-do.

I would also hope that we might be able to hammer out some more standard command key equivalents, although for the life of me, I cannot imagine why Command-K would mean delete. Could it stand for kill?

I would also like somebody—anybody—to show up with one properly conducted test report that shows that command keys are equivalent or superior to pull-down menus somewhere, somehow.

Menu ordering is another topic that should be raised at ID '89. Aaron is correct in assuming that items toward the top are accessed more quickly. In fact, our research showed that the fastest item of all is—drum roll—item two. Then there's the standardization of where items will occur on the menu bar: I am pleased to see that the new version of AppleLink 5.0, will actually open documents in the File menu. How revolutionary! Now if we can only get HyperCard to even have a menu bar. . . .

(The result of ID '89 was our adoption of a richer set of command keys, as published in the new Apple Human Interface Guidelines book, available at finer book stores and computer centers everywhere. One command key shortcut that remained undefined, however, was re-do. The problem is that every other command key has been used and reused so many times that there doesn't seem to be one that can be universally applied, thus again demonstrating the problem with command keys.)

In the Thick Of It

I received more mail in response to this column than any other. In fact, you will see that the letters hadn't stopped even one year later. Here are three letters I received shortly after the column was published.

❑ **Dear Tog:** As a developer and experienced user, I strongly disagree with your discussion on command keys. . . .

First, I disagree with the statement that keyboarding is slower than mousing. Bet you could see that one coming. I have absolutely no doubt that for most of the users, the non-power users (for lack of a better term that has been extremely over-used), mousing is faster. To me, this is a basic part of the Macintosh user interface. Users should *always* learn via the mouse and *only* in the most-used statements convert from mouse to keyboard. For example, I and many of my users and clients type at 75–125 words per minute. In their environment, they and I have set up key equivalents such as Control-B for bold. In typing their documents, it is far faster for the experienced user to press Control-B, type the word, then press Control-B to boldface a single word than it is to do the equivalent with the mouse. For the non-power users, it is far faster to select the mouse command. This is not because the mouse is inherently faster or slower than the keyboard, but because of the time spent switching between the two devices for the power user who types at extreme rates. I don't know how fast you type, but I know that some of my clients and myself no longer think of words as a series of letters. We actually think in a pattern of keystrokes. I don't think of 'the' as 't-h-e', I think of it as 'the'. Bottom line—key equivalents are, as you said, slower for anyone who doesn't type at an extreme rate. But, they are far faster for those of us who do.

Second, I'm glad that Apple thinks that Command-P stands for Plain, but let's not fight what is *clearly* the standard—and that is Print.[2] Most of my clients, users, and definitely myself Print far more times than selecting Plain. Now, you're probably sitting there saying "this guy is out of it," but think of this: Most of the time when you are word processing, you are typing in the Plain style. Occasionally, you may bold or underline something. If the formatting takes place while typing, most people will choose Bold, type some, and then choose Bold again. The other type of formatting takes place after the typing. In this case, the user rarely needs the plain command because he/she has selected only the relevant text. Now, the obvious exception to this is the user who frequently uses styles with multiple styles, but in my experience, this is much less common in everyday use.

Finally, what's the difference if Command-K does stand for kill, as long as the user remembers it?

—NEIL TICKTIN, *Truin Software*

■ Hi, Neil: I don't think most folks can touch-type 75–100 command keys per minute, particularly with the weird layout of the keyboard we've adopted, which often requires the user to curl the thumb underneath the other keys. Regardless, you have presented the standard argument that makes it seem logical that command keys would be faster. Unfortunately, experimental evidence does not support the argument.

---

[2] Recall that the original column announced that, contrary to all practice, P was for Plain.

You also argue that there is no need for a shortcut key for Plain, as there is for Bold, and so on. You have presented an argument based on most people writing in a very specific style and with no errors. I not only make errors when I type, but I play with the text, over and over, until it scans the way I want it to. As a result, I probably use the plain key equivalent in my word processor—Command-Shift-Space—at least thirty times per day. I print perhaps five times per day.

There are two things wrong with Command-K for kill. First, the menu doesn't say "Kill," it says Delete. Second, it violates an unwritten, but long-standing guideline:

➤ **GUIDELINE** *Words like "kill," "abort," and "default" have powerful emotional charges connected with them and have no place in the interface. Instead, use words like "stop," "cancel," and "standard."*

Your argument that P for Print is clearly the standard is well-taken: I hope we will change it soon.[3]

It's All In Their Minds   ❑ *Hi, Tog:* The August *Apple Direct* issue just arrived with your "Command Keys vs. the Mouse" article. I totally agree with you about keyboarders versus mousers. Keyboarders only *think* they are faster—I think it's because of the *sound* of the keys, and bosses think work is flying when they hear those keys pecking away. If the mouse had a motor in it so it made a sound like a motorcycle or a whoosh or a zip, maybe folks would think the mouse was faster.

As a result of my observations of users, there are *no* command key equivalents in my product, Smart Labels, except for Undo, Cut, Copy and Paste. The Clear and Escape keys will clear the label text edit box. Users may demand key equivalents, but I will resist them. One of my current interesting projects is software that will work with the keyboard disconnected, and, in fact, will not respond to any keystrokes. How's that for an interface challenge!

—KIM HUNTER

Or Is It?   ❑ *Dear Tog:* I have been doing some study and testing on the issues raised by your last article and would like to share some of my thoughts. (If they prove useful maybe you could cut me in on some of that $50 million you paid the guy to time the two-second "amnesia time slice"!)

Let me begin by saying I agree that the mouse should be the primary interface to any application and that any support of the keyboard should

---

[3]Neil's letter was particularly effective in catalyzing the change to P for Print.

in no way reduce the efficiency of the mouse or the aesthetic appeal of the graphical interface.

I disagree, however, with the premise that mousing is faster than keyboarding (notice that I did not say that I believe keyboarding is faster than mousing). I believe that making such assumptions will stand in the way of providing the user the ability to determine just how he will interact with the computer for any given function at any given time.

In your article you state "The keyboard users in this case feel as though they have gained two seconds over the mouse users, but the opposite is really the case." To the keyboard users, it may not matter that they were actually slower, because they have *perceived* a speed increase over using the mouse. It is the subjective nature of perception and the disparity between perception and reality that gives rise to the "religious" nature of these discussions.

I came across an interesting example of perception vs. reality while designing a small text editor: When scrolling the text horizontally in a window we would refresh the text by redisplaying each line starting at the top. This resulted in a wave of text rippling down the screen and many complaints that the screen refresh was too slow. The remedy was to scroll the bits already on screen and then redisplay each line from the top. The second implementation was actually slower than the first because we incurred the overhead of scrolling the bits before we even started to display the new text on the screen. However, the perception was that there was an immense increase in speed. We stuck with the second implementation because it increased the overall satisfaction of the user even though it actually decreased the throughput of the product.

In my mind, perception is stronger than reality. A user's perception of a product is what causes him to purchase it and influences his satisfaction with the product. . . .

I'm not trying to propose that Apple abandon the mouse interface. On the contrary, as I stated earlier, I believe that the mouse/graphical interface should remain primary. But I strongly believe that more needs to be done to allow for the experienced user who is willing to make an investment in learning to be allowed more keyboard access to the entire interface, not just menus. I think Donald Norman (Norman, 1988) put it best when he said ". . . the design should not impede action, especially for those well-practiced, experienced users who have internalized the knowledge. It should be easy to go back and forth, to combine the knowledge in the head with that in the world. Let whichever is more readily available at the moment be used without interfering with the other, and allow for mutual support."

—NOLAN LARSEN, WordPerfect Corporation

CHAPTER 7

Hiding the Menu Bar

❧ COLUMN 7: SEPTEMBER, 1989

❑ **Dear Tog:** Please bring this issue into the light of day: What is the guideline concerning hiding the menu bar? I think that hiding the menu bar is fairly rude to a user in most cases, but it can occasionally be justified. The general case where it can be justified is when the screen is being taken over for some special visual function like displaying a slide show or video.

What bothers me is that Apple has taken no official position on hiding the menu bar. Apple explicitly does not offer a method for doing it that is guaranteed compatible with the future, thus implying that hiding the menu is a bad thing. Yet Apple is (1) pleased to use PowerPoint slide shows in front of the public that hide the menu bar and (2) ships a product that hides the menu bar, even gratuitously on occasion.

Thanks for your help.

—DENNIS AUSTIN

■ Gee, Dennis, we thought we had been quite explicit about where we stood *vis-a-vis* the menu bar. And it worked out pretty well, too, until a certain Dennis Austin, author of PowerPoint, started hiding it! I wonder if he's any relation?

I must admit that when we wrote the guidelines, we never thought anyone would actually hide the thing, so we never actually said, "The menu bar should never be hidden." Instead we said, "The user must always be able to pull down the menu(s) and see the names of the operations . . .," thus rather forcefully implying that the menu bar would be there. It would be rather difficult to pull down the menus in the absence of the menu bar.

We were even more explicit in the discussion of "perceived stability," one of the ten Design Principles:

> The Apple Desktop Interface . . . defines a number of consistent graphic elements (menu bar, window border, and so on) to maintain the illusion of stability. . . .

Stability is shattered when the menu bar is removed. Users believe in the menu bar. The menu bar tells them where they are: in the safe, protective environment of Macintosh, where consistency reigns.

The menu bar is the most constant object in the Macintosh. When it disappears, non-computer-oriented users assume they, the users, have moved, navigated, to a different planet, a world where all the rules may have changed. They are no longer within their familiar Macintosh world. And their only known way back, Quit on the menu bar, has been stripped away.

I have seen, during user testing, the very real fear etched on the face of users when the menu bar disappears. I have watched them literally panic as they realize they are trapped in a strange world.

Even experienced, computer-oriented users find the absence of a menu bar to be disorienting and frustrating. Particularly our currently worshipped power-user contingent. These kids are not at all amused by someone trying to control their environment.

If you find all this a touch melodramatic, I would suggest you try doing a little user testing yourself. We tend to underestimate the power of that illusion of stability we have created.

Just to make things absolutely explicit:

➤ **GUIDELINE** *The menu bar should* never, ever, ever *be removed unless there is a* powerful, overriding *reason to hide it.*

I have seen only three circumstances that even remotely suggest the menu bar should be hidden:

1. Presentation vehicles, such as PowerPoint's

- The end-user, the presenter, receives a powerful, overriding benefit from being able to *temporarily* disable the menu bar.

- The end-user, the presenter, has made a conscious decision on his or her own to *temporarily* disable the menu bar by invoking the presentation mode.

- The program gives the presenter explicit instructions for terminating the mode before each and every invocation of the mode, thereby adding a measure of visibility. The methods for termination are based on the standard methods for termination: Command-Period and Escape. So even if the presenter fails to read the instructions, old learned behaviors will enable him or her to escape. (These programs should also give explicit instructions for advancing from slide to slide which many, including PowerPoint, currently fail to do.)

- The program never hides the menu bar at any other time.
- The hiding of the menu bar is hard-wired to the presentation mode so it cannot be misused.
- The method is valid as the audience would not be able to pull down the menus anyway—only the presenter could—so the audience does not suffer any lessening of control.

2. Applications designed expressly for public use, such as point-of-purchase displays

- Users are Macintosh-näive and will remain so.
- Users are not "going anywhere." Unlike standard Macintosh users, they have no need to get to the menu bar to quit, change applications, or return to the Finder.
- Use of application must demand close to zero learning time.
- The software designer goes through a lengthy design and testing cycle to ensure that close to zero learning time is being achieved. (This point should not be taken lightly: The last serious point-of-purchase application with which I was involved required over 18 months of interface development to achieve an acceptable learning time.)

3. Applications for the severely handicapped

Some forms of brain damage in particular require radical computer solutions. For example, people may only be aware of objects either on their left or right sides. Having a menu bar that stretched across the top of the display would effectively eliminate half the menus from their field of perception.

Apple does not support hiding the menu bar for the simple reason that we don't want people hiding the menu. We have all seen the excesses in the one environment on the Macintosh (known as application (2) in Dennis' letter) where amateur developers can get their hands on the menu bar switch. Like every other element in the Macintosh interface, if you really want and need to hide the unhidable menu bar, you will figure out a way. We just don't want to make it too easy for you.

Next month, I will devote the column to the excesses of Dennis' application (2). I have just received a letter devoted exclusively to the subject, and once the Cupertino Fire Department has thoroughly doused the flames, I will set to the task of responding to it.

Freedom of Choice

And a couple of readers commented about the issue of freedom of choice. . .

❑ *Dear Tog:* I look forward to reading your column in *Apple Direct* every month, and was interested in your comparison of mouse vs. keyboard shortcuts, and menu bar at the top of the screen vs. alternate menu access.

While it's hard to argue with the data you've presented, I would like to make an observation: One of the accepted tenets of the Macintosh interface involves giving visual feedback to the user when a lengthy operation is being performed. We all know that it takes extra CPU cycles to give visual feedback (beachball, watch cursor, and so on), meaning that the lengthy operation takes even longer. What's important, however, is the user's perception: having visual feedback makes it *seem* as if the operation takes less time.

You can probably guess where this is headed: If it *seems* to the user that using a keyboard shortcut, accessing a menu attached to a window, or using a command-click hierarchical pop-up menu is faster, they should be able to make their own choice.

Yours truly,

—DAVID STAUFFER, *Apple Computer, Inc., Cupertino, CA*

❑ *Dear Tog:* I really do agree with you 100% in principle except that user perception of speed is really, really important and under some circumstances the belief is more important than the fact.

In our office, some people still insist on hammering the arrow keys rather than mousing the cursor to the new location. Although it could be demonstrated that the mouse is faster, they still don't like to use it under some circumstances. True, these folks have come from other environments and are victims of the Control Key Mindset, but they do bring up the point of perceptions. They do perceive the keyboard as less hassle than moving the hands off the keyboard in many cases.

Lest I be perceived as a command key afficionado, I am not. I am a speed afficionado and do not like things to take longer than necessary and will do anything (within reason) so the users do not perceive themselves to be waiting on the machine. Paraphrasing *Inside Macintosh,* Volume 1, "Whatever is best done with the keyboard, do with the keyboard. Whatever is best done with the mouse, use the mouse" has proven to be the best rule for me—while remaining within our beloved Macintosh conventions.

—DAVID FOSTER, *PRT*

■ Moderate positions always seem so sensible somehow, although I've never taken one myself. These two guys are right: We should provide the mechanisms for people to work comfortably in their own style, regardless of experimental evidence of what is "right for them." That is indeed a fundamental tenet of the Macintosh. My purpose in taking a seemingly absolute position against function keys was to counter a disturbing trend toward interfaces that worked well for people who liked function keys, but no longer worked effectively for those who needed to use a more visible interface. (I also just love to generate controversy, but you've undoubtedly recognized that by now.)

Separating out all the sound and fury, my central advice still stands:

➤ **GUIDELINE**   *In developing command key shortcuts, do not short-change the user of the visible interface, either by creating command names that make little or no sense but fill the alphabet, or by expending resources on the "invisible" interface that are needed to do the visible interface right.*

And now that we're on the subject of guidelines, we should add two more, based on the principle that perception is more important than reality. The first one is drawn from Nolan Larson's letter at the end of the previous column:

➤ **GUIDELINE**   *In making design decisions, it is important to look beyond the objective facts. "Perception is stronger than reality. A user's perception of a product is what causes him to purchase it and influences his satisfaction with the product."*

➤ **GUIDELINE**   *The users' perceptions can only be found through user-testing. Guessing does no good.*

CHAPTER 8

HyperCard and the Apple Human Interface

For two years prior to the publication of this column, developers had been taking me aside to express their concern about the human interface, or lack thereof, in HyperCard. I received the following letter from Doug Miles that presented the developer's concerns perfectly. Getting his letter and my response approved for publication was quite an experience, but it said much for the openness of Apple Computer and the HyperCard team that it even happened.

❏ **Dear Tog:** I enjoy your articles in *Apple Direct.* You have a clear yet entertaining way of presenting useful information. . . .

I hope (but don't have much hope) that serious improvements to the HyperCard interface are in the works. I have gradually developed a violent antipathy toward HyperCard mostly on the grounds of interface; I am terrified of its becoming a more integral part of the operating system. I could go on and on, but I'll spare you the usual tirade. It boils down to two things, I think:

I see a similarity developing here with pre-Mac computers' built-in BASIC. I was delighted to avoid that in 1984 by buying a Mac and would hate to see a reversion occur. HyperCard has that message windoid that just sits there blinking, waiting for you to type in a command like on any command-line OS. To make things worse, most stacks hide the menu bar. How un-Mac-like! And in other ways, as in placing graphical buttons, HyperCard's too unstructured, forcing the stack developer to design his or her own interface. As a result, stacks have about as much confusing interface variation as different companies' software packages on the IBM compatibles. This is giving up the interface consistency that's been one of the main attractions of the Macintosh computer. Was releasing HyperCard like opening Pandora's Box?

—DOUG MILES, *Miles & Miles*

■ Boy, Doug, kind of pulling your punches, aren't you? On the other hand, your letter starts out so nicely.

HyperCard was certainly the most innovative product to appear on the Macintosh since its inception. It was the first embodiment of a brilliant, brand-new, and revolutionary class of product. It was as enormous a leap forward as VisiCalc, the original spreadsheet, was when it first made its appearance. So what's wrong with a little innovation? Just what is it that is making Doug froth at the mouth?

First of all, I think many developers may be under the impression that somehow the HyperCard (lack of) interface will somehow creep into mainline applications. That somehow we will open a dialog box in Word 8.0 and find a pull-down menu floating around in the middle of the dialog where a pop-up belongs. Or we may open SuperPaint 6.2 and discover that selecting the house-paint brush hides the menu bar.

A scenario that might have happened? True. But fortunately, the Human Interface Community at Apple eliminated such a possibility more than a year ago by publishing Apple Human Interface Note #3, which tells our dear developers, "Don't do that!" More specifically, it states:

> When elements of the Desktop and HyperCard metaphors are combined, confusion may result. In an interface with a mixed metaphor, a user can no longer predict the result of clicking an item in a list or clicking on an icon. Does a click select the object, as in the Desktop metaphor, or does it launch an action, as in the HyperCard metaphor? Clicking on an icon to select it and having it launch an action because it's acting like a HyperCard button is—at the very best—disconcerting. Such unpredictability destroys the comfortable feel that is essential to a good human interface. Users confronted with such unpredictability are likely to become lost, confused, and unhappy with your product.
>
> Do *not* mix the Desktop and HyperCard metaphors. . . . If you're writing a Desktop application, don't include (to take a real example) a house icon that takes the user somewhere when it's clicked, like the Home Card button in HyperCard. Desktop applications should not contain HyperCard-like interface elements.
>
> The most important point is this: It should always be obvious whether the user is in a Desktop application or a HyperCard stack. And this means obvious at a glance; users should not have to read text or remember whether an application or a stack was launched. If the context is obvious, the user knows the result of a click—without having to think about it.

I am happy to report that a hundred percent of the eleven developers who have ever seen this Note have conformed to its every provision. This should certainly relieve any who shared Doug's fears regarding Pandora's Box.

Although it is difficult to discern from Doug's diplomatic text, I feel his concerns may go beyond the simple issue of cross-fertilization. In fact, I think he may be a bit upset about the cacophonous state of the stackware itself. I share many of those same concerns, although I would argue that for the Macintosh interface to grow, a certain level of chaos needed to be infused into the community. HyperCard has been a grand infuser.

Still, it's time for second-generation releases and products to begin appearing and I, like Doug and the several dozen other developers who have buttonholed me on this issue, would like to see some gentle restraints applied to the enthusiasm of today's HyperCard developers. (Nothing involving electricity.)

In that spirit, I offer the following guidelines for all Hyper developers around the world and some examples of where I hope HyperCard will go:

➤ **GUIDELINE**   *Consistency with the Guidelines should be maintained unless a new solution is demonstrably and vastly superior.*

HyperCard was created with the express philosophy of going beyond Macintosh. Had Bill Atkinson and his team set out to make sure that HyperCard never violated the published guidelines, the product would have never happened. Indeed, many of the third-generation, powerful applications now being built on the Macintosh would not be usable if their designers were not looking beyond the Guidelines.

Ignoring boundaries and restrictions is a necessary part of early product design. Otherwise true innovation will not occur. For example, when Bill Atkinson first developed LisaPaint, he ignored the absolute law against modality by creating tool palettes. (A tool palette as a mode-selection object, with each tool being a separate and distinct mode.) Had he not, he would have crippled his application. He had some loud and powerful critics at the time, but they ultimately bowed to the correctness of his design: The modes are voluntarily entered by the user, they are made visually apparent by the change in pointer shape, and they empower rather than restrict the user.

So how does one gently guide programmers, particularly amateurs, into writing stacks that generally conform to the Apple Desktop Interface? By making it easier to conform than to not conform. A brand-new, amateur stackware developer, having never seen the Macintosh interface, should end up with stackware that bears a striking resemblance to Macintosh software. HyperCard and HyperCard-like products should offer standard dialog objects, radio buttons that interlock, scrolling lists that maintain highlighting as they scroll, and so on. This can be accomplished without seriously detracting from the ability of the seasoned veteran to create something truly innovative. How? Principle 2:

> ➤ **_GUIDELINE_**   _An interface system destined to produce consistent software is populated with standard, defined objects._

The Apple Human Interface is made up of defined objects. For example, the file folder object, which consists of not only a standard visual appearance, but standard behaviors: opening with a double-click, displaying contents in the user-selected view, and so on. The appearance element and behavioral elements are permanently bound together: Neither the programmer nor the user can (easily) create a file folder that acts like a trash can, an application, a scroll bar, or any other standard object in the interface. This ensures the end-user a predictable environment.

HyperCard has few natural bindings and none that cannot be easily broken. As a result, the application can be seen as element-oriented, rather than object-oriented. It features collections of elements that can be bound together in any form the stackware designer chooses: input fields that look like buttons, buttons that look like file folders, and menu bars that suddenly disappear when most needed because absolute visibility is not a bound behavior.

It is sometimes even impossible to bind behavior to visual appearance. For example, I can draw a picture of a stack with an exposed edge to show there is more than one card in the stack, but I cannot make the thickness of the stack dynamically vary according to the number of cards in the stack: Take a stack with 1000 cards, remove all but 10; and it will still appear the same thickness. This might seem like a nit, but it reflects the difficulty the serious designer faces in generating a true virtual reality rather than a counterfeit illusion when developing in HyperCard. It limits the designer's ability to generate an accurate, visible, system image.

The lack of binding in the interface is at once HyperCard's greatest strength and greatest weakness. It offers the practiced, responsible designer tremendous latitude in product design, while at the same time seducing the average HyperCard owner-operator into creating chaos.

An interface system designed for consistency makes it significantly easier to produce a standard object than a variation. (It also must allow for variation, so people don't end up having to "work around" the interface.) Macintosh was created with this philosophy in mind. I think all programmers will agree it is easier to create a standard dialog box rather than one with slightly differing behavior. In fact, it is phenomenally complex to vary the underlying behavior at all.

I think both the System Software team and HyperCard team at Apple could learn from each other: On Macintosh, for all the modularity of its tool kit, it's way too hard to create necessary innovation.

With HyperCard, the struggle is to avoid unnecessary innovation. If I choose to make a button look like a radio button—certainly a standard Macintosh interface object—it is my responsibility as programmer to link it up with other radio buttons so that it behaves correctly. SuperCard has turned these sorts of elements into true objects with inherent behaviors. I hope to see HyperCard follow suit, so that we can eliminate the current rash of radioless radio buttons and interlocking check boxes.

➤ **GUIDELINE**   *The user should be in control.*

In the past, the programmer was in control, guiding the users/rats through a maze of twisty little passages, slapping them when they were bad. Macintosh wrested control of applications out of the death grip of us programmers and put it in the hands of the users. (I don't know about you, but I didn't like it one bit—until I saw the real empowerment that occurred as a result.) HyperCard dragged that power back and put it in the hands of the amateur programmer, who immediately turned off the menu bar, just to make sure the uppity users didn't try to escape.

In what may seem like a contradiction, I welcome a BASIC-like environment on the Macintosh. I think we have been sorely lacking a friendly place where amateurs can exercise some control over their computers. My problem arises when they look up from their computers and decide to try and control *me*.

HyperCard's promise was giving power to the people. It started out as a personal tool: one human, one computer, one HyperCard. It was only after Atkinson and others recognized the enormity of what was emerging that they began to plan for Developers and Users as separate beings. I would like to see HyperCard return to the people some of the power that somehow got siphoned off to the developers. For example, that pesky menu bar. I want to be able to access the Apple menu bar any time I want without having to know special incantations or HyperTalk. It's great that I, as an end-user, can turn it off for presentations; just give me the power to turn it on. And if developers know the user can turn it on despite the developer's best efforts, they may stop trying to turning it off. (Not that any of my readers would even consider turning off menus. . . .)

The Future   HyperCard was the first release of a first-generation product, with refinements to be expected. It is to be excused for both its limitations and its excesses. Just the fact that it struggled into being is miracle enough.

The Macintosh Toolbox and all the bizarre computer languages, operating systems, compilers, linkers, and so on, that surround it are as insurmountable as Mt. Everest to "the rest of us." HyperCard has flattened that mountain into a smooth meadow that almost anybody can traverse. I suggest that we create some well-beaten paths through that meadow, so that design novices can find their way toward more usable, successful stacks. Everyone will win.

CHAPTER *9*

Short Subjects

Not all questions require my usual 87,000-word responses. Some can be handled rather quickly. . . .

When Down Means Up and Up Means Down

❑ ***Dear Tog:*** I have a complaint. You've probably noticed that you draw more than your share of fire, maybe it's the irreverent tone of your *Apple Direct* articles.

I draw your attention to the System 7.0 Compatibility Guide, published for developers on the 7.0b4 CD-ROM.

In the discussion of "Font Sizes" (page 8 when I printed it out), it says, "Applications should remove the typical 127-point limitation for fonts when running on 7.0. In addition, THERE SHOULD BE SOME METHOD FOR A USER TO INCREMENT OR DECREMENT THE SIZE BY 1 POINT. (Caps are mine.)

My complaint is that I don't think Apple should be suggesting a new feature that every application should implement in such a waffling way. In my opinion, the "suggested approach" hasn't been thought out very thoroughly at all, since the left bracket means "UP" and the right bracket means "DOWN". I don't know about you, but I've found that the right-hand key of a pair on the keyboard is "greater" more often than the left-hand key, just the reverse of what is suggested.

Also, is this the collective wisdom of Apple speaking? Are we as developers to accept this as the pronouncement of Apple's human interface group? If so, it should be more unequivocal. If not, it shouldn't be published until Apple has figured out what it really wants developers to do.

I sure would like to know what my application is supposed to do. . . .

—HUGH SONTAG, *3M*

■ Hi, Hugh, I try my best to draw fire; it makes for good letters for my column.

I cannot take any responsibility for the document and guideline in question. ([and] = up and down. Or is it down and up?) I'd never heard about them before I received your link. However, feeling this was a rather silly guideline, I brought the matter up at one of our weekly human interface meetings and got it changed. The guideline for the new, permanent set of shortcut keys is (drum roll . . .):

➤ **GUIDELINE**   *Command < reduces the size of selected fonts by one; Command > increases the size of selected fonts by one.*

Developers may also accept Command-, and Command-. on standard keyboards, as long as they remember to pull or change the shortcut on keyboards that don't have the <> above the comma and period keys.

Ellipsis Crisis   ❏ **Dear Tog:** Please settle an internal dispute going on in our development efforts.

I have a modal dialog box that has some buttons. (For sake of discussion, look at the LaserWriter 7.0 Page Setup, as it displays a similar situation.)

Some of the buttons dismiss the dialog box just like the OK and Cancel in the LaserWriter Page Setup. But other buttons bring up another modal dialog, just like the Options button in the Page Setup. My co-developers feel that since they bring up a modal dialog, these buttons should have an ellipsis (those three little periods), like the Options . . . button.

My feeling is that this messes up the button's aesthetics, and, as is obvious from Apple's own Page Setup dialog and from the fact that all the user interface guidelines do not mention it, that it is *not* recommended.

Yet, their feeling is that it does convey more information to the user about the buttons function *and* it is more consistent. They also point out that Apple's own DiskCopy program[1] *does* have a button (Load Image File . . .) that has an ellipsis. That button brings up a modal Standard File window asking the image to load. (I won't mention the fact that the File menu has an item that does the exact same thing but is labeled Load Disk Image. . . .)

Can you set us straight once and for all? Should the ellipsis be used on buttons that bring up modal windows?

We've looked in the following places:
System 7.0 Human Interface Guidelines
Apple Human Interface Guidelines: The Apple Desktop Interface
Thanks,

—THOMAS MYERS, *Interactive Television Associates*

---

[1] A copy program designed for producing hundreds or thousands of copies of the same disk. It's not exactly targeted for the average user, which is fortunate, because it is not exactly designed for the average user, either: I get hopelessly confused every time I try to use it.

■ Thomas, You were correct in calling upon me to answer such a critical question before storming off in what could have been a disastrous direction.

The current Apple Human Interface Guidelines cover ellipses in menu commands on page 69. The same guideline applies to ellipses in button commands:

> An ellipsis (. . .) after a menu item means that after the item is chosen, the user will be asked for more information before the operation is carried out. Usually, the user must fill in a dialog box and click an OK button or its equivalent. Don't use the ellipsis when the dialog box that will appear is merely a confirmation or warning (for example, 'Save changes before quitting?').

Under these guidelines, both the examples you mention are correct! (In the case of DiskCopy, this can undoubtedly be attributed to the power of random chance.)

DiskCopy, upon the user pressing Load Image File . . . , offers the user the chance to fill in more information before the operation is carried out, just as specified by the guidelines. It therefore correctly displays the ellipsis.

Options also generates an information-seeking dialog box, but does not have an ellipsis. So how can it also be following the guidelines? Remember that the guidelines talk of asking for more information "before the operation is carried out." "Options" is shorthand for "Show Me the Options," or, "Show Me the Options Now, You Stupid Hunk of Silicon!!", depending on one's mood at the time. Is the user asked for any more information before the operation is carried out? No. Because presentation of the dialog box *is* the operation.

Neat, huh?

If Options carried you to an intermediate dialog that inquired, "Left-handed options or right-handed options?," it would then need to have an ellipsis. As it stands, no ellipsis should be used.

We made a decision in the System 7 finder to violate one part of this guideline: Selecting Erase disk... from the Special menu does not ask for more information; it only asks for confirmation. We used the ellipsis anyway because we didn't want people to be inordinately fearful of accidentally choosing such a potentially damaging command. The ellipsis in this case lets them know, without trying the command, that they will have some way to get out in case they accidentally come to light on it. Without the ellipsis, people would have to select the command to find out for themselves whether it would destroy their disk, thereby facing the chance of replacing possibility with certainty. Catch 22.

—TOG

❏ *Hi Tog*: We're in a quandary. We're developing some network management software, and have come across an interesting HI problem: One of our windows calls for a group of radio buttons. This would be simple enough except that of the available five states, only three are user-settable. The other two can be triggered by the hardware, negating the user's setting.

How should we represent this? We've come up with some ideas, all of them unsatisfying:

1. Graying out the text of the radio buttons that are not user-settable. Though the easiest to code, this is the least desirable option because it'll send users scurrying into menus, manuals, or toll calls to find out how they can enable these grayed options.

2. Providing a passive indicator such as a light for each state. The user-settable states would have radio buttons next to them as well. Problem here is that I can't find for the life of me a standard icon for a passive indicator. I'm worried about reinventing the wheel and possibly confusing users who are expecting something else.

3. Creating another "highlight" for the button—that is, making up some kind of "halo" to float around the button when that state actually exists. The problem there is that the buttonless halos would likely look downright goofy.

4. Highlight the text itself somehow if the state is true. This would make the text of the radio button stand out somehow, but wouldn't interfere with the button. Not sure exactly how easily users would determine why the text was highlighted, though. . . .

5. Give up, go to Tahiti, and forget about all this software stuff.

We are trying to settle this and figured you'd be a good person to bounce this off of. An answer would be appreciated.

Thanks,

—KEN RESTIVO, *Product Manager / Fibermux Corporation*

■ Sure thing, Ken.

➤ *GUIDELINE* *Invent new objects, with new appearances, for new behaviors.*

I would keep the three radio buttons that can sometimes be selected among. I would create a "status" area that (1) tells the user the current status (which could reflect that one of the three buttons has been set or one of the two system-imposed states has overridden the user's selection) and (2) tells the user whether or not this state is the result of a user choice or a system choice. If it is a system choice, the message should spell out that the user cannot change it, and the three radio button objects should be grayed out.

> ➤ **GUIDELINE** *When you have an anomalous situation, err on the side of drawing excessive attention to it, rather than trying to slip it into some standard appearance.*

In the Macintosh, we try to be as sparing of words and extra visual clutter whenever possible, but sometimes we all overdo it. (Our original control panel, you will recall, had no words explaining what the icons stood for, and everyone was confused. The watchword around here, now, is that a word is worth a thousand pictures.)

—TOG

Multiple Text Selection: Against the Law?

❑ *Dear Tog:* Can you tell me why it seems illegal to allow multiple text selections? You are allowed to Shift-click individual objects to create a selected set. Why can I not add text objects to a similar set?

I can see that the UI gets interesting because of the decision to make Shift-click be the text selection extender. But is there a problem with the document model if it had the ability to have multiple passages of text selected?

It would seem that cut, copy, and paste would all work in a predictable way. Am I missing something?

—JOHN PAGE, *Quill Software, Inc.*

■ Yes, John, you are, but so is everyone else. Discontinuous selection has always been a part of the Human Interface Guidelines:

> To make a discontinuous selection . . . , the user selects the first piece in the usual way and holds down the Apple key while selecting the remaining pieces. Each piece is selected in the same way as if it were the whole selection, but because the Command key is held down, the new pieces are *added to* the existing selection, instead of replacing it.

This guideline holds true for text, graphics, arrays, or any other way that you folks might think up for presenting information. Few developers have been implementing this feature, and it is making life very difficult for those who do, since their users are unfamiliar with the feature.

It is time, ladies and gentlemen, for us to bite the bullet and implement the feature. Persons, start your engines. (Ah, the difficulties of avoiding sexism.)

❏ **O Great Guru of User Interfaces**: In the development of our
printer chooser driver software we have encountered the sticky realm of
"Excellent User Interface." The ensuing religious wars over proper
design have moved me to consult a higher spiritual source—you.
The first issue concerns the use of pop-up menus in the print dialog.
We have one called "Color Matching" for which the options are:

> SuperMatch
> Printer Table
> None

A second, called "Printer Table" has the options:

> Default
> G 1.4-B20
> Select . . .

The second option (G1.4-B20) is just the file name for the previously
selected table.

When "Color Matching—Printer Table" is selected, the table shown
in the "Printer Table" pop-up is used. However, when "SuperMatch" or
"None" is selected for "Color Matching," the "Printer Table" pop-up is no
longer valid.

One programmer suggested that the "Printer Table" pop-up should
disappear. I feel that the user interface in general should not have
controls appearing and disappearing. I suggested graying out the
"Printer Table" pop-up. The programmer thought that the user might be
confused if the pop-up was grayed out but still displayed the previously
selected table file name. The user might think that the table shown was
still being used, and that the pop-up being grayed out simply meant that
he or she could not change it. We decided that the best option would be
to gray out the "Printer Table" pop-up and change the displayed item to
"None" to let the user know that no table would be used.

Is this the best way to handle it or do you have any other suggestions
or thoughts? What is your opinion of controls disappearing?

The second issue is a moral opposition on my part to check marks
being used in menus for toggled items instead of toggled item wording.
The Human Interface Guidelines book takes a ho-hum attitude about the
whole thing and indicates that either is acceptable. I think that check
marks in menus are great for showing which item in a list is selected (like
font sizes or styles) but can be confusing when used as a toggle.

Case in point is an option we want to include in our printer server software for turning log-file recording off and on. The presently used method is to have an item in the File menu called "Record Log File" with a check mark to indicate if it is on or off. The problem I see is that a first-time user will see the menu item without a check mark on it. There is nothing to indicate that when selected, a check-mark-type item will be checked unless you have previously used it. A check-box item in a dialog clearly indicates what will happen even when it is not checked, but this is not the case in a menu item.

When I see "Record Log File" for the first time, I wonder if perhaps something will be recorded right now when I select the option. Maybe the server has been storing up all the log information in RAM and when I select this option it will be recorded to disk? In fact, even when I select "Record Log File," there is no user feedback to indicate that I have started a recording "mode" unless I go back into the menu and see the check mark. All in all, I see it as less than intuitive.

As an alternative, I would suggest using a menu item with toggled wording that states exactly what will happen when it is selected. It should initially say something like "Start Recording Log." Then when the menu is re-entered, it should say "Stop Recording Log." There is no room for confusion.

What is your opinion of this particular scenario, and in view of the "Good Book'"s indifference to the topic, what is your opinion of check marks for toggled menu items in general?

Hallelujah Brother!

—DAN KUCHTA, *Eastman Kodak*

■ Brother Dan, you have come up with the same solution I would have suggested for the first issue. I'm not sure the word "none" is the best choice, but you can measure that when you go to user testing. (You *are* going to do user testing, aren't you?) I would also try the word encased in parentheses, to indicate the system is commenting, rather than the user having chosen such an option.

One of the principles of the Macintosh interface is stability:

➤ **GUIDELINE** *Perceived Stability: Users feel comfortable in a computer environment that remains understandable and familiar rather than changing randomly.*

Having objects appear and disappear is in direct violation of this principle. There are times when it is appropriate to have an object no longer available in a given location. For example, if the system found that the printer table option was completely invalid for the printer being used (like the ROM group for the printer had forgotten that printer tables were necessary), it might be reasonable to not have the option appear at all. But to have it disappear several times per session, as another control is changed within the same dialog is way too unstable.

In answer to the second issue, I think we waffled on check marks. However, it is too late to do much unwaffling. You have made a compelling case for using toggles when the menu item in question is ambiguous. I'm confident that "Start Recording Log" and "Stop Recording Log" would prove to be far less ambiguous. (This is also a good candidate for a test: Just ask four or five people who are not hackers what "Record Log File," "Start Recording Log," and "Stop Recording Log" mean and see what results you get. These kinds of casual tests can save hours of arguing.)

The general drawback to toggling menu items is that they are always displaying the status opposite to the true status. Since menus are often used to find out current status, rather than alter it, this presents a problem: To detect I'm recording, I have to read, "Stop Recording Log," then translate it to mean that since I can stop recording, I must be recording right now. That's why we waffled.

—TOG

CHAPTER 10

Take Out
the Papers
and the Trash

➡ *COLUMN 11: JANUARY, 1990*

❑ ***Dear Tog:*** . . . I don't really know you, but I am sure as you say, you are the finest designer I have ever come across. . . .

Since Undo was one of the great features of the Mac, why was it not extended to recovering a deleted file? I suppose you will say that the trash can is a form of Undo for file deletion, but users do the "Put-in-trash-go-immediately-to-Special-menu:Empty-Trash" so fast that the Undo concept is lost.

I think the "swelling" trash can is a bad design. I think that the trash should never be emptied on launch or on shut down, but only on disk full and with a dialog such as "Make space by emptying trash?"

—KIM HUNTER

■ Kim, I couldn't agree with you more. The painful appearance of that trash can compels people to relieve it of its suffering when emptying it is the last thing they should be doing. But what about requiring users to throw their disks in the trash to eject them? That's a level of system image pathology unsurpassed by any other user interface feature anywhere. So what? I've been complaining about both these "features" forever. As far as the programmers are concerned, they work.

I am mentioning this because I think that you, the developer community, are letting both us and yourselves down. You have a high stake in the future of this interface, but you are sitting around being passive. You are not making yourselves heard.

I sat through a full day of MacWeek's InterfaceDesign '89 conference last fall, waiting for somebody—anybody—to rise up from the audience and call for some sort of concerted action. Instead, what I heard over and over was, "those people at Apple are so good that they must know all the answers, so we need to let them handle all the human interface stuff 'cause we might mess it up."

Poppycock! Yes we have more people and more hours to throw at human interface research. Yes, there needs to be a strong central focus if the interface is to remain consistent. But, we "know all the answers"? Ha! If you want new objects and behaviors in this interface, properly supported by tool kit extensions, you are going to have to make yourself heard.

Years ago the Apple Dealer Council was formed to let us know what the dealers really felt about what we were doing. We listened. It's time now for you developers to start talking. Is the tool kit providing everything you need? Do you like what we have done with the interface in some of our newer products: MPW, MacApp, HyperCard, AppleLink? Are you satisfied with the Macintosh interface as it is now embodied? Apple currently thinks you are, since they have not heard anything to the contrary.

As a community, you need to choose among yourselves, in whatever forum you find appropriate, those human interface issues that are really important to you. Then you need to see that Apple responds by talking to the people who can make it happen.

A Previously Unpublished Response

❏ **Dear Tog:** Your column in the last *Apple Direct* criticizes the development community for our lack of action regarding establishment of Human Interface standards. Perhaps if Apple were quicker to admit problems, you'd get more advice.

Doug Miles brought up some very germane criticisms of HyperCard in your 11/89 column (see Chapter 8), and you dismissed his suggestions with the argument that HyperCard was different because it was "a new interface" and therefore by definition fit a standard perfectly. You chose not to mention the obvious and serious interface problems that HyperCard does have.

For example, all scrolling fields have a scroll bar that looks active but usually is not. This is the sort of "feature" that is confusing to first-time users, aggravating to seasoned users, and a real waste of time for all. Paul Snively mentioned that he'd pointed that out to the HyperCard team more than two years ago, back before HyperCard was even released. If you don't listen to your beta testers, will you listen to your developers?

Then there's the text cursor. In every other application in the known Macintosh world, its "hot spot" is somewhere near the top of the I-beam. With HyperCard the hot spot is near the bottom, with the result that a casual user invariably selects the wrong line of text. Sounds insignificant, doesn't it? It's not.

One of the deadly inconsistencies is the lack of an explicit "Save" command. Press Delete, and you can lose a button, its script, and all its functionality with no recourse whatsoever. The Undo command looks active, but won't bring it back. And this is in an application aimed at computer novices? At least the graphic tools have a "Revert" command. But even that's not under the Edit or File menu where it should be.

Or how about the windows: Under MultiFinder, while a windoid is open, the main window's Title Bar is precisely the opposite of normal Mac windows. That is, when HyperCard is the active application, the window looks inactive, and vice versa.

There are other anomalies too numerous to mention. My point is, these are all important parts of the Human Interface that HyperCard has chosen to ignore for more than two years and four versions. Until Apple begins to respond to the feedback you've already received, there's not much sense in us developers wasting our time, is there? That's what those folks at InterfaceDesign '89 were saying.

—LLOYD MAXFIELD, *Infosynthesis*

Lloyd's letter reflects the frustration people outside the secret inner world of a large corporation like Apple often feel when they receive little or no acknowledgment about their complaints. The fact is we were listening: The System 7 team was plugged right into InterfaceDesign '89, my column, and every other source of developer feedback they could find, though none of us could talk about it. Apple's upper management was listening, too. Decisions were made. Decisions were changed.

In the face of continuing developer complaints, the philosophy of the HyperCard team changed drastically, too, and HyperCard 2.0 ended up a better, more consistent product.

PART II

The Process of Design

When I first joined Apple, we set up a procedure (I think we borrowed the idea from Hewlett-Packard) whereby the marketing people were supposed to whip up a specification called a Market Requirements Document (MRD), and the engineers were supposed to respond with an External Reference Specification (ERS). I saw several ERSs in my day—though none before the product shipped—but I have yet to lay my eyes on a genuine MRD. Robert Mulligan (Mulligan, et al. 1991) describes this process as the "waterfall model." It doesn't work.

➤ **GUIDELINE**   *The most successful designs result from a team approach where people with differing backgrounds and strengths are equally empowered to affect the final design.*

The developers I visit who have the most successful designs develop teams involving folks from many walks of life: programmers, human interface designers, graphic designers, marketers, salespeople, even customers! (See discussion of Time Arts' planning sites, Chapter 12.) They go through a product life cycle that produces results. Over the course of the columns, I talked about bits and pieces of this life-cycle. For the book, I have drawn them all together.

CHAPTER 11

Three Key Players

Software is theater, and like theater, there are a number of roles to be played. Three roles and their assigned players particularly affect the human interface: the human interface designer, the graphic designer, and the writer. Each of these roles has a key role in the success of any software product. Let me tell you a little bit about them and offer you some hints on what to look for.

Human Interface Designers

Human interface designers deliver the highest return on investment of any member of a software team, and I'm not saying that just because I am a human interface designer. Well, actually I *am* saying that because I'm a human interface designer, but I have some evidence, too.

Robbin Jeffries and company presented a paper at CHI '91 on a study they did at Hewlett Packard on the subject of user interface evaluation (Jeffries, et al. 1991). They took a software product that was at the user-testing stage and gave it to four different groups to be tested.

The first group consisted of four human interface specialists with backgrounds in behavioral science, as well as experience in the heuristic evaluation of real products. They were given two weeks to come up with a review of the product.

Second, an experienced user-interface tester ran six test subjects through the application and wrote up a report on the findings.

The third group was populated by three software engineers (I think this meant programmers) who applied a pre-written set of guidelines.

The fourth group was another three engineers who performed an intellectual exercise called a "cognitive walk-through," which, as far as I can make out, consists of mapping out paths users could take through the software, then "walking through" those paths to see how things are working out. (If this is an unfair characterization, I apologize: I have a thing about almost any human-computer interaction technique that starts with the word "cognitive." They always seem to me far too intellectual and likely to miss the gestalt of what is going on.)

The results of all this were rather clear and compelling as shown in Figures 11–1 and 11–2.

| | Problems found | | Person- | Benefit/ |
	Total	Core[1]	hours	cost
HI folk	152	105	20	12
Usability Testing	38	31	199	1
Eng w/Guidelines	38	35	17	6
Engineers w/Cogs[2]	40	35	27	3

Figure 11-1. Results of Jeffries Study

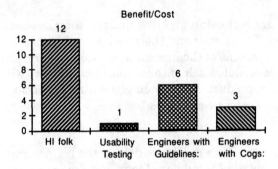

Figure 11-2. Results of Jeffries Study for Visual Thinkers

The Jeffries study is exactly in line with what I have witnessed during my years in this business: Having trained, qualified human interface people involved in a software effort produces a major benefit at a most reasonable cost.

Please do not read the usability testing result as an indication that user testing should be avoided; human interface designers depend on user testing to pick up problems that they can't find. And there are many. The best synergy arises from having a human interface designer and doing limited, very specific testing. You will learn more about doing inexpensive testing in Chapter 14, "User Testing on the Cheap." You can also get some insight as to my highly formal user testing methods in Chapter 36, "Case Study: One Or More Buttons."

---

[1] Core problems were those found to be significant problems with the product by a panel of an additional seven people—four HI experts and three HI people with a reasonable level of experience.

[2] OK, OK, I'm being excessively hostile about this whole cognitive thing. So shoot me.

Graphic Designer

➤ **GUIDELINE**   *The design of visual elements should be left to people schooled in their creation: graphic designers.*

Graphic designers can spin magic out of a handful of pixels. They are rivaled only by poets in their ability to communicate the most information in the least space possible. A graphic designer is an essential element of a crack software team.

If you need to hire a graphic designer, you are in luck: Graphic designers not only work for ridiculously low prices, you can quickly judge the merit of their work. This, in contrast to programmers (you may never be quite sure what they are up to) and to marketers whose relative success may be spelled in months, not hours.

Remember that the chief job of a graphic designer on a software project is to communicate, not decorate. Look for someone whose work communicates powerful images.

If you *are* a graphic designer, but new to computers, you should read *Graphic Design for Electronic Documents and User Interfaces*, by Aaron Marcus (1992). You should also, as should anyone new to the Macintosh, immerse yourself in the software until you "feel" the visual language of the Macintosh, because it has never been written down, and it's unlikely that it will be written down any time soon. It is not an intellectual language; it is a poetry of images, which most of us can only admire.

Graphic designers should be brought in at the beginning of a project, not the end; until the rest of the team sees the designer in action, they will not think visually. Those of us who lack the talent to draw have long since learned to avoid coming up with ideas that require drawing! Once having been exposed, people will start thinking visually and will get in the habit of doing quick place-holder graphics, to be worked up and worked over by the graphic designer later on.

The graphic designer will need to return several times during the course of the project to judge how things are progressing and to offer suggestions for increasing the "visibility" of the program. He or she will begin to create a characteristic "look" for the application that will give it character and form. Toward the end, he or she will want to review the whole design and confirm that the overall graphic design is resulting in clear, accurate communication of the conceptual model of the program.

Is all of this expensive? No. The total number of hours on a single project needed by a graphic designer is a small fraction of that needed by the programmers. Besides, the only thing more foolish and wasteful than having a bunch of engineers avoiding user testing by sitting around arguing about what users will or will not do is to have the same bunch of engineers spend their nights and weekends drawing icons that look like bugs and screen designs that look like a three-year-old's on a bad day.

Save yourself time. Save yourself money. Save yourself a whole lotta grief. Get a graphic designer. You'll be glad you did.

Writer   Whenever I come in on a software project in crisis, I immediately head for the manual writer. Writers know a program is in trouble as soon as they have to write a twenty-page explanation of a minor "feature" to keep people from stumbling over it. But writers are generally held in a second-class position in this industry, a position reflected in the amount of respect, involvement, and pay that falls their way. As a result, all too often in a project, writer's construct those twenty pages, feeling it is not "their place" to point out the problem.

Hire a writer early. Many independent writers like to have several projects going on at once. Getting one in early for short periods of time during initial design will usually not be a problem.

Make sure he or she is part of the design process, so you can be advised on what can and can't be explained to "normal humans." Take the time to let the writer know that his or her opinions are wanted. Educate everyone on the team that the project and the company are better served by their writer speaking up, rather than keeping quiet.

A number of years ago, I was writing the manual for Apple's implementation of the PILOT educational authoring system, SuperPILOT. I found myself at page fourteen of an enthralling treatise on how to mix colored text and backgrounds without disastrous interactions. I finally pulled back far enough from my deathless prose to realize that it would take the average educator at least three days to understand what I was saying.

I then reviewed the forty color mixtures we were offering, eliminated sixteen duplicates, knocked off an additional two (particularly ugly) mixtures that caused most of the problems, and recommended that we adopt only the remaining twenty-two. With the addition of some totally transparent rules (to the PILOT programmer) within the display program, the user was able to mix any offered text color on any offered background color. The necessary documentation was reduced from fourteen pages to two sentences. Many writers will not be able to work out alternate algorithms for a program, but they will know when to point out that an alternate algorithm is called for.

How do you judge a writer? Look at some previous work. Is the language clear and concise? Does it reflect a knowledge of the system and the domain of the application? Is it short enough to be usable, yet long enough to be thorough? Does the organization of the material promote ease of learning and ease of use?

Many good writers abound in Macintosh Land. Find one. Now.

CHAPTER 12

Field Analysis

➡ *COLUMN 26: APRIL, 1991*

➤ **GUIDELINE**   *Begin your project with field analysis.*

There is more to an application than its direct human/computer interface.

> The designer must know the subject he is presenting, and he must know the limits and opportunities of software technology. He also must immerse himself in his user's world. Only then can he see neglected possibilities, unworkable requirements, and the myriad details from which he can form a solution that has conceptual integrity. (Heckel, 1991)

How will your product be used? What problems are people likely to encounter other than obvious performance shortfalls? What is happening in the environment in which the product finds itself? The answers to these questions lie in a process called task analysis.

There are many excellent treatises on the full subject of task analysis, but I tend to favor Ben Shneiderman's as the most exhaustive (Shneiderman 1983). You may either fetch the original paper from your vast library or find the key excerpt on page 486 of Ron Baecker and Bill Buxton's exhaustive book, *Readings in Human-Computer Interaction, A Multidisciplinary Approach* (1987). (This book, by the way, is an absolute must for anyone involved in human interface design.)

In the next three chapters I intend to cover three important pieces of the entire analysis and design process, pieces that I have most often found developers giving little attention or leaving out altogether.

Let's Go Find Out . . .   During a field analysis, the team goes on location to visit various user populations. The sites must be representative of the full range of users and tasks. In the case of a communications application, for example, the team would want to visit a large installation, small installation, sole user at a company, sole user at a one-person business, groups receiving and sending large numbers of messages, and groups receiving and sending few messages. Each of these market segments would have their own special problems and needs, and carefully selecting representative groups from all critical population classes is vital.

Ideally, the entire development team would go on-site. If this is not practical, representatives from each profession should be there. You may certainly use contractors to select the population and write follow-up reports, but the development team needs to observe these sites first-hand. The visiting team must consist of more than product marketing and management people. It should include software engineers, the human interface designer, graphic designer, and manual writer, so they can get to know their users and see the product being used in its everyday setting.

The team will question users about their experiences with the product, eliciting what the users like and dislike about the product, what they would like to see changed, and what they think those changes should be. This alone is not enough, however, because users usually don't know what the possibilities are. In the six years I supported the Apple II interface before the advent of the Macintosh, not a single user complaining about the Catalog (file-viewing) function on the Apple II said, "Hey, you know what would be really neat? If you could see all your files sitting on like—oh, I don't know—a desk top or something."

When the AppleLink 2.0 team did a wish-list survey of AppleLink users around the company, most said they wanted to be able to do things like sort lists of files, pull in email messages faster, and turn off automatic scrolling. No one suggested that AppleLink should always be "live," represented by an in-box and out-box on their desktop, a superior approach to all this logging-in business that will soon become possible with the advent of ISDN.

The observers should get to know the people at each location, how they feel about computers, their jobs, and life in general. The observers want to constantly probe for emotions. What is making this person frustrated? What occurrences have made the person despair of ever accomplishing or even learning how to do specific tasks? What about the user's abilities? Can this person handle increasingly complex technology? What strategies does this user apply in using the software to accomplish the larger-context task? Where can this strategy be altered or strengthened by changes in the software design?

Failing to do field analysis often happens when the members of the team are also users of their application, because they assume that they are that magical "average" user and feel they understand all possible problems from their own experience. They don't.

Many vertical market applications violate the Guidelines; not being a mass-market product, they are insulated from the wrath of the media critics. Their producers, oftimes being small, may not attend the Apple Developer Conference and other forums where the Macintosh culture is passed on. However, developers supporting vertical markets are really good about doing field analysis. They are usually extremely aware of who their users are, what their strengths and limitations are, and exactly how they use the developer's software. They are also keenly aware of how their software package melds with the rest of the businesses' daily life, in which their software plays a small part. As a result, they end up with applications which, while violating some guidelines, are extremely functional and productive for their target group.

I find all this not surprising; when the software team fully recognizes they are not representative users, they will go out and find representative users. We must all go out and find our users, whether we use our own application or not. And, for heaven's sake, don't forget to observe a few new users: We have forgotten the initial pain of our learning our applications. We need to see new people squirming, to remind us.

➤ **GUIDELINE** *Field analysis doesn't end at the beginning. It continues with planning sites, alpha sites, and beta sites. All are vitally important to the design process.*

Field analysis doesn't end with the initial visit. Most developers today have "beta sites," locations with people who are part of their target population. To these beta sites, they send their alpha software, receiving in return feedback in the form of written responses and verbal abuse: "This stupid thing just ate my whole disk drive and I want you to know. . . ."

Time Arts, during the development of Oasis (see Chapter 35, "Second Release Software"), wanted to start with their feedback sites long before alpha. They made their customers part of the earliest design process by setting up planning sites: people who turned out to be willing to work with them from the very beginning, straight through to the end.

CHAPTER *13*

Brainstorming and Scenarios

We have our team, we've done our field analysis. Now it's time to design.

Brainstorming ➤ **GUIDELINE** *Brainstorming is vital to the task of casting off old ideas and embracing new ones.*

When I work with developers to launch a new software design, I begin with a group design session lasting from several hours to as long as four days, depending on the size of the project and the team's stamina. This session enables the team members to get to know each other and myself, lets everyone focus their energy on the new project, and helps establish an interactive design process for what will be an interactive product.

I get the whole team together: engineers, graphic designer, writer, marketing types, and, of course, the human interface designer. The meeting has to be away from the usual work space—in a different part of the building, town, or world, depending on your budget.

Three rules I like to follow are

1. No one is allowed to criticize another's ideas, and

2. Engineers are not allowed to say it cannot be implemented (even when they know it can't).

Both of these two rules are important if you are to walk away with anything worthwhile. Both free people up to think in new directions. One person's fanciful idea may very well spark a real breakthrough on the part of another, as long as a third person is not holding forth on how stupid the original idea was. And after you spend a few days hashing around the design, you will be pleasantly surprised how rational your design—which earlier required force-feedback steering wheels and a supercomputer—has become.

Use plenty of paper. Cover the walls with it. Draw. Scribble. Use lots of colored pens. You are there to create a visual, highly interactive user environment. It will spring most easily from a visual, highly interactive get-together. Which brings me to rule 3:

3. The graphic designer is not allowed to snicker at the engineer's drawings.

You can find a lot more about brainstorming in Edward De Bono's book, *Lateral Thinking* (De Bono, 1970).

You and your teammates have come to this meeting having done sufficient field analysis to have a good sense of your users, their work sites, and their goals. I like to think of users as occupying a space such as that shown in Figure 13-1.

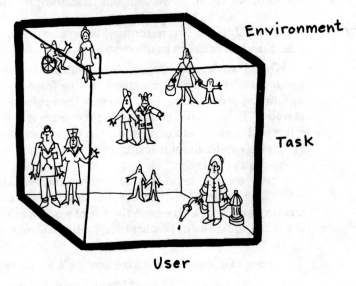

Figure 13–1.   *Dimensions of User Space*

The three dimensions cover the range of users, their work environments, and the kinds of tasks they will need to perform to achieve their goals. The object of the brainstorming session will be to identify these ranges in detail, in preparation for the process of building scenarios, which will follow.

Interleaf 5 for the Macintosh is the premier computerized publishing application, capable of handling documents in excess of six million pages with ease. At the beginning of the design of Interleaf 5, I spent several days with the software team going through formal brainstorming and scenario-building. The result was a solid design responsive to user needs and abilities, along with an enormous stack of giant wallcharts that the folks from Interleaf have graciously allowed me to share with you.

We first set out to identify who Interleaf 5 users might be. (I have taken the liberty of reducing the original font size of 786, as it was originally scribbled on the wall.)

Who are the users?

- previous Mac users
- previous TPS/Publisher users
- everyone in publishing
- middle management
- engineers
- typesetters moving to computers
- professionals, lawyers, consultants
- graphics people
- people who are writers
- technical writers
- word processor users
- large corporations
- naive users
- rich people
- sensories
- extroverts (who hate using computers)
- academics
- manufacturing industries
- CAD users
- CASE users
- the government
- government contractors
- foreigners
- small business folk
- Human Resources
- scientists/researchers
- programmers
- students
- editors
- project leaders
- financial industries
- system integrators
- marketing folk
- people writing highly structured documents
- churches, synagogues, temples, and so on
- country clubs
- newsletters
- people who must work within constraints
- people who need flexibility
- on the job location folk (maintenance)
- readers, not just publishers
- people who would have needed our training, but won't now because of our awesomely clever designs

There are people on this list for whom Interleaf, a super-high-end publishing package, is probably not appropriate: Newsletter writers and country clubs in particular would probably be as well off with a standard page-layout package. The list also reflects the light-hearted, humorous attitude prevalent in the room. In this early stage of brainstorming, people must be allowed to make mistakes and to keep things light—even sometimes frivolous—if people's creativity is to be turned on and kept on.

In order to begin exploring the range of users and their environments, we played with pairs of extremes:

User dichotomies

- Interleaf-only user vs. many applications used
- English-speaking vs. non-English-speaking
- American culture vs. other cultures
- users who choose vs. users who are forced
- specialists vs. generalists
- workers vs. management
- generators vs. readers
- creative vs. production
- unconstrained vs. constrained (CALS, MILSPEC, etc.)
- transitioning (typesetters) vs. non-transitioning
- creative writers vs. technical writers
- "what if . . ."/casual notes vs. straight description
- short stories vs. million-page new drug applications
- mathemagicians vs. Real People

- CASE vs. Real People
- CAD vs. Real People
- overkill vs. underkill
- structured document vs. unstructured document
- naive vs. experienced
  - in TPS/Publisher
  - in Macintosh
  - in publishing systems in general
  - in computers
  - in typography
- large company vs. small company
- techie vs. non-techie
- on the job vs. office
- visual (sensory) vs. text (intuitive)
- individual effort vs. group effort
- simple needs vs. complex needs

At this point, we had not yet chosen whether we would support either or both "ends" of each pair. We were merely identifying what the pairs were.

The users' previous experiences can either help or hurt in learning and using a new piece of software. The group decided to do a quick exercise to explore the range of those experiences we expected.

User experience

- education
- culture
- experience
- ideas
- deadlines
- outside constraints
- knowledge of audience
- knowledge of output medium
- help systems
- documentation

- hot-line
- training materials
- trainers
- other users of the application
- other users of the data
- other Mac/PC/Interleaf users
- other users of the same application configured differently
- sales people (we didn't say it would be useful information)

We then elected to explore tasks by working backwards from the users' goals.

What are their goals in performing the task?

- go home early
- produce great-looking documents easily
- reduce drudge work
- increase productivity
- increase revenue
- meet specifications
- meet deadlines
- save time
- demystify difficult concepts
- present ideas in an orderly, aesthetically pleasing fashion
- organize material well
- explore and retrieve information from huge amounts of data easily
- control access to information
- customize our product
  - ease-of-learning
  - conform to old learning
  - add/subtract features
  - for comfort
  - to do things we never thought of

- increase (and make easier) access to most frequent powers/features
- coordinate projects
- distribute workload
- maintain currency
- track
- standardize output
- "live" revision
- group mark-ups
- keep history
- get information from anywhere and output it any way/where
- play "What if . . ."
- use information efficiently
  - share
  - manipulate
  - store
- avoid errors
- have fun

Our attention turned to externals: The users don't exist in a vacuum, and neither does the information to be processed. We began there, then looked at what information would emerge from the process.

Sources of information used to perform the task

- spreadsheets
- databases
- word processors
- graphics tools
- Interleaf intermediary

- code listings
- scanned images
- OCR'd material
- templates (for format)

What information do users generate?

- Documents
  - short
  - long
  - electronic
  - CD ROM
  - printed
  - conditional
  - text vs. graphics
  - short life cycle vs. long life cycle
- intermediate results
- meta documents (templates)
- clip art
- custom tools

- voice messages
- sounds
- audit trail
- activity log
- attached memos
- "card catalog"
- marked-up ASCII
- PostScript
- true image
- plain ASCII
- standard export formats (PICT, TIFF, and so on)

We then looked at the classes of tasks users would need to perform to accomplish their work. Some of these would be done within Interleaf, others would be done using other programs, still others would be done by human-to-human communication, but we wanted to identify and explore them all. Users' needs and problems extend beyond the walls of our applications. We must design our applications to fit within the larger context of overall systems and solutions.

What methods do they employ?

- keyboarding
- mousing
- scanning
- OCRing
- getting clerical folk to do it for them
- parenthesizing
- writing
- editing
- drawing
- composing
- reading
- layout
- copying
- importing/exporting
- learning about the system
- configuring
- learning about publishing
- learning about content
- compiling
- collaborating
- experimenting
- trial & error
- exploring
- playing
- brainstorming
- talking/listening
- outlining
- plagiarizing
- theft
- designing
- sketching
- rough drafting
- polishing
- forms-/template-filling
- reading documentation
- calling customer support
- demo-ing
- hacking
- learning/teaching

With all these ideas displayed around the wall, it was time to identify the team's goals:

What are our goals?

- To easily produce great-looking documents
  - make the program easy to use
  - make it attractive to explore
  - make it easy to figure out
  - make it educational

We also boiled down what seemed to us to be the most important user needs for us to consider during the next phase of design. You will notice that we were now being far less flamboyant. Just as it is vital that the first portion of brainstorming sessions be free, open, and creative, the last portion should be a time of weighing possibilities and probabilities.

What are some user needs?

- large company vs. small company
- designing new documentation vs. maintaining existing documentation
- generating vs. reading (shop floor)
- unilingual vs. multilingual (both translated documents and side-by-side translation)
- long documents vs. short documents
- creative writing vs. constrained writing

- textual information vs. graphic information
- "active" documents vs. "traditional" documents
- content sensitive (reference manual) vs. layout sensitive (magazine)
- individual effort vs. group effort
- full cycle (everything in Interleaf) vs. production only (outside sources compiled in Interleaf)
- techie vs. non-techie

We were finished brainstorming. We now had a shared, internalized understanding of the user space. We also had a far greater understanding of each other, and what had been a group of individuals was quickly becoming an effective team. We were ready to move on to building scenarios, the final step before launching into the actual design of the product.

Scenarios ➤ **GUIDELINE** *Use scenarios to define and develop a sense of the user space.*

Several years ago, the Air Force carried out a little test to find out how many cadets could fit into what were statistically the average-size clothes. They assembled 680 cadets in a courtyard and slowly called off the average sizes—plus or minus one standard deviation—of various items, such as shoes, pants, and shirts. Any cadet that was not in the average range for a given item was asked to leave the courtyard. By the time they finished with the fifth item, there were only two cadets left; by the sixth, all but one had been eliminated. (Blake, 1985)

Design with only a single user in mind, and you will find that only a single user can use your program. Scenarios force us to consider a wide range of users, in a wide variety of circumstances. Scenarios are little "plays" that take place in various parts of the user space we explored during brainstorming. In choosing scenarios, concentrate on the middle areas of the user space, but don't forget the outside regions, either.

Let's take a look at the scenarios we came up with for Interleaf 5. Scenarios should be as specific as possible, identifying by name real people and real companies that the team have in mind as prototypical users. That's exactly what we did at Interleaf. However, I have disguised some of these companies and characters, since my aim here is to reveal the secrets of scenario-building, not the secrets of Interleaf.

Drawing from the material on the wall charts, we identified the following possible scenarios.

Possible scenarios

- new drug application
- U.S. railroad maintenance cycle
- Giant Accountants, Inc.: consultants doing financial presentation
- legal brief (small group/individual)
- Apple Computer, Inc.: technical documentation for hardware and software application
- book from small(?) university press
- Acme Service Bureau: pulling together information written outside
- Small graphics shop (need text flow and anchored graphics) (include in Acme scenario?)
- Lawrence Livermore: research and writing, including academic levels
- Advertising agency with glitzy material
- Borem Cilly, Inc.: Publishing math textbooks
- 2nd Wave Engineering, Inc.: Engineering Product Manager compiling monthly status report
- monthly newsletter
- Tog: writing a new book with publisher's close supervision

Of this group, we picked six to convert into full-fledged scenarios.

Final scenarios

1. New Drug Application (NDA)

Multinational Pharmaceuticals needs FDA approval for the synthesis and production of a new drug: Pixie Vitamins +.

- David, NDA Manager
  - needs to pull together data from university studies, chemical analysis, and so on
  - has a staff of 10 to organize, sequence, number, write, preface, index, and track sources
  - has 48 hours to prepare the information
- Alice, one of the staff members
  - receives late breaking study (machine-readable) and must incorporate it into the NDA

2. U. S. Railroad Maintenance

An entrée was accidentally cooked to perfection on the New York to Baltimore train.

- Eric, a writer at Dining Cars International, must document (in CALS format) a temperature-randomizer unit that must be added to the oven control to lower temperature accuracy.
- Each railroad receives the appropriate pages for the safety fix:
  - Lisa, a maintenance engineer at Amtrak in New York
    - receives the new page via electronic link
    - immediately adds the randomizer
  - Jean Luc, a maintenance engineer at the French National railway in Lyon
    - receives new page via express mail
    - discards it

3. Apple Computer, Inc. Technical Documentation

Apple is releasing the long-awaited Cray emulation card. They need:

- Collaborative editing by a group of software, hardware, etc. people from different locations (Cupertino & France)
- to import CAD drawings for the Hardware Installation Guide
- a project manager (Rudman) for Document Management task assignment
- a writer (Graham)
- a review process with group members from both locations (conference calls with online, live editing)
- a final English version (written in Cupertino) is given to native translators (in France)
- side-by-side translation in the final document

4. Acme Service Bureau

A service bureau of fewer than twenty individuals needs to pull together a document. Julie does the design and layout:

- working in Interleaf, she builds text and graphics from third-party sources
  - needs extensive (and highly reliable) import/export filters
  - wants text to flow around graphics locked to page position
  - needs kerning
  - multiple text streams
  - multiple windows of the same document while editing
  - needs to view pages side-by-side online
  - color separation
  - needs to output to typesetter, PostScript, and other standard output formats

5. 2nd Wave Engineering, Inc.: Compiling Monthly Status Report

Derek, the Heat Pump Project Manager, needs to produce a monthly status report with executive summary and expanded detail. Information will be culled from spreadsheet data, table format, and a Gantt chart. He wants to

- automatically pull in the Gantt chart and spreadsheet data from remote sources (hard disk, floppy, server, CD, anything)
- use "active" documents to compile information, create a "static" version of the document, print a copy of the new document for the executives, and mail electronic copies to staff members.
- prepare the active document template using routines written by Missy, 2nd Wave's LISP guru

6. Tog

Tog is writing a new book for Addison-Wesley. Tog writes the draft using a template supplied by the publisher. He sends it to the editor, Joanne, who edits an electronic version. She

- inserts standard markup symbols
- adds text (which appears in a different type style or color)
- deletes text
- uses voice annotation to ask for clarification and to explain the rationale for the changes that were made

Tog can view the draft in its edited state, its original state, or showing deletions in strikethrough (or color) and additions in underscore (or contrasting color).

With the scenarios completed, we had become a cohesive team with a shared vision and a clear goal, and we launched directly into the product design.

The scenarios were not dwelled upon during the design process, but were always in the background, ready to be referred to when pressing an argument or forming a new idea: "Yeah, but would Alice be getting enough information, or do we need to. . . ." "Well, Rudman isn't going to like it if we. . . ." "How about if Derek can simply. . . ?"

The usefulness of these scenarios doesn't end with the production of the first design: They can help fine-tune the choice of planning sites and will act as a continuing yardstick up to which design changes and ideas can be held.

Laurie Vertelney (1989) wrote a brief exposition of scenarios for a CHI'89 Panel on Drama and Personality in User Interface Design. It can be found on page 108 of the CHI'89 Conference Proceedings. While her paper focuses on scenarios in video prototyping, the same technique can be applied to more common design methodologies. The key is to infuse the design team with vivid pictures of a series of prototypical users, so that the entire team will focus on designing for those people, instead of for themselves.

And before you start any project, read Mulligan, Altom, and Simkin's paper on *Interface Design in the Trenches* (Mulligan, et al., 1991). It could save you a lot of grief.

CHAPTER 14

User Testing on the Cheap

➥ COLUMN 13: MARCH, 1990

One of the great myths of our time is that user testing is so time-consuming, expensive, and divisive that it should be primarily discussed, rather than actually undertaken. The truth is that user testing can be really, really cheap and really, really easy to do. It can even save you money—lots of it. And you don't need one-way mirrors and video cameras and all that other stuff that only keeps you from even trying. All you need is a couple of random people, a clipboard, and a computer.

User testing strikes fear into developers' hearts around the world. The conventional wisdom seems to be that such testing is (1) positively crippling and (2) properly reserved for the next release. The mighty "Communications of the ACM" once even published a paper claiming that the "costs required to add human factors elements to the development of software" amount to $128,330. (Mantei and Teory 1988)

Fortunately for the rest of us, Mantei and Teory are wrong.[1] You *can* spend that much, if you've got the budget and the time on your hands, but the major benefits of user testing can be had for a fraction of that cost. And this is not just my opinion. No, there are genuine scientists that agree with me! Before revealing their names, however, let us examine what might happen if the auto industry shared our hesitation over user testing.

---

[1] Actually, of course, they were right within the circumstances of their study, but most of us can't afford such expensive circumstances.

Low-Cost Dream Car Hits the Road, Pedestrians, Etc.
Four Months from Concept to Reality

Dateline: Detroit Auto giant Mega-Motors today introduced Mega Dream 1.0, the first of an exciting new breed of production dream cars. Whereas typical cars are first proto-typed, then tested, then redesigned, the MegaDream 1.0 went directly from the drawing board to produc-tion in under 5 months. Company spokesperson Clydesdale "Clyde" Snively credited the elimination of iterative design and testing with both the short time to market and a cost reduction in the $40,000 car of almost $300. "Consumers have always admired auto show concept cars. Now they have a chance to actually own one and save some cash to boot!"

We test-drove the new Mega-Dream and found the car just as exciting as all its Hollywood hype. With its smooth lines and distinctive design, heads are turned wherever you go. In fact, at least one head has to be turned: the driver's. The auto maker boldly attached the steering wheel to the left door, with the driver seated facing said door, "to make driving in reverse just as safe and comfortable as driving forward." (Company steering consultant Edward Harrow suggested they may change this side-saddle arrangement in the second release.)

The lack of user testing led to many of those endless and expensive meetings where groups of engineers close to the project sit around arguing over what naïve drivers will actually do, in the face of no evidence whatsoever. Arguments over the layout of the cockpit area were finally laid to rest by enabling the driver to decide his or her own configuration. Gas, brake, windshield wiper, and other functions are all easily switched around by a driver-preference function of the horn: one beep for brake on the left, two beeps for brake on the right, and so on.

This horn configuration system has so far caused eight fatalities this first week, as drivers in heavy traffic beep their horns to prevent collision, only to find the brake pedal they're stepping on has suddenly become the accelerator. An engineer close to the project admitted they had failed to consider that possibility but said they were planning an interim release that would instead tie the configuration to the current radio station. (No tests of this second design attempt are planned either: "Drivers have no business changing radio stations in heavy traffic, so they shouldn't have any more problems.")

We were impressed with the power of the new car, although the manual spark advance and choke, needed for every gear shift, were a bit daunting. Engineers pointed out, however, that bringing back driver-control over such features increased engine performance and versatility, and none of the engineers were hav-ing any problems adjusting them. (Spokesperson Snively admitted that making automatic spark advance a preference item is under considera-tion for version 2.0, "for the non-power-drivers.")

All in all, we found the Mega-Dream 1.0 to be a wonderful car, if a bit quirky. Even though it may have its critics, we feel the savings of $300 more than justifies the lack of testing. And for those few drivers who are unhappy with this first release, MegaDream 2.0 will be offered to surviving registered owners for only $36,000, with proof of purchase.

Pretty silly, huh? Meetings where engineers try to guess at how people will react, instead of finding out? Taking major chances at fundamental redesign, like reorienting the driver, with no testing? Assuming that if an engineer can do it, so can the average person?

Guess what, folks? We do it all the time at Apple, and I'm betting you do it too. It always shows, too, but, fortunately, we don't have to do it anymore. At last, we can all test consistently.

Jakob Nielsen of the Technical University of Denmark has recently published a paper entitled "Usability Engineering at a Discount" (Nielsen 1989). In it he refutes the findings of Mantei and Teory and offers a number of useful devices for reducing the cost of user testing to a quite practical level. Since his findings completely confirm the correctness of my own unbiased opinions, I recommend the paper highly.

The common perception of quality user testing is that it involves one-way mirrors, video cameras, and psychology drones in white lab coats, armed with clipboards. Nielsen's research found that usability testing can be done for about 50% of the regular price by eliminating all these elements.

My own experience (Tognazzini, 1986) has been that the chief need for video tape is to produce a propaganda piece that forces recalcitrant engineers to admit their grievous errors. This kind of testing is already expensive, because it implies an on-going war between the testers and the engineers, a war nobody wins, least of all the users.

➤ **GUIDELINE** *Inexpensive testing should be done by members of the design team as part of a cooperative effort to produce the best software possible.*

Testing Scenarios and Prototypes

Nielsen recommends developing testing scenarios: Create typical situations that users may face, then build prototypes that will enable exploration of those situations. Two types of prototypes can be built: horizontal and vertical.

➤ **GUIDELINE** *Horizontal prototypes display most or all of the full range of the application—menus, windows, dialogs—without going in depth on any one part. Use to test the overall design concepts.*

➤ **GUIDELINE** *In areas reflecting new design concepts and technology, build vertical prototypes that carry the user deep into the behaviors of specific parts of the system.*

This enables you to build and test those parts of the system that have potential problems, without having to build a working model of Standard File or some other area that is (relatively) immutable or previously proven.

> ➤ **GUIDELINE** *Prototypes can and should be created in a matter of days, not weeks or months.*

Prototypes should be built using rapid, inexpensive tools. Nielsen, saint that he is, recommends HyperCard. Some prefer SuperCard, because of its rich supply of standard Macintosh objects; others will prefer Prototyper or other tools of its class. The important thing is that you use a prototyping tool for design.

Test Subjects

Having built the prototypes, it's time to get the test subjects. Now, let's see . . . This is an accounting package, so in order to test whether people can use that new dialog box we will need to try it on Average Accountants. The most average Average American lives in Cincinnati, so we'll fly there and have a marketing research firm arrange a panel of sixty Average Accountants and the video equipment. . . .

Hold it! We are looking for interface problems, not accounting problems. While you want your application and prototypes to be reviewed by one or more accountants, they should be content experts on your team, not random folks in a far-off city. You will also get all the accountancy feedback you can stand during beta testing.

What we want to find, particularly in the early stages, are problems that anyone other than a member of the design team is going to stumble over. The only narrowing of the field I would suggest early-on is deciding whether you want people who are Macintosh-literate, not Macintosh-literate, or people from both groups. Neilsen has found that you need no more than three people per design iteration. My experience bears this out. Any more and you are just confirming problems already found. Better to spend the time iterating the next design.

We have historically used new Apple employees as our subjects. They tend to be a good mix of new and experienced computer users. Colleges are another good source. I have also used many people at computer stores. Stores will often cooperate in allowing you some space for a few hours during a slow time of the week. The test subjects will show up spontaneously, in search of a new computer or this week's hot software. As they come through the door, grab them.

Ten Steps for Conducting a User Observation

> ➤ **GUIDELINE** *"User observation through thinking out loud" results in our being able to "see inside" our user's conscious minds, to understand what errors in process are taking place.*

So far, things are looking pretty cheap and do-able here: We have created prototypes in a couple of days, and we've gotten one new secretary, one management type, and the guy who drives the sandwich truck to stop by for some testing. It's time to fire up the prototypes and do some testing. To explain how, I will turn you over to Kate Gomoll and Anne Nicol, Apple's resident "Thinking Out Loud" Gurus.

User Observation Through Thinking Out Loud[2]   The following instructions guide you through a simple user observation. Remember, this test is not designed as an experiment, so you will not get statistical results. You will, however, see where people have difficulty using your product, and you will be able to use that information to improve it.

These instructions are organized in steps. Under most of the steps, you will find some explanatory text and a bulleted list. The bulleted list contains sample statements that you can read to the participant. (Feel free to modify the statements to suit your product and the situation.)

1. **Introduce yourself.**

2. **Describe the purpose of the observation (in general terms).**

   Set the participant at ease by stressing that you're trying to find problems in the product. For example, you could say:

   - You're helping us by trying out this product in its early stages.
   - We're looking for places where the product may be difficult to use.
   - If you have trouble with some of the tasks, it's the product's fault, not yours. Don't feel bad; that's exactly what we're looking for.
   - If we can locate the trouble spots, then we can go back and improve the product.
   - Remember, it's the product we're testing, not you.

3. **Tell the participant that it's OK to quit at any time.**

   Never leave this step out. Make sure you inform participants that they can quit at any time if they find themselves becoming uncomfortable. This is not only an ethical testing procedure, it is required by law. Participants shouldn't feel like they're locked into completing tasks. Say something like this:

   - Although I don't know of any reason for this to happen, if you should become uncomfortable or find this test objectionable in any way, you are free to quit at any time.

---

[2] K. Gomoll, A. Nicol, "User Observation: Guidelines for Apple Developers," Apple Human Interface Update #11, 1988.

4. Talk about the equipment in the room.

Explain the purpose of each piece of equipment (hardware, software, and so on) and how it will be used in the test.

5. Explain how to "think aloud."

Ask participants to think aloud during the observation, saying what comes to mind as they work. By listening to participants think and plan, you'll be able to examine their expectations for your product, as well as their intentions and their problem-solving strategies. You'll find that listening to users as they work provides you with an enormous amount of useful information that you can get in no other way.

Unfortunately, most people feel awkward or self-conscious about thinking aloud. Explain why you want participants to think aloud, and demonstrate how to do it. For example, you could say:

- We have found that we get a great deal of information from these informal tests if we ask people to think aloud as they work through the exercises.

- It may be a bit awkward at first, but it's really very easy once you get used to it.

- All you have to do is speak your thoughts as you work.

- If you forget to think aloud, I'll remind you to keep talking.

- Would you like me to demonstrate?

6. Explain that you will not provide help.

It is very important that you allow participants to work with your product without any interference or extra help. This is the best way to see how people really interact with the product. For example, if you see a participant begin to have difficulty and you immediately provide an answer, you will lose the most valuable information you can gain from user observation—where users have trouble, and how they figure out what to do.

Of course, there may be situations where you will have to step in and provide assistance, but you should decide what those situations will be before you begin testing. For example, you may decide that you will allow someone to flounder for at least three minutes before you provide assistance. Or you may decide that there is a distinct set of problems you will provide help on.

As a rule of thumb, try not to give your test participants any more information than the true users of your product will have. Here are some things you can say to the participant:

- As you're working through the exercises, I won't be able to provide help or answer questions. This is because we want to create the most realistic situation possible.

- Even though I won't be able to answer your questions, please ask them anyway. It's very important that I hear all your questions and comments.

- When you've finished all the exercises, I'll answer any questions you still have.

7. **Describe the tasks and introduce the product.**

Explain what the participant should do first, second, third. . . . Give the participant written instructions for the tasks.

Important: If you need to demonstrate your prototypes before the user observation begins, be sure you don't demonstrate something you're trying to test. (For example, if you want to know whether users can figure out how to use certain tools, don't show them how to use the tools before the test.)

8. **Ask if there are any questions before you start; then begin the observation.**

9. **Conclude the observation.**

When the test is over:

- Explain what you were trying to find out during the test
- Answer any remaining questions the participant may have
- Discuss any interesting behaviors you would like the participant to explain.

10. **Use the results.**

As you observe, you will see users doing things you never expected them to do. When you see participants making mistakes, your first instinct may be to blame the mistakes on the participant's inexperience or lack of intelligence. This is the wrong focus to take. The purpose of observing users is to see what parts of your product might be difficult or ineffective. Therefore, if you see a participant struggling or making mistakes, you should attribute the difficulties to faulty software design, *not* to the participant.

Review all your notes carefully and thoroughly. Look for places where participants had trouble, and see if you can determine how your product could be changed to alleviate the problems. Look for patterns in the participants' behavior that might tell you whether the product is understood correctly.

It's a good idea to keep a record of what you found out during the test. That way, you'll have documentation to support your design decisions and you'll be able to see trends in users' behavior. After you've examined the results, fix the problems you found and test the product again. By testing your product more than once, you'll see how your changes affect users' performance.

Thank you, Anne and Kate.

The only thing left to do is to modify problem areas and retest—iteration. Most problems will disappear by the second or third iteration.

This all seems trivially easy, doesn't it. Guess what? It is. This is how Larry Tesler, vice president of Advanced Products at Apple, carried out the extensive testing that resulted in the Lisa computer:

> I've been personally involved in cheap user testing for about 28 years, including my tests for the Lisa. The equipment was me, a Lisa, two chairs, a note pad, and a pen. The subjects were right out of employee orientation. The tests ran one hour. I ran 3 to 5 subjects on each version of each application. I spent another few hours analyzing the notes and writing the report. Cheap. Effective.

How Testing Saves Time

Even when good horizontal and vertical prototyping and testing has been performed, you still need to test the whole application as it comes together in late alpha or early beta, due to Tognazzini's paradox:

➤ **GUIDELINE**   *Areas of an application where problems are expected have none, while areas known to be perfect are fatally flawed.*

Even though such late human interface testing sends chills up the programmer's spines, it does pay off in eventual time savings.

I experienced my most pathological example of Tognazzini's paradox while Dave Eisenberg[3] and I were working on "Apple Presents . . . Apple" back in 1979, the first time an in-box tutorial had been written for a micro. We had earmarked certain sections of the program as being hopelessly difficult, while others were hardly worth testing. Test subjects found most of the "hopelessly difficult" sections perfectly easy, while the one area we knew would have no problems at all proved fantastically difficult:

Problem:	In "Apple Presents . . . Apple, An Introduction to the Apple II Plus Computer," find out if the user is working with a color monitor.
User profiles:	New owner, customer in a computer store, or member of a class learning to use Apple computers.
Test user profiles:	Customers in a computer store, non-computerists in a classroom environment, friends, and relatives.
First design:	A color graphic would be displayed.
PROMPT:	"Are you using a color TV on the Apple?"
ANTICIPATED PROBLEM:	Those who were using a monochrome monitor in a classroom or computer store situation wouldn't know whether the monitor was black and white or was color with the color turned off. We reiterated the design.
Second iteration:	A color graphic was displayed.
PROMPT:	"Is the picture above in color?"
FAILURE RATE:	25%
REASON:	As anticipated, but incorrectly overcome, those seeing black and white thought their color might be turned down. They didn't answer the question wrong; they turned around and asked one of the authors whether the monitor in question was color or not. A decision was made that the authors could not be shipped with each disk.

---

[3] For those of you stretching back that far in time, Dave referred to himself in that era as "JDEisenberg." The lack of spaces between his initials led a great many users to conclude there was a problem with their computers. This amused Dave no end.

**Third
iteration:**   A smaller graphic with color names, each in its own
vivid color was substituted:
GREEN BLUE ORANGE MAGENTA

PROMPT: Are the words above in color?"

FAILURE RATE: color TV users: none
black and white monitor users: none
green-screen monitor users: 100%

REASON: Yes, well, you see, we hadn't exactly thought about
monochrome monitors with nice, bright green text.
After all, who could have predicted that users might
actually think green was a color? Silly twits! Actually,
we were extremely fortunate that we accidentally got
hold of a prototype green-screen monitor that day.
Otherwise, we might have shipped the software with
a fatal design flaw.

**Fourth
iteration:**   The graphic remained the same.

PROMPT: "Are the words above in more than one color?"

FAILURE RATE: color TV users: none
black and white monitor users: 20%
green-screen monitor users: 50%

REASONS: The black and white monitor users who answered
incorrectly admitted that they did so on purpose. (Our
methods for wringing their confessions shall remain
proprietary.) 50% of the green-screen folk considered
that they were looking at both black and green—two
colors—and answered the question accordingly.

**Fifth
iteration:**   Same display of graphic and colored text

PROMPT: "Are the words above in several different colors?"

FAILURE RATE: color TV users: none
black and white monitor users: 20%
green-screen monitor users: 25%

REASONS: By this time, the authors were prepared to supply
everyone who bought an Apple II with a free color
monitor, just so we would not have to ask the
question. It turns out that around 20% of the people
were not really reading the question. They were
responding to the question "Are the words above
several different colors?"

Sixth	
iteration:	Same display of graphic and colored text
Prompt:	"Do the words above appear in several different colors?"
Failure rate:	none

This was a highly interactive tutorial typically taking twenty minutes to complete. This was the only interface issue that required more than one iteration to correct. No matter how many engineers we had crowded into a room to discuss with what areas users were or were not going to have trouble, we would have never hit upon this as the major problem in the application. Had we not tested, we would have had a disaster on our hands: Instead of users having a wonderful first experience, they would have walked away thinking both they and our computer were awfully stupid.

My experience with this and other applications and systems have proven to me beyond a shadow of a doubt that testing can *save* time, rather than cost time because I don't have to work on things that aren't broken. I can instead concentrate my design talents where they will do the most good, on the things that actually need design work. And I don't have to release version 1.01 a week after ship date because of some major human interface problem.

I again put these methods to good use in a later experiment, captured in Chapter 36, "Case Study: One-Or-More Buttons."

PART III

The Goldilocks Theories

> *Those who are enamored of practice without science are like a pilot who goes into a ship without a rudder or compass and never has any certainty where he is going. Practice should always be based upon a sound knowledge of theory.*
>
> —LEONARDO DA VINCI

> *Dear friend, theory is all grey,*
> *And the golden tree of life is green.*
>
> —GOETHE[1]

> *Ooooh! This porridge is too hot!*
>
> —GOLDILOCKS

I have come to depend on three theories before any others: Jung's theory of psychological types, Shannon's information theory, and Norman's conceptual model theory (with generous additions on my part).

I've called this section "The Goldilocks Theories" because they remind me of the story of The Three Bears:[2] Engineers often at first find Jung's theory "too soft," psychologists and graphic designers find Shannon's theory "too hard[3]," and almost everyone finds conceptual model theory "just right." (Paradoxically, of course, engineers most need

---

[1] Faust, Part one

[2] For those not well-versed in English folk story tradition, "The Three Bears" is the story of a young juvenile delinquent who breaks into a neighbor's house, vandalizes it, and manages to kill herself while trying to escape. Good parents read it to their children, instead of letting them watch all that violence on television.

[3] "Hard" in this instance, refers to the solidity of the theory, not the difficulty of understanding it.

to read Jung's theory, and psychologists and graphic designers need to read Shannon's.)

Taken together, these theories form a framework for a deep and abiding understanding of human interface design. They have served me well for many years; I hope they will serve you too.

CHAPTER 15

Carl Jung and the Macintosh

➥ *COLUMN 9: OCTOBER, 1989*

This column begins an in-depth look at three theories that shed light on the most fundamental underpinnings of the Macintosh interface. My purpose is to offer succor, hope, and guidance for all who must embark on the frightening if necessary task of moving beyond (gasp) the current Macintosh Human Interface Guidelines.

Extending the Macintosh interface is not a simple matter of throwing together some stuff that looks really neat and shipping it. Extensions must be formed according to the same principles and the same visual and behavioral language from which arose the original interface. Without steeping yourself in the theoretical underpinnings of the system, achieving a Macintosh look and feel is a challenge indeed. Therefore, beginning this month, I shall slip each and every one of you into your own polyvinyl tea bag and dip you deep into the wonderful illusion that is Macintosh.

Carl Jung is known for both the founding of analytical psychology and for being the first person to publicly tell Sigmund Freud that he was a jerk. (Freud's wife had informed him he was a jerk in a private ceremony some months earlier.) Jung felt a deep-seated compulsion, arising undoubtedly from early childhood trauma, to begin dividing people into two kinds of people.[1] By the time he was finished, he had stumbled upon a most wonderful theory, and in this column, I shall share with you a bit of what he found.

---

[1] He was not actually carving them up like planaria, you understand: this was more in the nature of psychic surgery. And, I have it on good authority, absolutely no one was hurt.

Jung broke with Freud over Freud's belief that virtually all motivations were sexual in origin, believing instead that people carried internal tensions between opposing sets of ideas and beliefs. (How boring.) By the beginning of the 1920s, he had developed his theory of psychological types (Jung 1921). He defined four pairs of types that, taken together, enable you to assign people to one of sixteen different camps. The pairs are shown in Figure 15–1.

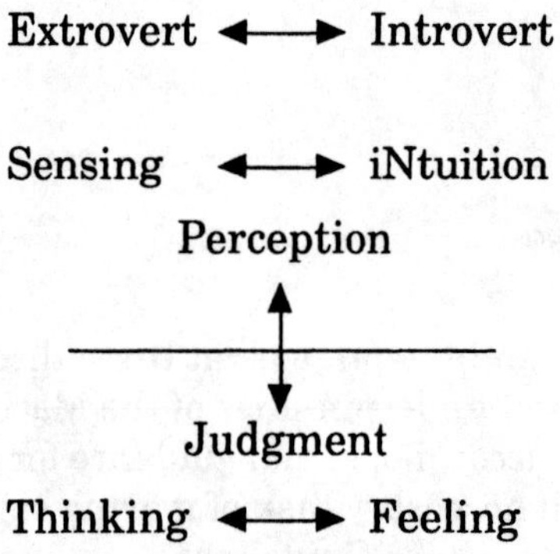

Extrovert ⟷ Introvert

Sensing ⟷ iNtuition

Perception
↑
——————————
↓
Judgment

Thinking ⟷ Feeling

Figure 15–1. *Jungian Types*

For example, a person might be an Extrovert-Sensing-Feeling-Judging type, or, quite the opposite, be an Introvert-iNtuitive-Thinking-Perceptive type. These types are generally reduced by researchers to just the capitalized initials, such as ESFJ. Because both introvert and intuition begin with the letter I, researchers decided to use N for iNtuition. Hence the second example above would reduce to INTP, rather than IITP (Settling on a scheme that uses the second letter of a word as an abbreviation is an error in judgment no modern software designer would ever make.)

During the fifties, Isabel Myers-Briggs built upon Jung's work, creating the modern Myers-Briggs personality typing system. By taking a simple test, people can measure their preferred methods of communicating, forming perceptions, and making judgments.

There is no implied value judgment to either end of a category. The system is designed so people can better understand themselves and their relationships with others, not to announce whether they are good or bad people. The results of the test can be eye-opening: The foundering salesman discovers he is an introvert and really doesn't enjoy meeting twenty new people every day. The intuitive suddenly discovers why she has always been totally unaware of her surroundings, being intensely involved with pictures and thoughts within her mind. All of a sudden there is a reason, an answer, and because the results carry no bias and no value judgment, people end up feeling good about themselves.

You can find out your own Jungian type a few different ways: Many companies have a career development person who is qualified to administer the Myers-Briggs Type Indicator Test (and will do so at no charge). If you do not have access to such a service, pick up a copy of *Type Talk* (Kroeger, et al. 1988). You will find an informal guide to discovering your own Jungian type, along with a great deal of information about how people of differing types interact in the family, in friendships, in school, and business. They will also help you find someone in your area authorized to administer the full Meyers-Briggs Type Indicator test. Another approach is to get a copy of Kiersey's book, *Please Understand Me* (Keirsey, et al. 1984). While the title may sound a bit wimpy, the book itself is fun to read, informative, and comes complete with the Keirsey Temperament Sorter, a self-administered Jungian test.

At the completion of the test, you are rather too easily dropped into one of the sixteen basic personality types. This is a sobering experience, particularly if part of your psychological make-up is a deep need to feel special. However, we designers must make sacrifices for our craft, and this test is an excellent way to understand your own relationship to others for whom you are designing: If you test as being way out on one end of a particular category vector, you need to be particularly sensitive to the needs of users who might test equally strongly on the other end. But until you take the test and understand your special position, you may very well not even be aware you are so far from center.[2]

Jung believed that we select our positions within the four categories early in life. We then spend the rest of our childhood fortifying those early decisions by developing the skills appropriate to the choices and by building a powerful belief system that our choices were correct. Often, part of this process of what is called "overcoming cognitive dissonance" is forming a belief that not only was our decision correct for ourselves, but it is the only correct choice for any right-thinking person. If this seems intolerant, keep in mind that these decisions are made quite early in life, and consider how tolerant the average six-year-old child is.

Now that we're grown up, of course, we can choose to be a little more tolerant. It's not a matter of giving up our belief that our choices were right for us, just that they don't have to be right for everyone else. Maybe we made up a rule that we choose to live by, such as being an

---

[2] I test out to be an INFP, a category populated by only a few percent of those who have been tested. It explained a lot.

introvert and remaining politely quiet unless spoken to. That doesn't (necessarily) mean that the next glad-handing salesperson we run across is an evil person.

Giving up such intolerance may sound simple and elementary, but take the test and then look up someone at the opposite end of the Extrovert–Introvert vector or the Thinking–Feeling vector, and see how difficult it really is to dump years and years of self-imposed conditioning.

Jungian Types Among Programmers and Designers

More than two million people have been tested for their Jungian personality type using one of several standard tests. The cumulative findings of one such test, the Myers-Briggs Type Indicator, has been published in a form enabling a researcher to track personality type by age, occupation, education, etc. (Myers 1985). In addition, a study has been carried out on programmers associated with the data processing industry (Sitton and Chmelir 1984).

The ranks of data processing programmers are filled with approximately twice the western world average of introverts and twice the average of intuitives. While those figures seemed startling, the figures (shown in Figure 15–2) in an informal study I completed in February 1987 on the then-entire engineering staff of 236 people at Apple were nothing short of amazing.

	Extrovert	Introvert	Sensory	Intuitive	Introvert *and* Intuitive
Myers	75	25	75	25	14
Sitton, et al.	50	50	50	50	N/A
Apple Engineers	58	42	25	75	25
Apple Writers	61	39	8	92	22
Apple Engineers & Writers	59	41	22	78	25

Figure 15–2. *Studies Compared*

Before speculating on how this high population of introverts and intuitives may be affecting human interfaces, let us review the meaning of these two terms, along with their opposite styles.

Extroverts are natural communicators, natural designers of effective dialog. Introverts converse when necessary, preferably with close and trusted friends. Extroverts have a head start when it comes to designing human-computer interactions. That is not to say that introverts cannot also be effective designers. Quite the contrary, many of the best designers, as many of the best actors and comedians, are introverts. It's just that introverts must compensate for their natural tendency toward withdrawal. Figure 15–3 shows the disproportionate number of introverts uncovered in computer industry studies.

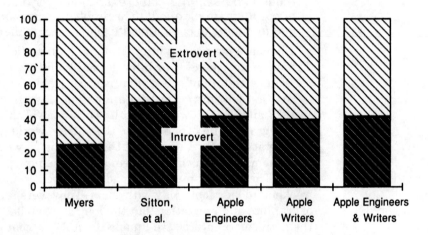

Figure 15–3. *Extroverts and Introverts*

Paul Heckel said, "The software designer must learn to think like a communicator," and wrote an entire book on how to do so (Heckel 1991). Communication is a skill that comes easily to the extrovert—sometimes too easily for any introverts in earshot. And yet it is a vitally necessary skill in the design of the human interface. If the designer cannot effectively communicate with people, it is certain that the program will not either.

This does not mean that if you are quiet you cannot remain so. There are very effective ways of communicating that do not require your donning a lamp shade and stepping out on a stage in front of 500 people.[3] There are many introverted people who successfully communicate through delayed-communication forms such as writing and drawing. Many others find an outlet in acting, where they can safely stand in the shadows behind their character. Software is one of the very safest ways to communicate as, by the time your audience begins to interact with it, you can be safely out of town.

➤ **GUIDELINE**   *While you are designing a program, continually remind yourself that you are designing for an audience. Think about them, think about their problems, and concentrate on how you are going to communicate your ideas to them.*

If you are not used to interacting with an audience, assemble one: Try out prototypes of your interface early and often with small groups of colleagues and friends. See what is working and what is not.

My first few microcomputer animations I wrote at home, alone, back in 1977 and 1978. (I was the Emily Dickinson of the micro world.) When the programs found their way to the outside world, people enjoyed looking at them for a while, but there was no way they could interact with them. They quickly set them aside. The next group of applications I wrote, The Shell Games, I dragged into my computer store every weekend to let people play with them. They were far simpler in terms of graphics and animation, but the longer I watched people play with them, the more interactive I made them. My elaborate animations were forgotten in months, but The Shell Games sold briskly for almost ten years.

After this experience, I learned to picture my audience in my head. I still subject my designs to potential end users as early as possible, but my first designs work much better, because I'm always imagining how they will work when people are actually using them.

Some programmers find out they are not cut out for designing interactivity. If you fall in this group, take heart: You are probably an awesome coder. Find yourself a communicator you can work with to slap you on the back and "get a little juice into the program." I have known excellent designers who were salespeople, executives, even amateur magicians. Marketers are particularly useful for this, if you can make them calm down. Search your organization for someone who seems to know how to communicate with people—including you—and also has a

---

[3] I am saying this only in theory: I've found I compensate best for my significant introversion by donning a lamp shade and stepping out on a stage in front of 500 people.

fair working knowledge of computers. Some of the top-selling programs on the market have resulted from partnerships between highly skilled, introverted programmers and competent communicators.

And as for you extroverts out there: Some of us do not appreciate bells ringing every time we make the simplest mistake. To us, it might as well be a public address system announcing, "Hey, everybody, Charlie just screwed up again!" We'd just as soon keep it quiet.

Sensories versus Intuitives

People choose to perceive primarily either with their immediate senses (sensory) or through mental imagery (intuition). Sensory people have a superior ability to instantly "size-up the situation." They are practical above all else and are highly observant. Sherlock Holmes was a prototypical observer, seeing what all others missed. Sensory people are firmly rooted in the here-and-now: If it cannot be seen, touched, felt, or measured, it simply does not exist. When Sensories drive to work, they are aware of the birds, the trees, the hills turning green. They notice a cow lowing in the field. Sensories are attracted to fields such as accounting, high-level management, and burger-flipping.

Intuitives live in their own private universe, depending on an internal model of external events. They are often unaware of or unswayed by the visual, aural, tactile world through which they move. Intuitives screen the real world into the theater of their own minds, adding extra color and detail where they see fit, creating a reality that is a mysterious blend of the here-and-now and the then-and-maybe-never. Theirs is a world of metaphor and images, run on its own time clock, powered as much by internally generated ideas and stored memories as external, immediate data. Intuitives are the absent-minded professors, the dreamers, explorers of internal worlds, the great discoverers, theoreticians, inventors. When Intuitives drive to work, they watch the tectonic plates, deep in the earth's crust, rubbing together. They run into the cow.

Intuitives are superb pattern-recognizers and highly imaginative. They make excellent clinical psychologists and thieves. They also apparently make excellent computer writers and engineers, as shown in Figure 15–4.

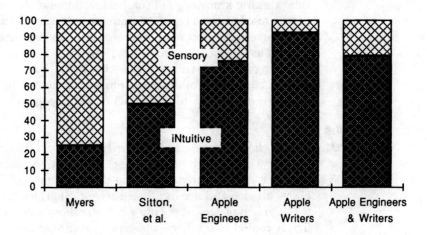

Figure 15–4. *Sensories and iNtuitives*

While the skew of programmers toward either introversion or intuition should produce some sort of measurable effect on human interfaces, the combination can be expected to have a profound influence.

Jung had this to say about people whose temperament is ruled by introversion and intuition:

> ...introverted intuition perceives all the background processes of consciousness with almost the same distinctness as it registers external objects. For intuition, therefore, unconscious images acquire the dignity of things. (Jung, 1921)

The introvert/intuitive types are remarkably adept at creating an internal reality that flows with and ceases to be distinguishable from the external reality around them. (I have some personal experience with this phenomenon, since I am an introvert/intuitive. I am told by my extrovert/sensing friends that these traits are very weird.)

Introvert/intuitive types

- are separated from external reality

- prefer to generate and depend on their own model of the external world

- can abstract and rapidly shift between concrete reality and abstraction

- tie past and immediate experiences together to form a whole

What kind of interfaces can the introvert/intuitives expect to do well with themselves? They are not dependent on a lot of immediate, real-world data. They should do well with human/computer interfaces that are very sketchy, expecting the user to maintain their own "reality," their own maps and models of the internal structure of the program.

The extrovert/sensation types are the exact opposite of the introvert/intuitives. Jung said of the extrovert/sensation types:

> No other human type can equal the extroverted sensation type in realism. His sense for objective facts is extraordinarily developed. His life is an accumulation of actual experiences of concrete objects, and the more pronounced his type, the less use does he make of his experience. In certain cases, the events of his life hardly deserve the name "experience" at all. What he experiences serves at most as a guide to fresh sensations. . . . (Jung 1921)

One can distill from this that the extroverted/sensation types

- are tied to the reality of immediate, external sensation
- strongly prefer concrete objects over symbolic abstractions
- are less willing to tie together objects or experiences that are temporarily distant

What kind of human interfaces can we infer would suit the temperament of the extroverted/sensation types? Interfaces that appear "real," that do not depend on the memorization of invisible behaviors, that appeal to the real-world sensations of sight, sound, kinesthesia, and so on.

Conversely, extroverted/sensation types can be expected to do poorly with interfaces that depend on the user to generate their own maps and models of the internal structure of the program.

Thinkers versus Feelers

"Thinkers" spend most of their time in their head, applying sound, logical judgment to the events of life. "Feelers" depend more on ethics than logic in forming such judgments. According to Myers, et al., approximately 60% of men tested depend primarily on logical conclusions, while 60% of women tested depend primarily on ethical considerations. These results explain a lot of insoluble domestic arguments.

The thinking/feeling scale may keep us from liking each other sometimes. However, I have seen no studies showing it to be an important factor in human interface design.

Perception versus Judgment

Perceptives spend more time and emphasis on gathering information than they do forming judgments. Judging people like to get to the point. Psychologists are often perceptives, digging, digging, digging, while offering few concrete opinions. Business executives tend toward the other end of the spectrum, gathering as much information as possible, then making a judgment, right or wrong. As in thinking versus feeling, I have seen no evidence that an inclination toward either perception or judgment, unless it is extreme, affects the design of computer software.

The Computer for the Rest of Them

The Apple desktop is very clearly a sensory interface: It is a visual, direct-manipulation interface in the form of a complete, stable, and consistent virtual reality. The miracle of its birth is that it was created by a long line of Intuitives, people just as happy with the "black cave" metaphor, where users are expected to formulate their own maps of the interface in the back of their minds.

Radio shows, "the theater of the imagination," were an Intuitive's paradise; they were swept away by the advent of television. The original text-based game of Adventure was swept away by the subsequent graphics-based games that let the Sensories see what was going on. The Sensory users, making up 80% of the population, want to see, feel, and understand what's happening. With the Macintosh, they are not expected to endure the torture of forming their own mental navigational models, a task that many of you readers do with painless ease.

➤ **GUIDELINE** *Understanding your own preferences, talents, and abilities is key to understanding your users'.*

If you have never taken a test to find out your Jungian type, I urge you to do so. And if you, like so many of us, are endowed with the desire to intuit, be aware that most of your users are not. Turn on the lights and let them see.

Improving Your Own Intuition

"To understand intuition, it seems necessary to avoid the belief that in order to know something the individual must be able to put into words what he knows and how he knows it. This belief, still common since Freud, is the result of what appears to be an overdevelopment of reality testing, which tempts some who are interested in psychology to think too far away from nature, and the world of natural happenings." (Berne 1949)

➤ **GUIDELINE** *Intuition is crucial to the task of software design. When we are creating the shape of our software design, we need to think in terms of big concepts, and we need to weave our design into a single fabric users can understand and feel comfortable with.*

Intuition is also a valuable tool in testing. Aristotle first wrote about the value of what he called "intuitive induction," what I would term "intuitive observation." Before the advent of the "thinking out loud" protocol for user testing (see Chapter 14, "User Testing on the Cheap"), I used to do all my testing through intuitive observation alone. Now, I combine the two methods. But before getting into a discussion of intuitive observation, let's talk more about intuition itself.

In the Western world, we have taken great pains to avoid the subject of intuition in our schools. The left hemisphere, a primary site of logic and consciousness, works with what psychologist Marcel Kinsbourne calls exclusionary sequences: You consider a group of possibilities, exclude all but one, then consider the resultant group of possibilities, exclude all but one, and so on (Campbell 1982). Intuition doesn't work with sequences, it works with patterns. It doesn't exclude, it includes, constantly shifting patterns to incorporate new information. It lies outside the human-as-a-computer model of one logical conclusion leading to another, to another.

That this would be distressing to programmers seems obvious. Programmers undergo a very subtle change in their thought processes as they learn to program—they become compulsive "branchers." You can usually find them wasting time at the head of the line at the airport asking such branching questions as, "But if the plane cannot land in Denver because of the weather, and it is re-routed to Utah, rather than Arizona, as you suggest, what would the effect be if...."

Western education is heavily biased toward intellect over intuition: Intuition is endowed with a perverse habit of delivering results most slowly when the need for speed is greatest. (You can learn to have some control over the speed of the results, as described in the following section.) Telling a bunch of kids to "think about it for a couple hours, a day, a week—whatever it takes—then get back to me" just doesn't fit into our lock-step educational process. Betty Edwards (1989): "The right brain—the dreamer, the artificer, the artist—is lost in our school system and goes largely untaught. We might find a few art classes, a few shop classes, something called 'creative writing,' and perhaps courses in music; but it's unlikely that we would find courses in imagination, in visualization, in perceptual or spatial skills, in creativity as a separate subject, in intuition, in inventiveness." (See Chapter 37, "A Glimpse of the Future." Some schools now do teach such "subjects.")

Even though many of the great inventions of the world arose out of intuitive illuminations, we are careful to teach them as though they were the result of plodding, logical experimentation. Somehow the proof that a brilliant intuition was correct is more important than letting children glimpse the creative act itself. How wonderful it would be if we would use computers to simulate the knowledge and conditions that let

Newton intuit the law of gravity, so every child could make the same discovery. Let children discover the inclined plane by having them try to lift a heavy object in the playground, rather than impressing the knowledge upon them in the classroom through abstract mathematical symbols. There is time to present the proof and the logical connections later. Perhaps we might even praise the child who, on his or her own, rediscovered one of the major advances of civilization, instead of saying, "That's stupid! Everyone knows that!" Do you remember someone doing that to you? Do you remember doing it to someone else?

With the empirical evidence of Western society's bias against left-handedness and intuition, with the clinical evidence of the struggle for dominance between the two lobes of the brain, one begins to understand why we know so little about such a profoundly powerful skill as intuition—our logical, verbal, conscious mind doesn't want us to know.

Defining Intuition

So what is intuition, what is it good for, and how do we use it? Eric Berne (1955) defined intuition as "a spontaneous diagnostic process whose end products spontaneously come into awareness if resistances are lifted." Intuition does not lend itself to intellectual analysis: we have to approach an understanding through metaphor, example, and shared experience.

Intuition operates in leaps. It churns away with no conscious thought and little conscious control and then suddenly springs forth with what is often described as an "Aha!" experience. An example of this takes place when you learn a new board game: You keep hearing and attempting to memorize the rules of the game and suggested strategies, but it is all very compartmentalized. You see no patterns. Every rule is a separate entity, and you must try to memorize each one before it slips away. Often, you are offered rules that seem meaningless at the time, further reducing your motivation to try and remember them at all.

Remember when you learned Monopoly?[4] You learned to roll the dice and move forward. You learned that picking a Chance card could land you in Jail. You learned that you paid $50 to get out of Jail, but you could hang around if you wanted, except they told you you didn't want to. You learned that if you landed on property, you should buy it. You learned that you should find out whether someone already owned the property before saying you wanted to buy it, because if a landlord noticed you were parked there, you must pay $8 or $10 for the privilege.

---

[4] Monopoly is an American game that lets the players gain a vast fortune in real estate in a matter of a couple of hours. Unfortunately, the vast fortune cannot be cashed in at your local bank, the currency involved being of somewhat dubious origin. Nonetheless, the game was a smashing success during the years of the Great Depression and continues to sell well today.

Finally, you built yourself a nice little split-level ranch house over on Mediterranean Avenue, all the time wondering whether you should spend so much money. A few moves later, you landed on "Go To Jail" and ended up in the hoosegow. You started gathering together your $50 so you could post bail, and you were preparing to hand it over to the banker when you happened to glance out the window of the jail house: As far as your eyes could see were beachfront condominiums—huge red buildings with grinning owners.

In the blinking of an eye, everything was suddenly all too clear: You knew that you had no desire to get out of jail. You suddenly understood that strange rule that requires that you to leave jail after three rounds whether you want to or not. In fact you understood, permanently and completely, the entire underlying strategy and purpose of the game. An illumination. An intuitive leap.

Those of you who are programmers have undoubtedly experienced working until 2:00 in the morning on a seemingly insoluble bug, only to finally give up and go home to sleep. Then, at 6:30 A.M., you woke up knowing exactly what was wrong and kicking yourself for not realizing it earlier—after all, it was perfectly obvious. Another intuitive leap.

Applying Your Own Intuition

As a designer, you need to recognize the needs of people who will use intuition in their attempt to understand your program. Such people are not using the visual elements you may have so carefully provided. Instead, they are depending on elaborate mental models they have intuited from both the underlying behavior of your program and what they perceive as similarities to other programs and events in their lives.

Cicero said, "The skill to do comes from doing." To understand how other people drive a car, first learn how to drive a car yourself. To understand how intuitive people think, first learn to think intuitively yourself. How do you learn think intuitively? To some extent you are already thinking intuitively. You have the power, however, to increase the effectiveness of your intuition and to gain a better understanding of the process. This will, at the very least, give you new insight into the needs of your users who depend on intuition.

The three steps to practical intuition that follow have been understood for thousands of years. From ancient Chinese Taoist priests to nineteenth century philosophers to the most modern psychologists, the message and the methods remain remarkably consistent. Only the vocabulary and emphasis shift. The three steps are presented here, verbally, to the conscious mind, with information as to what the conscious mind can do to improve the frequency and accuracy of the intuitive process. At the end of the chapter, you will find a set of quizzes designed to exercise the intuitive mind and let you actually experience this intuitive process.

Whether you choose to use this remarkable ability is up to you: In 1962, Eric Berne wrote in the *Psychiatric Quarterly* (Berne, 1962), "Engineers and psychologists are among the most highly educated individuals in modern society and at the same time have, generally speaking, the greatest resistance against intuitive cognition." Certainly, many of the readers of this book fall into this category. Berne found that those psychologists who made the error of telling their colleagues that they depended on such a sloppy ability as intuition in their clinical practice often received a lot of abuse. And yet, he found clinicians who didn't use intuition to be ineffective in the treatment of patients.

Foot binding was very popular in China until the beginning of this century. The fact that a woman was unable to totter across the room without falling on her face was clear evidence that her wealth was such that she didn't have to cross a room under her own power. Several years ago, Dave Eisenberg and I were in Canada, testing in a computer store a new French-Canadian version of "Apple Presents . . . Apple (see Chapter 14, "User Testing on the Cheap"). A well-dressed executive entered the store, and we invited him to try the program. He announced that he couldn't use computers, because, as he boasted, he didn't know how to type. Twentieth century foot binding: He was powerful enough that someone else could do his typing for him. He wanted to make sure that I and everyone else in earshot knew that. It turned out he was the owner of the computer store. Really.

Just as many an executive is openly proud of the inability to touch-type, many of us have been proud that we were so logically, "scientifically" oriented that we were willing to suppress this more mysterious half of our intelligence. In many individuals, reversing this early decision, with its many years of layered rationalizations, may be extremely difficult. If you are one of these people, and this is all sounding like a bunch of California psycho-babble, you might just want to jump to the end of this chapter and work with the quiz for a while. Then try the quiz on some of your family or friends, particularly with kids. If you find that they got answers quickly that you weren't getting at all, you might want to decide to involve yourself more deeply with this exciting ability.

The Three Steps to an Intuitive Result

Coming to an intuitive realization generally requires three steps: gathering information, incubating that information, and finally forming a judgment.

1. Gather information The information necessary for a successful result will typically be new sensory information coupled with old memories. Because intuition works on drawing together what is often logically unrelated data, you should make a conscious effort to be non-judgmental during this stage. Take in everything.

Intuition is an ancient ability, both in evolution and personal development. Dogs are no intellectual giants when compared to humans, but they are supremely adept at detecting and reflecting the mood of their owners from very subtle hints, often more so than the many psychologists who have abandoned intuition in favor of pure intellect. Children are also highly intuitive, often more deeply aware of the state of their parents' relationship than the parents are themselves. Family practice therapists, in the midst of a family therapy session, will report instances of children as young as six months old who detect and defuse fights between their parents by crying. The therapist, who has not yet recognized the subtle hints the child's intuition is drawing upon, then will turn around and use the child's crying as a useful indicator of an impending fight between the parents. As we grow older, we develop logic and are trained to push intuition away as an inferior, "childish" skill.

Most of the great scientists and inventors either failed to grow up "properly" and lose this childhood skill or relearned how to be a kid. Intuition works best when you gather information with child-like wonder and rapt attention. This does not mean you have to crawl around the floor making goo-goo noises. It does mean you have to open your mind, re-creating the simple wonder with which you took in new information as a child. Split apart perception and judgment: Take in the information, let it incubate for a while, then apply the judgment skills you spent most of your life honing and developing.

Archimedes had given up on his logical pursuit of how to measure the purity of the gold in the king's crown without melting it down. Then, one day, he stepped into his over-filled bathtub, absorbed the fact that he was splashing water out, and realized he was displacing exactly as much water as his own volume. Coupled with prior knowledge of the relationship between volume and weight, he had his solution.

As soon as you begin to prejudge the data streaming in, things begin to get lost. Eric Berne (Berne, 1949) carried out an experiment in intuition on 40,000 soldiers being separated from the Army. He attempted to guess their pre-army careers by gazing at them with rapt attention for approximately 10 seconds. His success rate was quite high—in the case of soldiers who had previously been farmers, he was able to guess their prior occupation 74% of the time. He then analyzed logically what he was doing to come up with these conclusions: studying facial muscle configuration, body position, eye movement, and so on. When he could analyze no more, he applied these rules to additional soldiers, while blocking the childlike attention that he had used before. His success rate immediately fell by half.

The conclusion? For intuition to have the kind and quantity of disparate information it needs to function properly, you must turn off your conscious, logical mind's attempt to filter and prejudge everything coming in. Relearn the art of being a child, of offering childlike, rapt attention to people and to problems.

2. Incubate   We have a lot of direct control over gathering information and judging the results. Incubating—letting the mind relax and stir around for a pattern—we have far less control over. When you went home with the program bug unfound and went to sleep, you were giving your intuitive mind the time and peace to incubate.

While you were sleeping, you were also casting about for a pattern that would solve your bug problem. Incubation can take anywhere from seconds to days. It stubbornly resists rushing, very much the way memory will perversely hold back someone's name if you really need it.

Incubation time can be shortened through relaxation, encouragement, and practice. It is likely you could have worked on your bug until noon the next day with no results. The intuitive leap came after you finally relaxed your conscious mind enough for intuition to be able to function. Some people go beyond relaxation: There is one prolific inventor living in the Midwest who eats an excessive amount of pizza whenever he wants to invent something. With the resultant light sleep on such a heavy stomach, he belches forth a new invention, regular as clockwork. While I would not like to accept the liability for suggesting such a regimen for solving design problems, I have found that most of my own large-scale intuitions become apparent during that period when dream moves smoothly toward wakefulness.

The discouraging thing about intuitive leaps is their resulting obviousness. It is childishly obvious, for example, that what goes up must come down (unless it happens to be exceeding around 18,000 MPH at the time). But when Newton intuited the law of gravity, it was a real breakthrough. When you do finally find that software bug, the tendency is to berate yourself for not finding it sooner. ("Aw! Why didn't I see that earlier! Any fool could have found that!") This kind of positive feedback goes a long way toward making sure your intuition never tells you anything again. Instead, try congratulating yourself for being clever enough to find the problem at all. Your intuition will be strengthened, and your needed incubation time reduced. You will also feel a whole bunch better.

For many of us, intuition is a rusty, repressed skill. Start out with the quiz at the end of the chapter, and then begin to apply intuition in your daily life. Pick up some books like Roger von Oech's *A Whack on the Side of the Head*, (von Oech, 1990) and re-establish rapport with your intuitive and creative mind. As you begin to listen to and congratulate your intuition, the number of intuitive leaps you experience will increase and your time for incubation will decrease.

3. Form Judgments   We commonly recognize two kinds of intuition. The first is "woman's intuition," a truly remarkable ability to understand human relationships and interactions. Western men will usually disavow any use of such intuitions, depending instead on what they call "hunches." So-called "women's intuition" is intuition with Feeling judgment, while traditional men's "hunches" are intuition with Logic judgment. "Women's intuition" and "hunches" both depend on the intuitive mind. However, "women's intuition" implies ethical, feeling judgment, whereas hunches imply logical judgment. These two kinds of intuition are different, but they are only gender-related in the West; in Eastern culture, both men and women develop powerful abilities to "look through" people.

Intuition usually delivers its results to the conscious mind in a convoluted, metaphoric fashion. It is very easy to ignore or misread the results. Back at the beginning of the '80s, Apple was developing its first database program for a computer with large mass-storage (five whole megabytes). No effort was spared in making every section of the program as "friendly" as possible. When a particular task proved somewhat difficult to learn or use, the task was reduced by picking up bits and pieces of it within other tasks. By the time the developers put it into an actual workplace, the program had slowly drifted toward being consistently and uniformly somewhat difficult to learn and use.

Someone came up with the bright idea of bringing me in to "simplify the interface," a task I found difficult. The original designers had done a really good job in making each section as simple as possible. The database program seemed to be a super-powerful program that had to be difficult to use because of its expanded capabilities and features. I struggled with the program for several days to no avail.

After the first day or so, I had a recurrent memory of an office manager I had once worked with. This guy used to tell all who would listen that he had to do "all the work around here," that he was the one holding the office together. I kept pushing this memory away, but it kept coming back, like a tune stuck in my brain. One evening I decided to let it in, hoping it might go away. When I closed my eyes and let the visual part of the memory come in, along with the words, I remembered the tiny detail that had been trying to push its way into my consciousness for days. The tiny detail that led to the redesign and ultimate commercial acceptance of the product was this: Whenever the office manager complained about his terrible responsibility and crushing work load, he always wore a tiny smile.

I suddenly realized that everywhere I had ever worked, there had always been one person—a secretary, area associate, whatever—who really held the office together. And, most importantly, they were proud of the difficult job they did; they tended to brag about it in a negative way because they received so little appreciation from those around them, and, of course, it is not polite to brag.

None of us had ever considered who our audience was beyond their being "office workers," so I did a field study of the kinds of people would be users of the system. I discovered three groups of people:

- The data-entry persons—These folk would be proficient typists who initially would be expected to enter a great deal of pre-existing information. They might be temporary help, or they might be people who normally performed a different job. Their needs were for a quick-to-learn, easy-to-use interface.

- The decision-makers—These people would be expected to draw information from the system, both by calling up data on the display and generating reports. They could be expected to be habitual users of the system. They could handle a long but gentle learning-curve that would give them progressively more power.

- The key operator—These people are the ones who, in real life, read the manuals. They can be expected to spend some time with the system initially and can be expected to learn how to perform the more technical operation and maintenance tasks of the system. This last one was the office manager my intuition was trying to remind me of.

Once the users of the system and their individual needs were identified, we were able to "unbalance" our equally difficult interface, so that each group of users had a level of difficulty consistent with their abilities and the amount of time they could spend learning the system.

A smiling, complaining office manager is a rather obscure hint to a program design problem, but it is typical of the way the intuitive mind communicates its results. Keep in mind that poor "primitive" intuition is quite incapable of speech and logic—even though, in this case, it knew the answer to the problem four days before my logical mind. Train yourself not to filter out thoughts and memories before you take the time to really examine them and consider their message. The finest intuitive leaps are utterly useless if you fail to listen. Learn to relax. When things look the darkest, you may already know the answer.

Relax. Open up. Let your intuition in. You have nothing to lose.

➤ **GUIDELINE** *Intuitive observation, the active gathering of
information through noncritical observation, incubation, and
eventual subconscious pattern recognition, results in insights not
otherwise obtainable.*

When I first became a bee keeper, I approached it very scientifically.
I graduated from bee school, did post-grad work at another bee school,
and watched a whole bunch of bee movies. They taught me that the way
to find out what was going on inside a hive was to go inside the hive.
That required a certain amount of equipment: giant white suit, hat, veil,
boots, gloves, smoker, prybar. The job of the prybar is to get you inside.
The job of everything else is to let you stay inside. Bees don't like people
pawing through their houses looking for their queen.

Ormond Aebi learned bee keeping from his father, Harry, who had in
turn learned it from his father, and so on, back many generations.
Somewhere along the line, someone didn't pay attention during the bee
movies and failed to learn the importance of tearing apart bee hives.
Instead, the Aebis learned to quietly and attentively observe their bees.

Bees are born gossips. If there is anything wrong with the queen bee,
everyone in that hive knows about it. And the bees don't just go about
their regular business. They start flying around agitatedly. Outside the
hive. Where the Aebis could watch them.

If the hive is producing a lot of new bees in the spring, as desired, the
young bees enroll in flight training, doing maneuvers worthy of Top Gun
school, right above the hive entrance. The Aebis didn't have to paw
through the hive to do a census on egg and larvae production. The
evidence was right there before them.

Scientific beekeepers, pawing through their hives two or more times
per year, manage to get their bees to produce around 45 pounds of honey
per year, per hive (Root 1980).

The Aebis didn't use them fancy new scientific methods. They used
intuitive observation. And they did OK: They managed to capture the
world record for honey production several years back, a whopping 404
pounds from a single hive with a single queen.

The thinking-out-loud protocol described in Chapter 14, "User
Testing on the Cheap," is a very effective method of eliciting information
from the user, but it still only goes so far; the users are not always
aware on a conscious, verbal level of what is confusing them. By
combining thinking out loud with intuitive observation, much more of
the picture becomes available.

Intuitive observation is not a passive activity. "The chief requisite
seems to be a state of alertness and receptiveness, requiring . . . intense
concentration and . . . outwardly directed attention. . . . ." (Berne, 1949).

By gathering information through completely opening your mind, avoiding snap judgments and giving your mind time to incubate the information and draw patterns from it, you will achieve insights that you will otherwise filter out of existence.

The power of intuitive observation argues for direct participation by design team members in the testing process, by their being either in the room or behind a one-way mirror. It also argues, when such a "live" presence is not possible, for videotaping the procedure. Any attempt by the testing crew to verbalize the results of testing will automatically filter away intuitive information important to design team members. It is fine to write a report, but people must see their users in action.

If You Think this Is All Nonsense

You probably hail from one of two fields:

> "Engineers and psychologists are among the most highly educated individuals in modern society and at the same time have, generally speaking, the greatest resistance against intuitive cognition." (Berne, 1958)

The methods I have described do work. A great body of literature exists on them in the world of clinical psychology. They draw on an intelligence that some have identified as inhabiting fully one-half of the human brain. Intuition is a powerful tool, and it makes no logical sense to suppress it.

Intuition Quiz

Here is a set of exercises to give your intuition a jump start. Few people can answer more than half the questions on their first pass. Most people need a period of incubation before the answers will pop into their minds. You may realize some answers an hour, a day, or a week after reading the problems, as your intuition finds patterns that work. This is expected and even useful, as the process of solving the more elusive questions—and your reaction to that process—will offer you insights into your own intuitive function and clues as to how to improve it.

Run through the test now and answer the problems that jump out at you. Then write the other problems down and carry them around with you for the next couple of days, glancing at them periodically. As you come up with solutions to the more trying problems, think about the experience in terms of these questions:

- Did answers always come while you were working actively on the quiz, or was your attention sometimes elsewhere?

- Did pushing yourself help?

- What time or times of the day were you most successful?

- Did you find answers through logical analysis, by figuring out one letter or relationship at a time? Or did answers usually just suddenly appear, whole, with your mind left feeling as though it had always known the answer—a sign of intuitive process?

- When answers appeared whole, was your first response to bask in the glow of happiness and relief, or to turn on yourself for having been such a fool in taking so long?

- If you improved at rewarding yourself during the course of answering the questions, did the exercise become more pleasurable? Did you notice future answers were easier?

All of these problems are based on the shared experiences of people in the English-speaking world. None are technical; none are esoteric. The ones you get right away someone else may struggle with for days. Intuition is like that: powerful, but quirky. Relax and enjoy it.

> Example: 4Q in a G (4 Quarts in a Gallon)
> 1:   64S on a CB
> 2:   1 P on FT
> 3:   90 D in a RA
> 4:   7 W of the W
> 5:   32 DF at which WF
> 6:   1 H on a U
> 7:   3 BM (SHTR)
> 8:   18 H on a GC
> 9:   88K on a P
> 10:   26 L in the A
> 11:   12 S of the Z
> 12:   24 H in a D
> 13:   1000 W (what a P is W)
> 14:   54 C in a D (with the J's)
> 15:   1001 T of the AN
> 16:   29 D in F in a LY
> 17:   57 HV
> 18:   9 P in the SS
> 19:   For Americans only: 200 D for PG in M
> 20:   For everyone but Americans: 14 D in a F

CHAPTER 16

Information Theory

COLUMN 20: OCTOBER, 1990

Now that we've got all that fuzzy-headed psychology out of the way, we can move right into a light-hearted discussion of the **second law of thermodynamics** . . .

("Good Grief, Henry, he's at it again! The great 'I-write-non-technical-stuff-for-all-you-non-technical-types' is beginning to blather about the second law of thermodynamics, ferevensakes!")

. . . which I will present to you, of course, in non-technical terms.

The second law, as I'm sure you all remember from high school physics, is the one that says that energy tends to become less and less interesting—ice cubes become warm water, electricity ends up as heat, jogging contributes to the greenhouse effect, and so on. Eventually, the universe will "run down," by reaching maximum entropy, at which point everything will be uniformly warm. All energy transfer depends on a potential energy difference: The earth is cooler than the sun, so it can absorb solar energy. Water runs downhill. Electric current flows from positive to negative. Baseball players slide into second, lessening their velocity and warming their posteriors in the process.

So much for the second law.

In 1948, a young mathemagician by the name of Claude Shannon was working at Bell Labs, attempting to figure out how to shoehorn more telephone calls into a single line. Having a background in mathematics, rather than optics, he was unable to finesse the problem by coming up with the fiber optic cable. Instead, he fell back on his own high school physics—*he* was paying attention—and applied the second law of thermodynamics to the question of how to get Grandma's and the president of General Motors's phone calls through the same twisted pair. ("Twisted pair," we are informed, is a technical term at Ma Bell referring to standard group of telephone wires and in no way reflects on any relationship that may or may not have existed between Grandma and the president of General Motors.)

The result of Shannon's theorizing was a breakthrough that has revolutionized the way we look at information. It has proved valuable not only in the multiplexing of telephone calls, but in interplanetary satellite transmission, the unravelling of DNA, and understanding human-to-human communication strategies. It is this last area of application that can, with the slightest of twists, be applied to our own problems in human-to-computer communications. In fact, Shannon's breakthrough is the cornerstone of a strategy that will enable you to add major new powers and capabilities to your applications, while maintaining solid consistency. Shannon's breakthrough was, of course, information theory.

Shannon proved that no matter what you did to a pair of telephone wires in terms of filtering, shielding, and so on, you were going to lose information and gain noise. He referred to the process as entropy. (Shannon was originally going to call it "uncertainty," but the mathe-magician Von Neumann counselled him, explaining that since no one understood what entropy means, no one would be able to challenge him.)

Information theory states that information tends toward entropy. What's that got to do with computers? This theory has been one of the driving forces behind making everything digital, from computer data to sound data (compact disks) to even moving picture data (CD-ROMs, digital video recorders). Why? Because Shannon not only identified the entropy problem, he offered a solution: redundancy.

Redundancy, as we all learned in grammar school, refers to repeated repetitions of the same information. Saying the same thing over and over, perhaps in a slightly different way. Repeating one's self by delivering the identical message couched perhaps in slightly different terms. Redundundancy, we learned, is a drag.

As it turns out, they lied to us. Redundancy, like staying up late and partying all night, is actually cool.

Let's see if you'd be in favor of this redundancy: You are caught behind enemy lines. You have three means of calling for help. You can release a homing pigeon, you can send an SOS on your shot-up radio that probably transmits but no longer receives, and you can pick out the smallest guy in the outfit and tell him to sneak through enemy lines. The redundantly minded will do all three (unless you are the smallest guy in the outfit, of course).

This form of redundancy has to do with sending the same message through multiple channels. It is applied constantly in the Macintosh interface where the user, rather than being confronted with a single channel of information, such as command line interfaces offer, instead finds messages conveyed through pictures with accompanying words and behaviors. Redundancy is why we redesigned the control panels to have labels (a word can be worth a thousand pictures). Redundancy dictates that grow boxes and zoom boxes should not look the same. Even though their positions in the window structure acts to communicate their difference, having a different visual appearance reinforces the communication, making people more comfortable.

Rules Within a single medium, redundancy takes the form of rules. Rules, by their very nature, limit the range of possibilities. Limits make interpretation of information easier. For example, let's say you have requested a number between one and ten and you think you hear someone say "sex." Since your possibilities are limited to digits, you can not only safely assume the information was garbled in transmission, but you can "heal" the error by finding the closest match, the number six. Imagine your embarrassment were there no rules and you had attempted to act upon the transmission error.

("Hey, Henry, come on in here. This here is gettin' inerestin'.")

While they told us in high school that rules were cool, they offered no evidence to support such a finding. Most of the rules we came across in high school were restrictive and coercive—known as primary rules. We were constantly being limited in our free expression by such pronouncements as "Don't squirm in your seat; don't kiss in study hall; don't light the school mascot on fire." It is a wonder we ever survived such a repressive experience.

An example of restrictive rules is the rules of etiquette. For example, when eating a lobster we are admonished to crack the claws slowly, lest we squirt an adjacent diner in the eye with the juice. Furthermore, in those Japanese restaurants that serve actual live lobsters, we are likewise admonished not to release our lobster to prey upon adjacent diners. Sounds just like high school, doesn't it? "Don't have any fun, whatever you do!"

Restrictive rules on Macintosh give Macintosh users a chance to feel empowered in their operations with the computer. For example, by our obstinately requiring that all modal dialog boxes have thick and thin concentric outlines around them, users grow ever more certain of what is and is not a modal dialog. Through the seemingly capricious and arbitrary rule that says that windows with grow boxes can be grown, users have become confident that when they see a grow box, they will be able to grow the window.

The day the Amiga computer was introduced, it sported (at least) four different cursors, each with its own set of rules, depending upon which application was running at the time. This led to a madcap adventure to identify what would happen when various keys were pressed. For example, pressing delete might or might not delete the current character from the text file. Pressing delete might or might not delete the current character from the screen. Whether it deleted it from the screen was in no way predictive of whether or not it had been deleted from the text file. Fun! Fun! Fun!

The Macintosh, after six long years, still offers only a single text pointer, with one set of rules. Does this limit the user's options? Yes. Does it make the computer more boring? Yes. Does the user have a clue as to what might happen when the delete key is pressed? Yes. Can the user get work done efficiently? Yes.

Secondary Rules

The restrictive, or primary, rules that make up the bulk of the Human Interface Guidelines are demonstrably necessary, but hardly cool. Fortunately, there is a different kind of rule, called a secondary rule, that is downright awesome. The United States Constitution is filled with secondary rules. The Bill of Rights is exclusively secondary rules. These rules are used to derive and modify primary rules. Without such rules, there would be no framework for adaptation to new conditions, and an organism that cannot adapt is doomed.

A rapidly emerging theory of evolution, based on the concepts of primary and secondary rules, holds that we evolved not through some plodding course of one-small-change-at-a-time, but in sudden jerks and starts. Whereas we used to consider that man must have evolved from his primate ancestors through a vast series of tiny changes—"get rid of that grown-together brow"; "kill the fur on that dude's back"—we are now beginning to put faith in a concept known as *neoteny*.

We carry a secondary rule in our DNA that dictates at what rate we will mature. At some point in the distant past, a mutation threw off our time scale, so that when we are all grown up, our attributes are those of a fetal ape. This slowing down of maturity is known as neoteny.

A fetal ape and an adult human look remarkably alike: The fetal ape's brow has not yet grown together. It has no fur on its back. On top of its long neck it carries a round head with a face that looks remarkably human, right down to its small teeth. It has an oversized brain and has not yet developed the bone configuration requiring it to hunch over. It could stand upright, like us. Thus a single, tiny change to a piece of DNA code carrying a secondary rule is capable of the most profound effects.

We are not the only neotenous animals: Dogs are neotenous wolves. Ostriches are neotenous, explaining the baby feathers that adorn their adult bodies.

How About Some Evidence?

"OK, so you say that people want lots of rules, they want redundancy, they want screens with pretty pictures instead of just a couple of green words at the top of the screen. Do you have any evidence?"

Yes! We need look no further than the English language. Where are the rules? We all know the ones we learned in high school, but let's look at some more fundamental ones we were never taught but just learned. These are the rules governing the frequency of letters.

One of the simplest forms of encryption involves offsetting the alphabet, so that every *e* becomes *g*, each *s* becomes *u*, and so on. The key to decoding this encryption lies in letter frequency: Since *e* is the most common character in English, discovering a sheet of paper laden with the letter *g* indicates that *g* is the substitute character for *e*. Armed with that, it is quite easy to work out the offset being used.

William Bennett, Jr., a Yale professor of engineering, decided to take a look at English letter probability to see how much these rules affected the nature of our vocabulary (Bennett, 1976). He fed Act Three of Hamlet into a computer and analyzed how often each letter occurred. Then he began printing things out based on those probabilities. If groups of letters to be printed out were based on nothing more sophisticated than how long the words in Hamlet were, output like this would result:

LAQ NRY WERWL GUHAUX WEH M LTA U CK JS ZSFZ MRD AQA XHJ BTGNSL J FHTU IKI ARMRW . . .

It doesn't look a lot like English. But by tempering this purely random formula with simple letter probability, he got this typical result:

NCRDEERH HMFIOMRETW OVRCA OSRIE IEOBOTOGIM NUDSEEWU . . .

Next, he decided to get fancy by including the probability of each letter succeeding the previous letter. In other words, if a *t* occurs, there is a good chance a vowel or an *h* will follow, but little chance an *s* will follow. If a *q* occurs in Hamlet, we can pretty much assume that a *u* is not far behind. The following is a typical printout:

ANED AVECA AMEREND TIN NF MEP FOR'T SESILORK TITIPOFELON HERIOSHIT MY ACT . . .

As it turns out, good old Anglo-Saxon expletives are among the most probable words in all of English: Once two-letter probability rules were in force, the computer started swearing like a sailor. Spurred onward by such exciting results, Bennett entered his final phase, probabilities based on the previous three letters. Late one night, he got this result:

TO DEA NOW NAT TO BE WILL AND THEM BE DOES DOESORNS CALAWROUTOULD.

In the final analysis, English text, with its rules of letter probability, word probability, spelling, grammar, and so on, carries better than 75% redundant information (Campbell, 1982). So does German, French, Italian, Japanese, and Chinese. Even languages with more limited vocabularies, such as Hawaiian, carry the same ratio of redundancy.

In short, every human language studied has 75%+ redundancy. Coincidence? Hardly. Transmission of information is rife with possibilities for error. The transmitter can missend the message, the medium can add so much noise that the message becomes garbled, or the receiver may hear it wrong or even interpret it wrongly. Only through redundancy do we readers and listeners have a chance to heal, or correct, the message.

Redundancy can also serve as a memory device: There was a reason that epic tales in the time of Greece were told as poems. Poetry is an extended-redundancy version of prose, offering rhyme and rhythm as additional clues for healing. From the beginning of Book VI of the Odyssey:

> While thus the weary wanderer sunk to rest,
> And peaceful slumbers calm'd his anxious breast,
> The martial maid from heaven's aërial height
> Swift to Phæacia wing'd her rapid flight. (Homer)

The storyteller, having reached the word "anxious" would be hard-pressed to avoid remembering the word "breast":

> While thus the weary wanderer sunk to rest,
> And peaceful slumbers calm'd his anxious left forearm.

"Heaven's aërial height," "swift," "wing'd," "rapid"—all lead inexorably to "flight."

Now take the pop quiz[1] in Figure 6–1. How many F's can you find in this sentence? Most people can only find three. (Answer at the end of this chapter.)

---

[1] Teachers in the United States give short tests, called pop quizzes, any time they are confident that you did not do your homework last night.

FINISHED FILES ARE THE RE-
SULT OF YEARS OF SCIENTIF-
IC STUDY COMBINED WITH THE
EXPERIENCE OF MANY YEARS.

Figure 16–1. Now you see it . . .

Multiple-channel Redundancy

An interesting loss of redundancy has taken place in the stark vocabulary of television news, where nouns, in the form of gerunds, have replaced verbs, and articles are cast aside as so much excess baggage. How can they get away with this in the face of people's need for redundancy? They are offering extra channels of information. When I mention to you in personal conversation "the Persian Gulf" and you hear "the Persian Golf," you are able to correct the error because "Persian Golf" would not be preceded by "the." When the TV newscaster says "Persian Golf" without the "the," the screen is displaying a huge, ocean-like thing. While hard-core golfers might simply be impressed with the immensity of the course's water hazards, most of us would be able to muddle through and figure out we're talking gulf here.[2]

Three media that people use for human-to-human communication are visual, vocal, and verbal. Of these, sighted people depend most heavily on the visual. In one test done by Dr. Albert Mehrabian at UCLA (Mehrabian, 1967), the effects of an affective conflict between the contents of a verbal message, vocal tone (tone of voice), and "body language" were measured. Where such conflicts existed, 55% of the time the subject placed his or her faith in the visual message, 38% of the time in the tone of voice, and only 7% of the time in the actual contents.

Three Forms of Communication

Explicit Communication The verbal content of a conversation, in almost every instance, is explicit: The communicator has consciously assembled a message he or she hopes you will believe. Tone of voice and body language can be explicit communication. The same words said with

---

[2] The other factor allowing TV newscasters to get away with the desecration of the language is complexity. The more complexity involved in the message, the more redundancy required to "heal" it. Because TV news deals in the simple "sound bite," rather than the whole story, it can get away with a more stark language construction.

a sarcastic edge on your voice take on a whole different meaning. Every culture has a "vocabulary" of standard gestures which either supplement the verbal exchange or stand in place of it.

Involuntary Communication Tone of voice and body language can also be involuntary communicators: The person who claims to be feeling fine and dandy on a Sunday morning may have a slumped posture and scratchiness of voice that indicate he or she is actually suffering greatly from the effects of Saturday night.

Back-Channel Communication According to Chris Schmandt of MIT's media lab, beyond the explicit and involuntary aspects of human-to-human communication is what has been dubbed back-channel communication:

> People help each other, using what are sometimes called back channels, giving cues, perhaps visual, perhaps spoken, though not necessarily lexical ("un-huh") that indicate their degree of understanding (as well as interest in the topic and the talker, among others) (Schmandt, 1990).

As I'm writing this, I'm watching my ten-year-old daughter, Rebecca, talking with her friend, Julie. The amount of back-channel communicating going on is amazing. They approach. They avoid. They squirm in annoyance. They snort and chortle. They look away in boredom. They clap their hands in appreciation. They are performing an elaborate, communicative dance.

Audiences provide back-channel information as to their enjoyment of a performance. In the U.S., they clap to show approval and they boo loudly if they think the act stinks. They may add some whistles in either case. (In Germany, they whistle if they like what you are doing. There is no clapping at all for approval. The first time I gave a talk in Germany, I almost left the country after the first round of applause—I assumed from the absence of clapping that they were "boo-whistling" me.)

The back channel is vital to high-speed transfer of information among people. Consider what happens when it is limited: In the game of contract bridge, players are allowed to communicate with their partners, but only explicitly through a bidding process. Think of how much better things would go if only they could occasionally lift an eyebrow, wink, or just squirm in their seats when their player promised a bidding outcome that could not possibly take place.

Poker goes in the opposite direction from bridge: Players routinely send back-channel communications to their competitors—all of it the most egregious lies.[3] Actors, politicians, used-car salespeople and other similar types learn to manipulate the back channel to produce an impression in the spectator that is far from the truth.

As software designers, we have concentrated on generating explicit dialog on our computers. For a long time, we had no choice: With nothing but thirteen characters per second on a green screen as our medium, there was little room for explicit communication, let alone back-channel communication. Now we have lots of "bandwidth," and we should make full use of it.

The Human Interface and Information Theory

The job of most microcomputers is to accept information from a human, manipulate that information, and deliver the results back to a human. The human interface acts as the communications channel between the computer and the human. By applying information theory, we can begin to see anomalies in the interface as sources of noise and determine how to minimize their number and their effect.

Rules, such as those of grammar, of punctuation, of letter probability, of upper/lowercasing, are the fundamental counterforce to information entropy in human-to-human information. I propose that rules will also prove to be the fundamental counterforce to loss of consistency in the human interface.

➤ *GUIDELINE   The job of the interface is to provide as broadband a communications channel as possible.*

➤ *GUIDELINE   The broader that communications channel, the more intolerable is "noise."*

Morse code has a very narrow band. It is transmitted by radio by alternately turning the transmitter completely on or completely off. Morse code can get through where voice fails because there is nothing subtle about it. It is strictly binary, either on or off. Variations in the pitch or signal strength of the transmission can be tolerated to a great degree because the operator is interested only in two conditions: any receivable transmission and complete cessation of transmission. Problems begin to creep in when one increases the bandwidth of the information, when one begins to vary the intensity or pitch of the carrier wave in order to impress voice or picture information. Then, any minor variations in the carrier wave, which the receiver assumes is stable, end

---

[3] The ethics of poker are confusing at best: It is acceptable and even encouraged to lie to the greatest extent possible, but get caught doing a little simple cheating and you are likely to be executed on the spot.

up being misinterpreted as information. As this new, spurious "information" mixes with the real information, both become lost in the resulting noise.

One can see how the redundancy inherent in the English language can overcome even the most extreme ambient noise conditions by listening to rock music. One can often discern ill-enunciated lyrics amid tumultuous noise. This exercise also displays the difficulty of "healing" (reconstructing) defective information. The process of trying to figure out the lyrics is usually an intellectual strain, requiring playing the piece repeatedly while trying to separate out the words from the wildly pitching carrier wave of the music. Contrast this with the banality of yesteryear, where the lyrics rode gently on the drifting strains of one hundred violins and the only threat to understanding was encroaching sleep. Our interfaces could use a little banality. When we provide a wide bandwidth communications channel in our human interface, we must make every effort to ensure that all perceived variations are reflective of transmitted information and are not spurious noise from the interface itself. The interface needs to have all the stability of a constant carrier wave.

The Macintosh interface has a very broad band. It uses not only words, as in the old days, but graphics, screen layout, the behavior of the mouse, the actions of the cursor keys, and so on. We assure our users by implication and through our manuals that every element that appears on that screen or emanates through the speaker is there to communicate useful information. Any variation among applications is directly related to the task being performed. The Macintosh promises consistency, and it is a promise that is dreadfully hard to keep.

Sources of Entropy in the Interface

Developers expect and encourage their users to buy software. They want them to own lots of it, and so do we. The development community makes money, Macintosh customers find new uses for their investment, and Apple hardware becomes more versatile, valuable, and desirable. Consistency is the critical feature of the Apple interface that makes our users feel free to pick up new software. Consistency promises that the user buying a new program will already know how to use it because Macintosh and the newer Apple II programs look alike and behave alike.

Given that it is vitally important to those of us within Apple as well as independent developers to maintain this consistency, where is this gradually encroaching "noise," or inconsistency, coming from? You and me, of course. We are the ones writing the software.[4] We are being

---

[4]This "we" most emphatically includes Apple—divergence has been even more rampant within Apple than without.

neither foolish nor wicked; the only evil character in the piece is Shannon's entropy. We are, rather, reacting to what I have labelled the desire, compulsion, and need to diverge.

The Desire to Diverge

Developers want their software to have a unique look. They have tremendous incentive to make a new word processor look different from the next guy's; how else will the customer be able to tell them apart?

There are many consumer products—foods, drugs, and cleaning agents—sold in this country that are chemically identical. Yet their manufacturers spend millions of dollars in packaging and advertising to imply differentiation that doesn't really exist. These companies would stampede Washington if there were the least hint of an impending law mandating standard, "generic" packaging.

Developers need to be able to differentiate, too. Fortunately our industry is not in the position of the standard product manufacturer; we have the opportunity to create a substantially improved or at least different product. We are hardly so mature an industry that everything is perfect.

Each of us needs to remain aware that varying the interface to imply differentiation of product hurts everyone, including ourselves. Every rule that is changed, however slightly, requires the user to form a new, more generalized rule to cover both situations. It means a learning burden for them now, and adds to their increasing wariness about any future purchases.

We have failed, within the Apple interface, to provide a means for the independent developer to visually "trademark" his or her product on screen. We have had a standard pull-down menu item called "About [program name] . . ." that lists copyright notices, author credits, and so on, but because the user need never look at it, this is much like making watching TV commercials optional. Now at least we have provided a standard location for an identifying icon or title at the head of the Applications menu. In the future, as screen definition increases, Apple will need to enable developers to alter standard interface elements to provide a unique look.

The Compulsion to Diverge

The microcomputer industry in general and Apple in particular were built by nonconformists who had no interest in the conventional wisdom of what was and was not possible. The independent software development community is filled with rare geniuses who sit on mountaintops dashing out code that routinely changes the world. Such people do not take kindly to being dictated to on any subject, let alone what their interface will look like. Today's average, competent programmer will often take it as a badge of honor that the stamp of his or her personality be put upon every facet of the program, especially the human interface.

This is a problematical aspect of an otherwise invaluable individual, and it is an aspect so deeply intertwined with the individual's genius that we are loath to meddle with it too much. We have absolutely no desire to kill the goose that laid the golden eggs; we should only like that the eggs stay gold instead of showing up in designer colors.

I talked to one developer who had introduced what appeared on the surface to be a minor change to the way scrolling works, but that rippled throughout the interface causing great confusion. I asked him why he would change such a fundamental behavior of the system. He replied with casual innocence that he thought he might do it our way, then he thought he might do it his way, and since it didn't matter, he decided to do it his way. It did matter, and his employer paid for it in lost sales.

The Need to Diverge

A living system must grow, and the Macintosh interface is no exception. It is the reason for this series of columns, and the chief source of "noise" in today's interface. The counterforce is consistency, continuity, and careful growth. The counterforce is the Guidelines and the human interface principles and, I hope, these columns. The counterforce is the people, like you, who take design seriously and care about the user.

The Proof Is in the Pudding

Information theory predicts that an interface like the Macintosh, rich in redundancy, should enable people to perform far more complex tasks than could be accomplished in the more abstract interfaces of old, and the evidence is certainly there to support such an assertion. Contrast the typical text editor of ten years ago with the complex word processing, page layout, and graphics tasks that users perform with ease today. Consider Vellum, rich with back-channel communication and other forms of redundancy, enabling a ten-year-old child who has never seen the application to accomplish drawing tasks in a fraction of the time that an experienced draftsperson takes using older, more abstract, "power-user" packages.

➤ **GUIDELINE**   *People don't want the most abstract interface. They want multiple channels of information. They want neither just words nor just pictures. They want both. The more visual, verbal, vocal, and tactile the interface is, the more natural it feels, the more feedback and response it provides, and the more confident the user becomes.*

Climb into the Hard Drivin' arcade game from Atari and experience the redundant kinesthetic feedback provided by steering wheel, clutch, and brake "feel." This is a driving game that literally cannot be played without the force feedback transmitted to the wheel and pedals: When the designers disconnected it, even the very best players spun out almost immediately. And yet, all information necessary on road position is provided visually on the screen.

Answer to Pop Quiz

(F)NISHED (FI)LES ARE THE RE-
SULT (OF) YEARS (OF) SCIENT (F-)
IC STUDY COMBINED WITH THE
EXPERIENCE (OF) MANY YEARS.

Used with permission of the Exploratorium, Copyright © 1990

Figure 16–2. *Pop Quiz Solution*

"Of" is a throwaway word, there simply for redundant cuing. We never even see it unless something goes wrong.

Conclusion   The first time I read about information theory, I set the book aside and thought, "Gee, that was interesting, now what?" But two months later, I realized I had a new model for looking at a lot of the processes of the world. Start measuring some of your observations against information theory. I think you'll find it a real eye opener.

CHAPTER 17

Conceptual Models

And now, at last, we get to an explanation of the structure of the system image of the Macintosh. (Uh-oh, I think I hear people inquiring, "Huh? What's a system image? Is it written in C++? Do I have to have more than 2 megs to run it?" I see we'd better begin at the beginning.)

Professor Donald Norman, chair of the Department of Cognitive science at UCSD and highly respected sage of the human-computer interaction community, has devised a wonderful model for designing and gauging the success of an interface (Norman 1983b, 1986, and 1988).

Norman cynically (and accurately) finds there to be two quite different conceptual, or mental, models at work in a product. First, the **design model**, the concept we, as designers, have about how the application works. We attempt to translate this design model into a physical form integrated into the application itself, into what Norman terms the **system image**—what lawyers might describe as the "look and feel"—and what Richard Rubinstein and Harry Hersh (1984) call the **external myth**. All is working quite well up until this point, when in walks the dreaded user. This poor fool, rather than reading the manual, wherein you have described in detail what you had in mind (the design model), will insist on building his or her own conceptual model, called, appropriately, the **user model** as shown in Figure 17–1.

Assume this user is an Actual Human, such as your accountant, dry cleaner, or even Mom or Dad, rather than a seventeen-year-old kid who has been programming more than 237 hours per week for the last twelve years. Actual Humans may have been quite negligent in their studies of such fundamentals as system heaps, but are usually acutely aware that pulled-down menus will roll up rather suddenly if the mouse button is jiggled too much. In other words, they maintain not a model of the inner workings of the modern electronic computer, but a model of the inner workings of mice, menus, and dialog boxes—the illusions we have created for them.

Figure 17–1. *From Design Model to User Model*

The function of the designer is to communicate the design model accurately via the system image. The function of the user is to form a user model that bears as little resemblance to the design model as is humanly possible. Users will add to what is so clearly communicated on the display every past experience that they have had, relevant or not. If the interface carries any trace of ambiguity, the user will find it out and jump to the wrong conclusion. In short, the user will insist on doing everything wrong, wrong, wrong! (A key reason for user testing applications is to expose this perversity among the user population at an early stage.)

Don Norman states:

My observations on a variety of tasks, with a wide variety of people, lead me to a few general observations about mental models:

1. Mental models are incomplete.

2. People's abilities to "run" their mental models are severely limited.

3. Mental models are unstable: People forget the details of the system...especially when (the system has) not been used for some period.

4. Mental models do not have firm boundaries: Similar devices and operations get confused for one another.

5. Mental models are "unscientific": People maintain "superstitious" behavior patterns even when they know they are unneeded because they cost little in physical effort and save mental effort.

6. Mental models are parsimonious:...People...are willing to trade off extra physical actions for reduced mental complexity. (Norman, 1983b)

What we have here is an uncontrollable, cantankerous receiver. We are trying to transmit information via the medium of the system image to this user who is just not trying. But we have no control over this person. We will just have to try harder.

Tog's Conceptual Model Guidelines

The occurrence of design model/user model incongruence can be reduced or eliminated in various ways. Among the less obvious ways are several that do not require physical assaults on particularly obstinate users, assaults that certain unsympathetic juries could interpret as criminal in nature.

➤ **GUIDELINE** *Develop a simple, smooth design model, reflective of the needs of the user, not the limitations of the hardware or the difficulty of the coding process.*

For the design model to be simple in no way implies weakness. Quite the contrary. The lines of a Lamborghini sports car are quite simple, more so than many boxy compact cars, but those lines fairly scream power. One would swear that a parked Lamborghini was worthy of a speeding ticket. In the same way, the friendly simplicity of the Apple desktop metaphor belies the power in the hands of the user: In a glass-Teletype[1] environment, transferring a file can often take fifteen to twenty minutes of effort—leafing through utility disks, booting the proper one, identifying the operating systems of the source and destination, and on and on. With the Desktop, you "grab" the document with the mouse pointer, "move" it to the disk you want, and let go. Done.

To avoid the underlying "reality" of the hardware mixing into the system image, it makes sense for the software design team always to include more than just the programmers. It is extremely difficult for programmers, actively engaged in battling the system software, to keep from having the rough system image of the System software "bleed" up

---

[1] Early computers used printers as their sole output. When programmers at various large traditional computer companies were first give monitors, they immediately duplicated the printer interface on their green, glowing screens, giving rise to the term "glass Teletype." With this lavish investment of more than 20 minutes of design time behind them, they saw no need to update the interface for the next thirty years.

into the illusion being created for the user. Besides, those of us who no longer have to code (or never did code) can be ruthless when it comes to the painful trade-offs between ease of coding and ease of use.

➤ **GUIDELINE** *The system image is an illusion designed to convey the design model. Have it communicate the design model clearly and concisely.*

People don't interact with Macintosh system software directly; they do so through the system image. This illusion, derived from the design model, should conform to the power of the underlying application like the sleek skin of a sports car. It should reveal the power, guide the users towards gaining that power, but do so without intimidating them.

Notice that I talked about the power of the underlying application, not its form: The form of a Lamborghini with its skin taken off is not a pretty sight. (Well, actually it is a pretty sight, but only to those of us who are really into technology.) The goal is not to put gold paint on all the wiring and tubing, but to create a completely separate illusion that in its own universe of visual space is as powerful as the underlying automobile is in its universe of technology and power.

The system image should make visible every structure, concept, and feature within an application. For example, if users may have difficulty understanding the order in which tasks need be done, the menu bar titles can bear the name of each task, arrayed in proper order. Or, if the more likely confusion will be the structure of the resulting documents, the menu bar titles can display the names of those structures.[2]

Any object or element of the interface that does not add to communication is subtracting from it. The most aesthetically pleasing interface is one in which all elements communicate most efficiently.

➤ **GUIDELINE** *Make the application memorable by making the design model, and hence the system image, correspond to the past experiences and expectations of your users.*

For example, if you are writing a spreadsheet application (as if we are all really desperate for another spreadsheet application), consider

---

[2]This example was inspired by some recent consulting I had been doing with the Xerox Ventura Publisher team on their then-unreleased Macintosh product. Their menu bar had been originally categorized by function, but after I experienced difficulty figuring out the structure of their documents, we reorganized the menu bar according to document structure. This resulted in the menu titles Chapter, Frame, Tags, plus a title at the end that switched among Text, Graphics, and Tables, depending on what kind of data the user was manipulating at the time, in the manner of SuperPaint (see Chapter 33, "Making an Interface Articulate"). Coupled with some well-executed drawings in their manual, these menus made the invisible structure of their specialized documents apparent and accessible.

using a sort of gridlike structure of cells, instead of clouds of animated dancing bubbles.

Our market research has always shown that people taper off their software buying. One of the chief reasons for this is that people tire of having to learn new software; often their last piece of software was so difficult for them to learn and memorize that they lost interest.

Programmers in particular have a superior ability to remember abstractions such as numbers, and disconnected details such as lists of key words. If you have a superior memory, you should be particularly sensitive to the needs of more average people.

The greatest aid to memorization is familiarity: If people already know how something functions, they don't have to memorize anything. By using a standard human interface, you save your user from having to remember anything about your interface—he or she has learned to use it already. The second greatest help is a good conceptual model. The simpler the model, the easier it is to grasp and remember.

Current theory of memorization, as reported by J. Campbell (1982), holds that people remember not the event but a simplified set of rules that allow the event to be reconstructed. Every new event is coded in terms of previous familiar events, or schemas. This phenomenon can be seen with crime witnesses, all of whom have different recollections of the same crime. One witness will remember that the criminal had a bald head "just like my Uncle Harry." A teenager may not have remembered anything about the criminal except that he was old, but will be prepared to discuss in detail the rattling of the overhead cams on the criminal's 1957 Ford.

While details of such reconstructions will be selective and sometimes conflicting, the primary event will usually be uniform: The man came into the bank, he robbed it, he left. By building your program on one simple conceptual model, regenerable by a few powerful rules and concepts, your user will be able to form an accurate user model and be able to memorize the few rules necessary to reconstruct it.

➤ **GUIDELINE** *Make the application memorable by reducing the user's need to memorize.*

A group at Stanford did a study of Macintosh users in 1986, asking them to describe exactly what went on when they used their computers. The researchers were surprised to discover that, while subjects explained in detail many of the more technically difficult aspects of the interface, not a single subject mentioned the desktop. Not one. The researchers ascribed this to some fundamental failure of the desktop—after all, it didn't seem to have made much of an impact—but when I saw the data, I saw it as confirmation that the desktop was working perfectly. People didn't remember the desktop because they didn't have to remember it.

The display of a computer [can act as] an external memory that is an extension of the user's own internal memory, one with which he can remember and keep track of more information than otherwise. (Card, Pavel, and Farrell, 1985)

I often do follow-up questioning after user tests, where I ask people what they remember. Then I try to rework the design so the next group of subjects won't have to remember.

The system image can act as an external memory of the data and its structure, not just the application and its structure. When following up on field testing, keep a sharp eye out for instances where users have found it necessary to repeatedly refer to the manual or their raw data for structural information. Then figure out how the system image can be modified to present or represent those missing relationships.

➤ **GUIDELINE** *Prototype, user-test, and iterate.*

Every one of Norman's six observations cries out for user testing. It is the only way to find out what weirdly warped interpretation of your perfectly marvelous design users are bent on making. Only by carefully following this process can you hope to succeed in fulfilling the other guidelines above. (See Chapter 14, "User Testing on the Cheap," and Chapter 36, "Case Study: One or More Buttons.")

Components of the Macintosh System Image

We are now prepared to dive into the system image of the Macintosh, keeping ever in mind that we are looking at the system, not from the viewpoint of the programmer, but the user.

Objects   The Macintosh interface is made up of objects designed for direct manipulation[3], so that people can communicate with their environment through physical actions that produce immediate response. These objects, such as buttons and sliders, have standard visual appearances and respond to a characteristic form of movement, such as clicking or dragging.

---

[3] Direct Manipulation: As defined by Ben Shneiderman:
- Continuous representation of the object of interest
- Physical actions or labelled presses instead of complex syntax
- Rapid, incremental, reversible operations whose impact on the object of interest is immediately visible
- Layered or spiral approach to learning that permits usage with minimal knowledge (Shneiderman, 1983)

You will find more information about Direct Manipulation in *The Apple Human Interface Guidelines*.

These objects are not equivalent to the objects defined by object-oriented programming; they're objects from your Mom's or Dad's point of view, not a hacker's.

Large objects, such as windows, are formed from other, smaller objects, such as drag regions and scroll bars. These in turn are made up of even smaller, indivisible objects, such as close boxes and scroll arrows. The process of expanding the interface is virtually synonymous with the process of creating new objects out of new and existing building blocks, called elements.

Elements A Macintosh human interface object is formed from several distinct elements. Any new object must be constructed out of these elements, with careful consideration and design of each element. These elements are drawn from and feed into four important aspects of the system image.

Models of the System Image

For many years, broadcasters scoffed at the idea of stereo television because TV screens were typically less than two feet across, and it seemed to make little sense to provide people with a sound field more than eight feet across (to say nothing of the fifteen or twenty foot deep sound fields provided by surround sound). Today, we not only know that people do not need their visual field and sound fields to overlap, we have found that people given two pictures with no difference other than the size and quality of the sound field will report that the picture with the better sound was larger, sharper, and displayed more faithful color reproduction.

Like television, with its separated sound and picture, the system image can be considered to be built out of several separate models. Four I will discuss in detail are the visual and general sensory, kinesthetic, feedback, and resulting action models.

Visual and General Sensory Model

The original game of Adventure appealed to Intuitives. It was strictly text, and there was very little of that. It was indeed a black cave. Adventure games entered the mainstream when someone added the element of graphics. All of a sudden, people could look around and see where they were! They loved the new games, even though it was slow, cumbersome, far more limited in scope and complexity, and did away with all imagination. (Programmers hated the new games.)

While most programmers have no need to actually see objects, due to their most wonderful ability to use their "mind's eye," most human beings are utterly lost in a system sporting the so-called black cave metaphor, as they crash around desperately seeking a way out.

➤ **GUIDELINE**   *All Macintosh interface objects can be seen, heard, felt, or otherwise directly sensed by the user. There should be no abstract, invisible objects in the interface, ever.[4]*

The Sensories want to see where they are, where they've been, and where they can go next. The visual model must convey that information to the user in a manner that is as natural as possible, with the least encroachment on and distraction from the user's attention to the task. That dictates high bandwidth graphics (high resolution, depth of gray scale, color, and so on) and artistic, communicative design.

➤ **GUIDELINE**   *Any element that does not communicate information that the user may need right now is superfluous.*

The visual model begins to breathe life into the system image. It needs to be bold but restrained, with menus that are unseen until needed, but instantly available. With icons that communicate rather than adorn. With multiple tasks that can be moved among easily, but without the abandoned clutter of many of the window systems of today.

➤ **GUIDELINE**   *Objects must be designed to encourage and facilitate specific user behaviors.*

For example, if it looks like a button, a Macintosh user will press it. This means that objects that act as symbols—for example the exclamation point within a triangle object used in alerts—should not look like a button, as clicking it will do no good. On the other hand, the OK button should look like a button, not a salmon, so the user will know that this is something that should be pressed.

---

[4] This does not mean that every object must be some great bloated thing: A great bloated printer is represented by a tiny icon. A menu structure with hundreds of items is represented by a thin bar stretched across the top of the screen. A list of twenty attributes is represented in a pop-up menu by a small drop-shadowed box surrounding the currently active attribute. Subtlety, not invisibility.

➤ **GUIDELINE**   *The design of visual elements should be left to people schooled in their creation: graphic designers.*

Kinesthetic Model

The user's physical actions in directly manipulating the interface objects cause the user's muscle and skeletal systems to move in certain characteristic patterns. The user's sense of these movements is called "kinesthesia."

Kinesthesia, like cyan, is not mentioned in school because none of the teachers know how to pronounce it. (Oh, yes, I know this is pure conjecture, but what other possible explanation exists?) Kinesthesia is the sense that makes pointing devices like the mouse work for people. Sensories, in particular, enjoy pointing and choosing. They enjoy the physical feeling of moving, clicking, dragging, and the resultant sense of power and control.

Kinesthesia is the sense that lets us clasp a tiny, living creature between our fingers without crushing it. It is that sense the nice police officer is testing when a motorist is asked to locate his or her nose using only an outstretched finger. Kinesthesia is the second sense to go in the presence of ethyl alcohol (immediately after common sense).

Kinesthesia feeds into **motor memory**, the memory of body positions that enables you to find your way back to your dentist's office by getting in your car and driving the route again, even though you might be at a loss to identify what town she lives in before you set out. When a user wants to access a given menu item for the twelfth time, the user will often depend on his or her memory of what it felt like when the hand and arm had moved a certain distance down the menu from the top the last eleven times through. Try switching around a couple of items, like New . . . and Open . . . and see the number of errors that result. Even better, rig an application so that the first item says Open . . ., but does New, and see how few errors result!

Sony Corporation made wonderful use of kinesthesia in an object on many of their VCR remote controls. Instead of recording being initiated the usual way, by holding down the record button while simultaneously pressing the fast-forward, rewind, play, and doorbell buttons, they have a single record button. Normally, this would be a recipe for disaster, but their record button is on a spring-loaded slide switch with a good, stiff spring. Rather than pressing the button down, as with every other button on the remote, the user must slide the switch to the right. This physical action is so different than pushing a button straight down that it is all but impossible to accidentally trigger the button. Even if the user did manage to slide the button, the resulting kinesthetic feedback is so powerful that the user can hardly avoid noticing the error.

As a general rule, the kinesthetic model should track the visual model: Move the mouse, and the mouse pointer should move a scaled distance in the same direction. Sometimes, though, good visual design will dictate exceptions. For example, as shown in Figure 17–2, one effective paint program found it desirable to have a palette all but hidden off the bottom edge of the display. When the user moves the pointer down to the bottom of the display, the palette suddenly pops up onto the screen, and the pointer now appears at the top of the palette, in the same position relative to the palette as it was before the jump. The user continues moving down and clicks on an appropriate palette object. Upon moving back up, when the pointer reaches the top of the palette, both the pointer and the palette return to the bottom of the display again.

Figure 17–2. *Moving Palette*

In this case, the visual model is neither smooth nor stable, but the kinesthetic model is both: From the standpoint of the user's muscle movement, they moved down linearly, clicked on the palette object, and moved back up linearly. I strongly suspect that, as a general principle, the stability of the kinesthetic model is more important than that of the visual model.

Feedback and "Feel"

Many of the rules of the metaphor can be discerned by the information presented directly to the senses: sight, sound, touch, and kinesthesia. Other rules have to be discovered from the behavior of the system. If the user clicks a mouse button while poised over an icon and then drags downward, will the icon come along, will the pointer simply move away, or will an apartment house in the next block suddenly burst into flame? Until the user tries an action, it's unpredictable.

The following four guidelines are cardinal rules to an effective behavioral model.

> ➤ **GUIDELINE** *Keep it simple. People can only remember so many rules. The more of them that can be conveyed graphically, the better. Anything displayed and available doesn't have to be memorized.*

> ➤ **GUIDELINE** *Keep it safe. Don't let the users fall off the edge of the earth: One dark little corner with a shortcut key that lets the users initialize their hard disks will permanently undermine a million programmer-hours of friendly software design.*

> ➤ **GUIDELINE** *Keep the system's behavior consistent. The same class of object should generate the same type of feedback and resulting behavior, no matter in what part of the program or release of the software they appear.*

> ➤ **GUIDELINE** *Interpret user behavior consistently. Consistent interpretation of user behavior by the system is even more important than consistent system behaviors.*

Manipulated objects must inform the user that the user is successfully or unsuccessfully manipulating them. Usually this is done visually: When the zoom box is successfully clicked, a zooming rectangle immediately fires off as the window shrinks or grows to the rectangle's new size. A good slide mechanism will let the user drag the slide up and down, with the slide bar tracking mouse movement in real time.

Sound and voice are other popular feedback mechanisms, particularly when a manipulation has not been successful: "That's the third time you've messed that up, Douglas Bartholemew, the second, right over here in the red shirt. Why don't you let one of those other people now clustered around your cubicle try to help you out, if you can be helped."

In time, we will undoubtedly see commercially available force feedback devices added to visual interfaces, letting users directly feel as well as see the objects on the display. Consider feeling the cell walls as you slip from cell to cell (or bubble to bubble) in your 1995 spreadsheet application.[5]

---

[5] Someone has already developed a prototype for a "sticky mouse." It moves on a metal mouse pad and contains a large electromagnet. Whenever the mouse pointer encounters a black pixel, the electromagnet turns on, sticking the mouse to the pad. The effect is that the user can "feel" the screen.

Objects with poor feel tend to offer sluggish feedback and an indistinct or abstract feel. It is hard to become emotionally involved with the object of one's desire if it never indicates it did anything important or takes twenty seconds to show it got the message. One application I recently witnessed being demo'ed took as long as three seconds to reflect that it understood the user had triple-clicked a paragraph of text with the mouse. By the time two and a half seconds went by, the poor woman showing the product couldn't resist clicking the mouse one more time "just to make sure," so that when the paragraph was finally selected from the first three clicks, it was instantly deselected because of the fourth. It took the woman six tries to perform the selection correctly.

Shneiderman (1987) writes: "In most situations, shorter response times (less than a second) lead to higher productivity. For typed data entry, mouse actions, direct manipulation, and animation, even faster performance is necessary for each individual step."

Resulting Action

➤ **GUIDELINE**   *The action that results from manipulating an object is just as much a property of that object as its appearance.*

Toasters toast, barbecues burn, dishwashers remove everything but tomato seeds. Should a dishwasher begin toasting or a barbecue fail to convert all food to carbon, we would be shocked and amazed.

Consider people's delighted reaction to objects that produce unexpected results, such as the telephone disguised as a shoe (snort, chortle) offered by a leading magazine.[6] Or, my personal favorite, the box of chocolates that turns out to be harboring a summons. I'm sure you have your own hilarious examples, but the important thing is that all elements of an object, including the resulting action, are important to that object. Therefore, all the elements should work together, reinforcing each other, making that object a unified, believable whole.

And a Reader Response

❑ *Dear Tog:* I've read your articles for quite some time now and have never been 'hit' quite so hard as by your last one. We are in the process of creating what we believe is a new market niche application. Some of our partners just don't seem to understand the Macintosh or the

---

[6] In an effort to hawk magazine subscriptions, this magazine ran late-night ads featuring people with room-temperature IQ's expressing amazement and surprise that a an ordinary-looking shoe with a wire the size of a garden hose coming out the back was actually a telephone. It's a sad commentary on our times that the only way to get people to read a quality magazine is to sell, instead, telephones disguised as shoes.

ideology of the Macintosh or its market. That has created a problem for us. Some of these individuals blessed with closed minds have given us programmers insight into how they think by simply being dumbfounded at what we profess to be logical. It wasn't until we sincerely took a step back from our personal involvement in areas of the project that we realized that if they can't understand it, how are our end users going to understand it? The previously mentioned article is, to us, one of the most important you've ever written. It reminds (hopefully) all of us Mac developers that even though we are "blessed" with a wonderful mind's eye capable of seeing the unseen, we often see the unneeded or unwanted.

We do have nonprogrammers test and make suggestions on our applications. Non-computer-oriented spouses are a good example. They seem to have been given, somewhere along the road, the ability to sit down, point out this—and this—and that—and get up and not want to be bothered about it anymore. Aside from frustration, we must remember how many users (not just spouses) are out there doing the same thing.

—DEVON

PART IV

The Natural Interface: Principles to Design By

One of the most serious problems confronting psychology is that of connecting itself with life. . . . Theory that does not someway affect life has no value.

—LEWIS MADISON TERMAN,
GENIUS AND STUPIDITY (1906)

CHAPTER *18*

Natural Law

➡ COLUMN *21: NOVEMBER, 1990*

"186,000 MPS: It's not just a good idea, it's the law"
BUMPER STICKER PARODY OF HIGHWAY PATROL AD

Several summers ago, after a particularly pernicious stint of compulsive programming, I quit cold turkey by going up to a lovely valley in the Cascade mountains with nothing more than a canoe, a backpack, and a programmable pocket calculator. I spent many happy hours frolicking among the trees, racing through the meadows, and studying the local insect populations. I returned to civilization a week later with 32,767 bites from mosquitos and a program that reads out temperature in Fahrenheit, Celsius, or Kelvin, based on nominal cricket chirps per minute.

When I got home, I noticed a strange, new phenomenon: I kept crashing into walls. (I had crashed into walls on several previous occasions, but not at 10:00 in the morning.) I'd been living in this house for more than two years. Why was I suddenly slamming into things?

By careful analysis of the frequency of electrical discharge by certain sensory nerves in the afflicted areas of my body, I was able to determine my approximate velocity at the moment of impact, a value higher than observed previously. (Translation: It hurt like hell, so I must have been going really fast.)

After a relaxing week in the valley, I shouldn't have found myself careening around the house. I should have been movin' kind of slow, reflecting my newly mellow self. What was happening to me? Further analysis led me to the conclusion that I wasn't moving at such a high speed at all. I was moving at a very natural speed—for the Cascades.

What enables people to move faster in the wilderness than in their own homes? What is it about a strange, natural surrounding that makes it safer at high speed than the most familiar artificial surrounding?

Simple, consistent, stable rules.

The rules of redundancy, at the risk of repeating myself, are vital in human communication if people are going to comprehend the message and feel comfortable doing so. They are vital in computer interfaces. We as designers are charged with the task of communicating to the user, via the system image we create in our software, our conceptual model (the design model) of the software. If communication is cloudy, if it is not supported by rules, users will not understand how an application works, and if they don't understand it, they will surely fail.

We, as designers, are not simply assembling dialoguing systems, we are building worlds, carefully crafted virtual realities, in which users will live and work. We are the deities of these worlds we build, and, while many interfaces show no evidence of determinism, these worlds we build our users are, in fact, determined. We are not the first world builders, of course, and we can learn a lot from the Architect[1] of the world we currently occupy.

The architecture of our cities is also a virtual reality of sorts (particularly on Saturday nights), but differs in one giant way from the reality we create within the computer: gravity. Actually, not just gravity, but a whole lot of other physical and economic laws that limit the range of the architect's expression. Computers wiped out all those limitations, leaving us to design our own natural laws. Of course, with programmers being the anarchistic group they are, the first thing they did was repeal the law of gravity. (In fact, for many years, computers were endowed with anti-gravity, as text and everything else floated inexorably toward the top of the screen. In the modern era, of course, everyone has abandoned this silly law, with the exception of AppleLink.)[2]

---

[1] For millennia, people have argued about whether the world we occupy was determined, occurred through completely indeterminate processes, or was the result of some of each. Even though I am an evangelist, I am of the secular variety and claim no special knowledge of the way things came to be. In fact, I claim no special knowledge of why I wanted corn flakes last Tuesday. I shall therefore offer no opinion on either of these subjects. However, for purposes of comparing the determined world we create for our users to the natural world outside, I have found it useful to speak of the natural world as being the product of a single, determined deity, whom I have called the Architect. I do so with apologies to those of you who are poly- or atheistic.

[2] As mentioned in Chapter 32, AppleLink is an electronic mail service used by Apple employees and developers. Prior to release 6.1, it had a particularly pernicious habit of displaying the mail as it was retrieved at several hundred words per minute. The result was that users had to sit there and wait until the entire message had disappeared off the top of the display before being able to drag it back down to where it could be read.

Before delving any further into natural laws and computers, let's compare mountain rules with city rules, from the standpoint of the user:

Lassen National Park

- Always look down. Surfaces may change suddenly, posing danger.
- You need look horizontally only if you see something growing out of the ground
- You need look up only if you've seen a tree trunk or notice the sun disappear.
- Slow down in thickets; speed up in meadows.
- Don't pull branches back and let them go so fast they hit the person behind you. The person may retaliate.

- Whatever you do, don't go out after dark.

San Francisco House

- Always look down. Surfaces may change suddenly, posing danger.
- Always look horizontally. Things like walls are "growing out of the ground" everywhere.
- Always look up. Heaven only knows what might have been left dangling.
- Everything is a thicket. Speed kills.
- Don't leave shoes on the stairs.
- Don't mix ammonia and chlorine bleach.
- Don't run into an unexpectedly open door.
- Don't get your fingers stuck in drawers.
- Don't stick your tongue in a light socket.
- And so on and so on.
- Whatever you do, don't go out after dark.

Notice how much simpler the park users' rules are.

Now let's look at the rules followed by the *architects* of these two environments. As you'll recall from Chapter 16, "Information Theory," primary rules form the specifications of an environment, while secondary rules are used to generate the primary rules.

Some primary rules:

Lassen National Park	San Francisco House
• Plant trees only in the ground	• Put up walls anywhere, dangle stuff from the ceiling, make corners sharp.
• Don't shock anyone without first whipping up some wind and darkening the sky.	• Put electricity all over the place, always on. Make it interesting for little kids to stick paper clips into electric plugs.
• Make water a constant temperature	• Pipe in scalding and cold water to every sink and bath. Then make it so no one can tell for sure which faucet is which. (Using words on the faucet in some foreign language, like French, is particularly good.)
• Make large areas of the land flat, so people needn't constantly worry about falling off cliffs.	• Put stairs in all the houses, then make them attract roller skates and baseball bats, so people will fall down and go boom.
• Have it seem scary outside at night	• Have it be scary outside at night

The architect of the house has taken far greater liberties (followed less restrictive rules) than the Architect of the wilderness. Unfortunately, that liberty has resulted in an environment where the user's liberty has been proportionally curtailed, since the user must be constantly alert to avoid crashing into walls. Or falling down stairs. Or scalding himself or his child in the bath.

The Natural Law Interface

Several years ago, when the Apple Human Interface Group had distilled the human interface principles, we all breathed a sigh of relief and went back to our normal jobs of trying to get System Software to do something about the Chooser.[3] Unfortunately, we were still holding on to our old idea that the interface was done, finished, perfect forever, and we were going to be of little help to our developers until we let go of that old idea completely.

---

[3] The Chooser was probably the most confusing feature of the Macintosh interface. Designed in an era when people needed to choose among perhaps two printers and a single file server, it was pressed into service for handling networks featuring thousands of users and hundreds of devices. Similar to the weather, it became something everyone talked about but no one did anything about.

Macintosh was never intended to be a static, standardized environment. That is why the Guidelines are not called the "Standards." And like the original principles, the instructions for expanding and adapting the interface had always been there, as long as you came to Cupertino and sat at the feet of the original designers. This has long since ceased to be a useful strategy for our now 10,000-plus developers, many of whom have a healthy aversion to other people's feet.

Fortunately, your very own human interface evangelist, having abandoned all hope of ever reforming the Chooser, has spent much of his free time the last two years staring at the wall and thinking about this very problem. (Least you feel sorry for my Spartan existence, this particular wall is washed with the light from a commercial video projector fed by three VCR's, a satellite dish, and a video disk player.) As a result, I have gained a clear understanding of how to evolve and adapt the Macintosh interface while maintaining strict consistency. (As a side benefit, I have also gained an in-depth knowledge of "Hee Haw," "The Beverly Hillbillies," and "Charles In Charge.")

The heart of this great, guiding principle is this:

➤ **PRINCIPLE**   *The real world is a complex, adaptive structure formed from a few simple, driving principles, and humanity, through millions of years of evolution, has become attuned to its every nuance.*

If we want our own artificial worlds to communicate most effectively, we will model them after the real world, following its rules wherever appropriate.

The Macintosh, like the wilderness, is at once a widely varied, evolving, animated, exciting environment while, paradoxically, it remains strikingly consistent, predictable, and dependable. The wilderness enabled me to move faster, more surely, and feel more comfortable than I had in my city environment. It did so through strong, simple, secondary rules (principles). Similarly, the Macintosh has empowered me, through its own secondary rules, to accomplish things I simply could not in older systems. Next, we'll take a look at the secondary rules of both nature and the Macintosh and how they enable you to go beyond the Guidelines.

Reader ₁sponds   One reader was quick to point out a precedent for my concept of the "simple, consistent, stable rules."

❏ **Dear Tog:** Your November HI article brought to mind William of Ockham, a fourteenth century philosopher. Ockham's Razor is the idea to which you refer in the article:

"The medieval rule of economy, that 'plurality should not be assumed without necessity,' has come to be known as 'Ockham's Razor'. . ." (*Encyclopedia Britannica* 15th ed.)

This has become known as "the law of parsimony" (among other things) and in the human interface rule-making scenario is exactly what you prescribe. Personally, I kind of like the sound of Ockham's Razor slicing away the assumptions to the minimum required to achieve a desired result.

I learned of this idea from a SciFi novel in the '50s, and it's kind of amazing to observe (as I have observed) the incredible capacity of the human mind for creating the unnecessary complexities that prompted Ockham's Razor.

Regards, —BRUCE A. FAIRMAN

■ Hi Bruce, I knew I was ripping someone off in my November column, but I didn't quite know whom. I am aware of William of Ockham, that great forerunner of King C. Gillette, however, I had never realized I was ripping him off in my great twentieth century theory. Oh, well, I guess it's better to be discovered ripping off Ockham than Desi Arnaz or a back issue of *TV Guide*.

—TOG

CHAPTER 19

The Evolving, Adaptive, Consistent Environment

❧ COLUMN 22: DECEMBER, 1990

[*Apple Direct* editor's note: This column of Tog's series will present the principles he has found benefit developers faced with having to move beyond the confines of the published Macintosh Guidelines. We recommend that those readers who have not read the previous three columns—and are endowed with an unusually high threshold of pain—get ahold of them. They can be found in the wastebaskets of finer corporate libraries everywhere.]

You have to come up with an interface for some brand-new function not covered by the Guidelines. The engineers need it by last Tuesday. The users need to grasp it quickly and intuitively. How do you do it? Simple. Just use my critically acclaimed theory of natural human interface design:

The real world is a complex, adaptive structure formed from a few simple, driving principles, and people, through millions of years of evolution, have become attuned to its every nuance.

If we want our own artificial worlds to communicate most effectively, we will model them after the real world, following its rules wherever appropriate.

[We feel it our duty to report our inability to find any critics who have "acclaimed" Tog's latest theory. The critics, while grudgingly acknowledging the validity of the theory, have ascribed its "discovery" to Tognazzini's keen sense of the obvious.—*Apple Direct* Editor]

By applying a few simple principles, you can easily build new objects and behaviors that users will immediately understand; objects and behaviors built on the visual and behavioral language of the Macintosh.

The Macintosh is at once a widely varied, evolving, animated, exciting environment that, paradoxically, remains strikingly consistent, predictable, and dependable, just like the natural world. Let's look first at a few of the principles observed in nature. They will lay the foundation for the Macintosh principles that follow.

Some Principles of Planet Earth

➤ **PRINCIPLE** *Possibilities are limited, making the world predictable.*

Nothing is fastened to the sky. Water never runs up hill. Fire never causes frostbite. Birds cannot fly through the ground. If there is no water, there are no fish.

The number of possible events is finite and predictable. Night follows day. Winter follows summer. While the timing of some events, such as earthquakes, is left seemingly to chance, the Architect notifies the more deserving animals in advance. (Scientists report that dogs and other beasts detect the release of radon gas, a precursor to major earthquakes. My dog seems to respond by falling into a deep sleep, a response similar to that she displays at the sound of breaking glass in our living room in the middle of the night.)

➤ **PRINCIPLE** *The world is populated with consistent, predictable objects.*

Solid objects, such as granite, are considered quite stable. Liquid objects, such as water, conform consistently to the law of gravity in everything they do. Our atmosphere will generally not fling you into the sky if you avoid natural attractors of tornadoes, such as trailer parks.

Organic objects can be divided into plants, animals, and relatives. Plants are usually green and grow upward from the ground, never down from the sky. Animals move around a lot, but usually announce their intentions: lions roar; bees buzz; rattlesnakes rattle; and relatives, bearing luggage, ring your doorbell.

➤ **PRINCIPLE** *Objects can be easily perceived, discriminated, and manipulated.*

The only invisible objects are country air and hungry mosquitos. People have become specialized for objects that are visible.

Every object is coded through such characteristics as color, texture and density. This coding is directly and inextricably bound to the character and behavior of the substance being coded: Land is hard and brown, trees and plants are supple and green, water is very, very supple and blue (except in Cleveland). If the surface of the earth changes from safe to dangerous, the color and texture change with it: From soft brown dirt to hard white rocks. From green meadow to blue water. From firm red soil to dark brown quicksand. Trees are never plaid, and water never looks like a chicken (exception: the Sunday buffet ice sculpture down at the good-old Bowl 'n' Chew).

Guidelines for Expanding the Macintosh Interface

➤ **GUIDELINE** *If it ain't broke real bad, don't fix it.*

Tree kangaroos still have huge hind legs—rather useless in trees, but not so detrimental it can't continue to survive. The ostrich, though permanently grounded, still retains its wings.

Survival must usually be threatened before radical change takes place. One classic example involves the white birch tree moths of England: With the arrival of the black soot of the industrial revolution, white moths were suddenly silhouetted against the blackened tree trunks. Within months, all the white moths had become bird food, and the occasional mutant black moths that used to get picked off by the birds were fruitful and multiplying.[1]

Some fool back in the '20s decided that batteries put in radios should alternate polarity: Face the first battery up, the second down, the third up, and so forth. This saved the guy two cents worth of wire and five cents worth of labor. People have gone through a confusing learning process ever since. In the late fifties, a few companies decided to help people out by having all the batteries lie the same way, much more in keeping with people's naïve mental model of how electricity works. The unfortunate result was that people, through habit, alternated the batteries and turned their radios into hot plates.

Macintosh users expect certain objects for certain manipulations. People expect scroll bars for scrolling. They have historically rejected any attempt to get rid of them. People look forward to the menu bar. They become dazed and confused when it has been replaced by 255 check boxes and something that looks like a steering wheel.

If you don't have something to replace a standard object that works a whole bunch better, as proven by extensive, objective testing, forget it! Remember the Dvorak keyboard? It was better, but not nearly enough better.

---

[1]Actually, as reader Maury Markowitz pointed out to me, "the darker moths are no more 'mutants' than short or tall people are 'mutants.' Averages exist, and the average for the moth population was a light colour, but the darker individuals always existed in the population. When a new selection pressure was applied, the change was that the average moved. There were no new moths created, a new mutation did not suddenly appear to help the moths out. The ability to survive was always there. Boy, I hate the word 'mutant'!" (Maury's words. I personally love the word mutant.)

➤ **GUIDELINE**   *Reflect the illusion of the interface, not the realities of the hardware.*

We are an animal, evolved to spin illusions around the realities of nature: We sit in awe of a "sunset," though we know the sun doesn't set. We yearn to sit on a cloud, although the reality is we would meet a rather ugly death within ninety seconds.

The battery industry finally learned about illusion: Alkaline cells by nature have the opposite polarity of standard cells, a fact carefully camouflaged by making the (now negative) center post look like the flat negative end of a standard cell, and raising a post on the back end of its now-positive outside case. As a result, people blissfully load the cells into their tape players, never realizing they are putting them in "backwards" from the viewpoint of actual physical construction.

If you are a programmer, you must deal with the realities of the hardware and operating system. Be careful not to transmit that reality into the user's world, and be sure to user-test to measure the purity of your illusion.

➤ **GUIDELINE**   *Build on existing visual/behavioral language.*

When the Earth's Architect decided to whip up a snowstorm, he cooled the rain until it turned into white crystals. He didn't start dropping sodium chloride on everybody. While that would also have resulted in white crystals, it would have made for a very complex meteorological model.

When first designing for the Macintosh, use key end user applications until you can "feel" the computer's delicate system image. Then design. Otherwise you will create an application that looks "Mac-like" but feels and acts like MS-DOS, Amiga, or some other foreign interface, and no one will touch it.

➤ **GUIDELINE**   *Use big concepts.*

It is very easy to get caught up in the details. Every once in a while, we need to step back and see the connections. Is there one concept growing within the system that will enable users to understand a whole bunch of things at once? Can we make it even more encompassing, universal, and apply it to a range of objects and behaviors?

➤ **GUIDELINE**   *Depend on precedent.*

One of the safest methods of extending an interface is by use of precedents. The basic components of this method are, as applied to new objects or behaviors:

- What other applications have solved this or a similar problem?
- Are they major applications?
- Are they designed for the same target users?

- Is one of their solutions as good as ours? Would changing ours to exactly conform to theirs lessen the effectiveness of ours?
- Can we come up with a super solution that could replace all of theirs, resulting in a single Big Concept?

➤ **GUIDELINE** *Invent new objects, with new appearances, for new user behaviors.*

The magnifying glass on the Macintosh is a tool that can be "grasped" by clicking on it. Once grasped, the mouse pointer becomes a magnifying glass and the user can click on items of interest to be magnified.

Lately, a few developers have pressed the magnifying glass into service as a content-zoom button: Users click on it expecting to end up with a tool and instead end up with a zoomed-in image in their window. We have icons for this function, shown in Figure 19–1. Using the visual element of a tool to represent a button causes the worst sort of confusion.

Figure 19–1. *Zoom Icons*

➤ **GUIDELINE** *Invent new objects, with new appearances, for new resulting behaviors.*

When fish came out of the ocean, the Architect stripped them of their fins and gave them lizard legs and bad breath. Not only were they able to move around a lot easier, people could tell a dragon from a trout, an important distinction.

The ellipsis object (. . .) on the Macintosh means a dialog box requesting more information will be revealed. The right-facing triangle object used in hierarchical menus means that a submenu will appear. A tool in a palette that will reveal a subpalette of tools if held down should be marked with a right-facing triangle, not an ellipsis.

➤ **GUIDELINE** *When possible, evolve objects, rather than starting from scratch.*

New natural objects are evolved from old objects, retaining important characteristics. Meadows routinely evolve from lakes, retaining their flat surface. Birds—egg-laying, warm-blooded, and feathered—evolved from an earlier species of dinosaur with these same characteristics, just adding flight to their repertoire. (Their direct ancestor apparently used its feathers to scare the hell out of potential enemies, a lesson not lost on Native Americans and other early cultures.)

At Apple, we evolved the modal dialog box by making it movable. (see Chapter 5, "Making the Most of Modes") To reflect that new ability, we glued the drag region of a modeless window to the double outline form of a modal dialog. People knew instantly what it was for and how it would act.

➤ **GUIDELINE** *Make changes clearly visible.*

An unfortunate piece of conventional wisdom holds that by making something radically new appear similar to something old, people won't be frightened by it. Problem is, they also won't understand it. What if the Earth's Architect had made camels look like cacti because people already knew about cacti? A desert denizen might not be frightened by the first sight of a camel, but it would be a long time before he attempted to ride one.

If an object is new, people need to know it's new, so they can learn what it is and how to use it. The more differently it acts than what came before, the more different it should look. Naturally.

➤ **GUIDELINE** *Interpret users' responses consistently.*

One thing the Architect settled on early was absolute stability in the way the environment interprets the activities of the individual: If you strike a bush with a branch, it recoils. It does not turn into a rabbit. If you strike water with a branch, it recoils. It does not change into a serpent. (If you strike a rabbit with a branch, it does turn into a serpent, so don't ever strike a rabbit.)

Macintosh users expect the Delete key in every text editor they ever come across to delete the last character from the screen and from the text buffer. They like to avoid the adventures offered by some of our competitors that seem to come up with some new and exciting interpretation for a press of the Delete key in every application. (See Chapter 16, "Information Theory.")

➤ **GUIDELINE** *Multiplex meanings.*

Natural objects have different perceivable characteristics, among which people can easily discriminate. Take the bristlecone pine. The oldest living thing on earth, it has been formed and shaped by the wind and scarred by thousands of years of existence. The youngest school kids look at it and know there must be a lot of wind around there. They know the pine may be even older than their father. They also know, to a certainty, that it is a tree.

Kristee Kreitman Rosendahl, responsible for not only the graphic design of HyperCard, but also much of its spirit, created a collection of Home icons that shipped with the product, as shown in Figure 19–2.

Figure 19–2. *"Home" Icons*

No one has ever shown confusion at seeing various little houses on various cards. Never once has someone turned around and said, "Gee, this little house has three windows and seems to be a Cape Cod. Will that take me to a different Home card than that two-story bunk house back in the other section?" People are designed to handle multiplexed meanings gracefully, without conscious thought.

In System 7, we multiplexed the meaning of system extensions, by developing a characteristic "generic" extension look, (shown in Figure 19–3) to which developers can add their own unique look for their specific product. As the "bandwidth" of the interface increases, these kinds of multiplexings will become more and more practical.

File Sharing Extension   FinderHelp   DAL   Network Extension

Figure 19–3. *System 7 File Extensions*

CHAPTER 20

The Advent of Agents

If you are associated in any way with design, and you have yet to study Vellum from Ashlar, you had better go directly to your local computer store and buy a copy. This CAD application has solved, in a single stroke, a problem that has kept poor souls like me from being able to use graphics programs with any kind of facility.

The problem I have with all drawing programs is that I can't seem to tell very well where the exact center of a circle lies, or whether I have bisected a line accurately. Vellum has installed an agent[1] they call the Drafting Assistant, who lies beneath the drawing sending me verbal messages whenever I hit any logically related targets:

Figure 20–1 is taken over time, showing the Drafting Assistant responding to my movement across the square. My task will be to draw a line from the top-right end point of the square to the upper tangent of the circle. The cross (+) is the actual location of the mouse cursor, the x is the location the Drafting Assistant is guessing I really want to be.

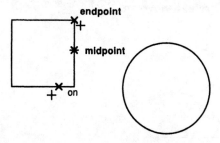

Figure 20–1. *Vellum messages*

---

[1] Vellum makes no claim that the Drafting Assistant is a real agent, probably for fear of raising the ire of the AI community, since the Drafting Assistant makes no use of AI technology. It certainly fulfills the general definition, however, as encapsulated by Alan Kay: "Computer processes that act as guide, coach, and as amanuensis." (Kay 1990)

As I approach the bottom of the square, the Drafting Assistant jumps to the bottom line and announces (via words on the screen), "on." I continue my sweep upwards and to the right, with the Drafting Assistant cruising along the lines of the square, until he[2] leaps to the center of the vertical line and announces, "midpoint." At the moment captured in the figure, I have also reached the midpoint, and the agent and I are occupying the same spot.

Again I move upward, this time sweeping too far to the right, but the agent makes an educated guess as to what I want and sticks to the vertical line until he comes to rest at the top corner, announcing, "end point," at which time I can press down and begin to drag out my line.

What we have here is a rapid-paced dialog going on between the Drafting Assistant and myself. He is making reasonable suggestions as to what I want, and giving me instantaneous feedback as to what those choices are. I, in turn, am giving him feedback as to the success of his choices by moving toward and away from where he is leading me. Using Vellum, it feels as though the Drafting Assistant is on a short leash, like the organ grinder's monkey. And it is as adept at suggesting geometric relationships as the monkey is at extracting money from your pockets.[3]

In Figure 20–2, I have stretched the line down until I am inside the circle. The agent has noticed an emerging relationship: I am close to a 45° angle from the beginning point of my new line, and I have just crossed the intersection of the bottom of the square. To better communicate his thoughts on the matter, he has drawn the two dotted lines, demonstrating the relationship. Releasing the mouse button at this point would result in a line drawn to the intersection of the lines. (The agent's location, rather than the user's, is the "real" location from the point of view of the program.) Since, however, I'm looking for the tangent of the circle, I move on.

---

[2] Yes, the Drafting Assistant in my copy of Vellum is definitely male. Others have reported their Drafting Assistant to be female, while those sticking to a position of strict anti-anthropomorphism cling stubbornly to the notion that their agent is an "it." I will present a counter-argument to this last, most unromantic position later in this chapter.

[3] For those who have never experienced an organ grinder's monkey and may thus assume that I am putting the Drafting Assistant down, let me rush to assure you that I am not: Organ grinder's monkeys are marvelously intelligent and adept at what they do.

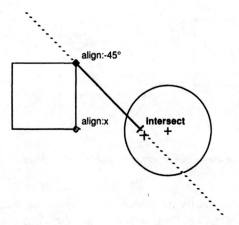

Figure 20–2. *User stretches diagonal line*

In Figure 20–3, the agent has now discovered that I am crossing the intersection of the midpoint of the square and a vertical line passing through the center of the circle. I push on.

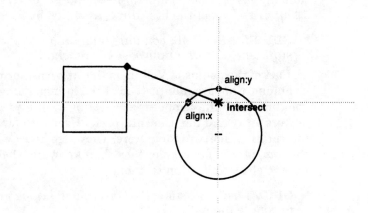

Figure 20–3. *Drafting Assistant "notices" an interesting relationship*

In Figure 20–4, I have moved close enough to the tangent that the Drafting Assistant has suggested that is my goal. We are in complete agreement and I release the mouse, completing the line.

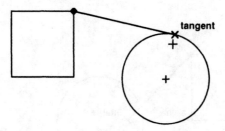

Figure 20–4. *User achieves goal of finding tangent*

You really have to see it to appreciate the sheer elegance, but the net effect is that I am suddenly in complete control of my drawing. The agent is light and nimble. Instead of my issuing a cumbersome series of absolute commands, as required by other CAD packages, I am engaged in rapid conversation with a knowledgeable and cooperative ally.

The Nature of Vellum's Dialog

Susan Brennan offers us guidelines for applying the laws of human-to-human conversation to human-to-computer conversation (Brennan, 1990). Let's look at the first three, as stated by Brennan:

➤ **GUIDELINE**   *Don't continue until an understanding that is sufficient for current purposes is reached.*

Part of the genius of Vellum is that it turns normal human/computer communication around: Instead of the human doing most of the "talking," with the computer attempting to interpret, the computer jabbers away and the user interprets. Users are far better at interpreting than are computers. They also know when they understand the computer; a far simpler task than knowing when a computer (or anyone else) "understands" them.

➤ **GUIDELINE**   *Assume that errors will happen and provide ways to negotiate them.*

➤ **GUIDELINE**   *Articulate the answer or response in a way that preserves the adjacency with (and apparent relevance to) the question or command.*

These first three guidelines describe well the functions of the Drafting Assistant.

Brennan continues:

➤ **GUIDELINE**   *Represent the interface in a way that invisibly constrains the user to act in ways the system understands and to stick to the application domain.*

This guideline, in this instance, is fulfilled by the very nature of the program: This is a CAD package, and the "intelligence" of the Drafting Assistant is limited to, but covers well, the subject of CAD things.

➤ **GUIDELINE** *Integrate typed input with pointing and other input/output channels.*

This guideline suggests that dialog between user and computer should not be constrained solely to the user's typing in natural language. Vellum does not depend on the user entering any natural language; the user communicates via movement and gesture. The Drafting Assistant, however, is constantly communicating in natural language, through the pop-up labels announcing recognized relationships (intersect, midpoint, tangents, and so on). But the Drafting Assistant also communicates with visual information, such as its construction lines and the markers indicating the position of the Drafting Assistant and the user. Using just the labels without the additional visual feedback would seriously affect the confidence and productivity of the user.

Add to Brennan's list a guideline from Chris Schmandt (1991) about synchronization, which I've rephrased:

➤ **GUIDELINE** *Provide feedback to the user so that the user knows whether the computer is keeping up or lagging behind.*

The Drafting Assistant presents the user with continuous evidence of synchronicity, through what Brennan has dubbed "animated language."

One way to make a natural language interface more conversational is to integrate it with a graphic interface that, when appropriate, provides the user with additional clues as to how her utterance has been interpreted with respect to the application. The goal is to make these clues analogous to (though not slavishly imitative of) back channels in human/human conversation. For more information, see Chapter 16, "Information Theory."

And now a few guidelines from me:

➤ **GUIDELINE** *Make the response time snappy. The more rapid-fire and closely coupled the dialog, the more the user will feel and be in control.*

Many Macintosh applications fulfill the first six guidelines. The difference in Vellum is that the rich back-channel communication on the part of Vellum's Drafting Assistant occurs virtually instantaneously. As a result, the user, being presented with evidence of continuing synchronicity, works surely and rapidly, thereby complying with the requirements of the last guideline.

I developed a technique for entering times on my old microwave oven which consisted of converting the time into the nearest multiple of 11, 111, or 1111. Thus, something requiring 3:30 seconds of cooking time, I entered as 333. This was faster, if somewhat less accurate, than thinking about each integer to be entered.

I noticed a few days ago that I no longer do that with my new microwave, and I wondered why. The answer turned out to be pretty simple; it takes my new microwave almost ½ second to feedback, with a beep, its acknowledgment of a digit entered. The oven thus had trained me to take at least ½ second to enter each digit. With all those half-seconds lying around, my subconscious apparently decided there was no longer a reason to strive for speed rather than accuracy, so it returned to following the package directions.

When I experimented with the oven, I discovered that, in fact, it will accept any number of presses as fast as you can make them; it just doesn't bother acknowledging them until later. Vellum's Drafting Assistant doesn't make such a mistake. Its response time appears instantaneous, with wide-ranging and useful feedback. Indeed, if the agent were slow, the user experience so marvelous in this program would drop away to nothing.

In the following letter, developer Kim Hunter reports his experience with response time.

❑ **Dear Tog:** I was looking at the latest CD-ROM with talking heads in various languages. This multimedia stuff is fun but *no good* for the public because of the delay in loading.

I recently watched people using a kiosk in the county courthouse in Pasadena. A HyperCard stack could be clicked to get info on the court building. In typical HyperCard fashion, when someone clicked a button, it didn't highlight until a few milliseconds later. The general comment was "It must be broken" or "Boy, I hope the taxpayers didn't have to pay for this piece of junk." It had a color monitor and was probably a Mac II.

I am sure you'll agree that the response speed of the interface is most important, and frequently overlooked by designers in the flush of the latest clever trick.

I've been using computers for thirty years (I'm older than Sculley) and they have always been too slow. Hunter's law: "In computers, demand always rises to slightly exceed supply." The result of this is that computers will never be acceptable to the general public but only to us nerds.

—KIM HUNTER

You will find more on response time in the kinesthetic model discussion in Chapter 17, "Conceptual Models."

Let's turn now to a subject that is a perpetual hot button: anthropomorphism[4]: One of the reasons that people tend to become angry at attempts to anthropomorphize computers has to do with what I would characterize as the "ethics" of anthropomorphism:

> A useful point that has perhaps not been made in the course of the ongoing controversy is the distinction between the personification of the computer and the representation of anthropomorphic agents within larger representational contexts supported by the computer medium. (Laurel, 1991)

Thus we can extract:

➤ **GUIDELINE** *Don't pretend the computer is human; create a character, separate from the computer, that displays human characteristics.*

Another reason for people's anger is that the pseudohuman inside the computer is so damned stupid! "Artificial intelligence" (AI) has taken on the task of making agents as smart as people—and not just any people, but Nobel prize winners. This is a truly wonderful pursuit, but much can be done with agents that fall far short of this lofty goal, as long as those agents do not pretend to be that which they are not.

I would extend Brennan's "invisible constraint" of the user to an equally "invisible" constraint of the user's expectations:

➤ **GUIDELINE** *Constrain the user's expectations to match the abilities of the agent.*

The Drafting Assistant very clearly lives in the domain of the document window itself. The user has no expectation that the agent will suddenly begin helping the user remember where other documents were stored on the disk, or carry out any other activity within the application or computer other than its chore of carrying on a dialog during drafting.

A couple years ago, I hired a worker to help me add some outdoor electrical outlets in my Japanese garden. All day, he regaled me with stories of all the wonderful things he knew how to do: He was not only a master at electrical work, but could handle some particularly difficult plumbing I was installing for the fish ponds in my garden, and was an expert at the care and feeding of *koi*, the colorful Japanese fish that would occupy the ponds, as well.

At the end of the day, I paid him off. The next day, I redid all his electrical work; none of it was to code. Not only had he failed to constrain my expectations, he had violated the next guideline:

---

[4] Literally, to make something appear in the form of a human being.

➤ **GUIDELINE** *Constrain the agent to performing tasks it is capable of performing.*

This might seem rather obvious, but to some designers, it's not: I used a text editor with an "agent" about as competent as my "electrician" back in the early days of the Apple II. This program, in the name of offering me protection, was constantly in my face, constantly preventing me from doing what I needed to do.

The designers had set out with the best of intentions to develop a protective environment for their users. Unfortunately, they didn't have a clue as to what their users' needs would be and, therefore, designed automated services that were not only counterproductive, but were impossible to work around. It was as though their "agent" was some demented Dudley Doright, constantly just one step ahead of you, saying, "Wait a minute! Stand aside! *I'll* open that door!" and then, at the last minute, slamming it in your face.

Contrast that with another early Apple II program called Hormuz, written in SuperPILOT, with children as its intended audience. Sporting a fully anthropomorphic character, it was designed to carry on a dialog with the child, interspersed with references to the child's name and gender. And therein lay the problem: It is within the bounds of kid-etiquette to ask a child for his or her name—after all, that cannot normally be deduced from appearance—but there are few insults greater than to ask a nine-year-old standing right in front of you whether they are a boy or girl.

The Hormuzian "agent" set the user's expectations well, however, and no boy or girl ever complained. The character started by introducing himself, then asking the child to "come closer to the fire, where I might see you" setting the mood as outdoors at night in the desert, and the character as one having trouble with his vision. The character would ask the child's name, then say, "I am old, and my eyes grow dim. Tell me, are you a boy or a girl?"

Here then was the secret: The author first established the character as a grandfather-of-the-desert, then endowed him with an expected limitation of an older person's vision. Having set the user's expectations of the agent's abilities and lack thereof, it then asked about gender. Afterwards, it proceeded to carry out a warm, delightful conversation that left people feeling good about the agent and good about themselves.

Many colorful animated applications appeared in SuperPILOT, but I never saw one that captured people's hearts the way Hormuz did. Agents need not be geniuses, they need not be Nobel prize winners. They do need to act in a constrained environment, they do need to constrain the user's expectations by the nature of the character itself, and they do need to be honest, reflecting the true nature of the agent-as-character and the limitations of the design.

Given conformance to these rules, designers can be much bolder in adding intelligence to their interfaces. I, for one, do not need a Nobel prize winner in my computer. But I could sure use someone who would organize my desktop once in a while.

For now, stay tuned: You will find a discussion of agents used as guides in the next chapter.

CHAPTER 21

Designing
"Natural"
Multimedia

❑ *Dear Tog:* I just read with great interest your article in *Apple Direct*, "Learning From the Natural World." I am certain that you are on the right path by recognizing our evolutionary roots. I once knew a young woman who drove off the road trying to swat a wasp in her car with her pocketbook. I suspect her fear of the wasp (triggered by its yellow-striped warning coloration) was instinctive, and that fear of going off the road was not instinctive.

After a few million more years of driving cars, even entering one will seem like walking into a lion's mouth. As for warning coloration, it clearly works! Hence we have wasp-mimicking insects who trade on the wasp's reputation. Our instinctive fear of warning coloration may be generalized. Any brave, gaudy animal can be assumed to be bad medicine, from a tiny red tropical arrow frog to an overweight skunk in a northern trash pile. For desert dwellers, the gila monster's brightly colored beaded markings are a multilingual sign that says "Step on me and I'll bite your backside!" Perhaps should we pattern our warning dialog boxes like the wasp or the gila monster.

Your wilderness observations are valuable and well worth pursuing and building on as principles for interfaces.

For the past twenty years, Peace River Films has produced natural history documentaries for public TV. We were part of the team (with Apple and WGBH-Boston) that produced a HyperCard-driven "Interactive NOVA" about animal migration. The computer interface has been a major interest for us. Natural models and the exploration of real places through "surrogate travel" have been the core of much of our multimedia work. Decision-making while following a natural game trail is satisfying and fluid. Trail branching most often entails one choice at a time and at shallow angles so you don't have to slow down.

Often interactive media is driven by multiple-choice screens that act as deadly, screeching halts, such as we meet when driving in the city. The Mac is a great machine and System 7 is especially good, but what about the natural world? In the wilderness, multiple cues, including sounds, help us to know where we are and to decide where to go.

We have begun to find some interface solutions, and the best have come from nature. Your article rang a bell. There should be few computer walls to bang into. The conditions in nature that we have been steeped in for millions of years have tempered us.

Thanks for an interesting article. Your trail will lead to the top of the mountain, where there is a satisfying view—and a strategic advantage.

—JOHN BORDEN, *Peace River Films*

■ The walls in multimedia have always bothered me. In fact, I have tried few multimedia presentations built around a video disk that I haven't ultimately "experienced" by slapping the disk on the player and watching it end to end. There is something wrong when the chief task of the driving program is to slow you up.

For forty years, TV stores have been selling indoor antennas for the tops of TVs that consist of a pair of rabbit ears protruding from a box with a rotary switch on it. By rotating the switch to just the right position, you can get the best possible reception from the rabbit ears. In the industry, this switch is called the pacifier switch. It is there to give people something to do—and to justify the $24.95 cost. In that one position you finally discover works best, both rabbit ears are attached to your TV in-phase, just as God intended them to be. In every other position of that switch, that antenna is being crippled: One or the other rod is either disconnected or thrown out of phase. None of these antennas ever came with instructions that said, "If you want to get decent reception, make sure you put the switch in position number 37." No piece of multimedia ever came with instructions that said, "If you want to get through this thing during your lifetime, just slap the disk on the player and sit back and relax." Wonder why?

The folks at the Exploratorium in San Francisco did an interesting project where they recorded thousands of images of the Golden Gate Bridge, all taken at the same altitude, all with the bridge dead-center in the image. The images were shot from a helicopter flying along the pathways of a five-square-mile grid with one-mile spacing between lines. The result is an interactive view of the San Francisco Bay Area, in which the user can fly all over the San Francisco Bay Area by spinning a track ball. The main screen shows the view of the bridge from the currently chosen point in space, while a secondary screen displays a map with the grid lines and current location of the user. This and other such projects demonstrate that multimedia can be built around the idea of having a constantly alive environment, with the user moving from place to place within it by direct manipulation.

Several years ago, I was attempting to achieve a flat-line state by watching back-to-back episodes of "Happy Days" when my finger accidentally slipped on the remote control, hurling me without warning into the "NBC Nightly News." The fusillade of thirty-second sound bites brought my brain back to life. Alas, while exciting, these "bites" did little but whet my appetite, thereby forcing me to read an actual newspaper to find out what had really happened.

When I watch news, I want to click on my remote control and instantly pursue more information about the current topic. (Meanwhile, the rest of the show would get shuttled off to my VCR or held down at the phone company, ready to be re-sent via fiber-optic cable.) I want to print out articles on the subject or laterally related areas from a variety of newspapers. I want to be able to explore what led up to today's event. I want multimedia to be used to offer additional information, rather than making the original information cumbersome enough to access that it seems like there must be a real lot of it. I want multimedia to supplement linear presentation, rather than obstructing it.

Kids start out naturally curious. Through the miracle of today's education system, we are often able to cure them of this destructive bent. Those who persevere are usually those who have been able to find answers to their questions. I grew up with *The World Book Encyclopedia* at my beck and call. I was able to find answers, so I kept making up questions. I think if people can satisfy their curiosity, curiosity will become a powerful force in their lives. My multimedia system would mean a lot of extra information must be created and a lot more branching between pieces of information must be available, but what a pay-back! What the heck, we have nothing else of importance planned for the twenty-first century. Let's do it.

In the meantime, there is much we can do to increase the quality of today's multimedia products. Let's look at a few guiding principles.

Principles of Multimedia Visible Interface Design

Of all the forms of information delivery, multimedia has the greatest potential for clear, error-free communication. It also has one of the highest potentials for causing utter confusion. Here are four principles of interface design drawn from "natural laws" of the original Macintosh culture that are particularly applicable to multimedia. They are not the only principles, but they are four I have found to be particularly useful in creating clear, easy to use, powerful multimedia products.

The reason for discussing the principles is simple: There are problems arising in graphical user interface applications, problems for the first time making it difficult for people to understand and use them. By understanding the underpinnings of effective multimedia interfaces, designers can produce better designs, and buyers and users of multimedia products have improved criteria for judging an application's effectiveness.

Making the interface of a multimedia application visible is not a simple task. The richness, diversity, and sheer bulk of the information often rules out use of a productivity interface, such as the Macintosh interface. Instead, developers must use such environments as HyperCard and SuperCard which, while they do offer some finished objects, expect designers to create other objects and tie them all together with their own, visually apparent structure.

Making an interface visible costs: It can mean giving up screen real estate that might be used for yet another button, and it can reduce the apparent efficiency of an application. Yet it pays handsomely, for users are far happier when not confused and far more productive when not lost.

Guidelines to Reduce or Eliminate Navigation

➤ **GUIDELINE**   *Avoid elaborate menu trees.*

Users are far more comfortable in an environment based on **user-centered design**, where objects are brought to them, instead of requiring them to go searching. The menu bar on the Macintosh, with its hierarchical menus, enables users to access more than 6000 menu commands without ever leaving the current display, without ever scrolling the menus. (Anyone bent on using more than 6000 menu commands should not be allowed anywhere near a multimedia design.) By using the menu bar or whatever equivalent is supplied by a particular interface environment, navigation for purposes of menu access can be totally eliminated.

➤ **GUIDELINE**   *Put away the cards.*

The cards in card-based development systems such as HyperCard are the central theme to the developer's environment. They need not and, in many cases, should not be the central theme to the user's environment. Users cannot see what is going on when the entire screen is always filled with a single card, any more than a library user could see around the library if someone were constantly shoving books in his or her face. Users want to see the big picture.

Opening the card catalog need not replace the image of the library. Instead, clicking on a file drawer might only pull the file drawer out into full and expanded view, so the user can now leaf through cards. The illusion is one of information being brought to the user, rather than the user moving around some unfathomable space. Designers know what they are really doing is moving from a card showing the library to a card showing the library with a file drawer open, but the user believes the drawer has simply opened. Card movement remains the designer's "reality," but it is now no longer the user's.

➤ **GUIDELINE** *Consider the information space as well as the system image.*

People also have to navigate within the **information space**, a collective term for all the data they want to access. "Information space" is a good term, because it implies a single, unified structure through which people can zip around. Unfortunately, enabling people to zip around is one of the great challenges facing designers right now, and we have yet to come up with the best answers. Still, we will eventually be able to apply a lot of lessons from books.

People don't find a familiar book by looking for the book that says, *Call of the Wild* on it. Instead, they look for that little red book with the ink blotch on the back, or that tall green book with the worn leather cover. If we select a volume from an encyclopedia, we don't type in the name of the article we are seeking, we flash pages by at the rate of several hundred per minute until we near the one we want. If a book has been designed to stimulate curiosity, as the *World Book Encyclopedia* has, we may never find the initially wanted entry, as fascinating diagrams and pictures flashing by draw our attention, just as videodisk projects, if the designer has allowed rapid, single-frame searching, will encourage people to explore and learn unexpected things.

Guidelines that Make the Interface Visible

➤ **GUIDELINE** *People want clear, visual communication.*

As with all other software endeavors on the Macintosh, developers should always have a graphic designer as a member of their team. (See Chapter 11, "Three Key Players.")

➤ **GUIDELINE** *Use objects and make them visible.*

In the Macintosh interface, objects such as the menu bar, window frames, and scroll bars have their visual appearance, methods of manipulation, feedback, and resultant behaviors bound together. Other graphical user interfaces depend on the designer and programmer to do this binding. Users depend on an object having a consistent appearance and behavior. If the designer needs an object to act differently, she should turn it into a new object by creating a different visual appearance for it.

➤ **GUIDELINE** *People need visual landmarks to act as anchor points.*

Beyond the standard visual landmark on the Macintosh, the menu bar, designers should add their own stable, visual landmarks within their applications. User-centered design fails rather miserably when users no longer feel centered.

➤ **GUIDELINE** *All movement to subordinate windows should leave the primary window open and visible.*

If the subordinate window lies within a panel of the primary window, it is then analogous to your opening a book while seated in the library, and no navigation is felt. If the window zooms open to cover up most, but not all, of the primary window, the user has navigated to the new window, but it's navigation made visible by the animation of the zooming and by the continued visual presence of the anchor point—the primary window.

➤ **GUIDELINE** *If all else fails, offer maps.*

Comedian Steven Wright once reported that a friend had given him a map of the United States—and it was actual size. Applications are actual-size maps, too, and if the designers have followed the other guidelines for turning on the lights, people will likely be able to do any necessary navigation without the aid of interface maps. However, should user testing indicate that people are still getting lost in the interface, something will have to be corrected. The first approach developers should take is to make their actual-size map more enlightening. Only after they have exhausted this avenue completely should they offer the user a map of the interface.

Maps to the information space may prove more necessary. When I visit a large library, I am able to get a map to the various rooms, since I can't zoom up in the air several hundred feet and view them directly, but I can also see a map to the information space: the layout of the Dewey decimal system. This can be a most helpful guide to effective browsing.

➤ **GUIDELINE** *Provide a unifying theme.*

Robert Abel has produced two seminal multimedia projects, one based on a Picasso masterpiece, "Guernica," and the other based on Tennyson's poem, "Ulysses." In each case, the showcased work acts as a central, unifying theme to the data space, offering users a powerful anchor point in their explorations. In each case, Abel takes us far beyond the featured work by not only covering the work itself, but the issues surrounding and raised by the work. Here is a wealth of information about the worlds of art and literature, and the great themes of life itself. One comes away with new insight into such existential issues as war, peace, life, and death. One would be hard pressed to walk away unmoved after hearing the rumbling voice of a great English actor recite Tennyson's stirring words on the nature of heroism, joined with images of a single, unarmed Chinese student holding back a tank near Tiananmen Square. It is multimedia at its best.

Abel could have simply talked about a bunch of different things, like life, painting technique, death, bickering drama critics, war, dramatic speaking, and the plight of Chinese democracy, but by tying them together with a famous work at their center, he helps users not only to avoid getting lost, but also to build a strong framework for retaining the information they have absorbed.

A couple months ago, I worked on a multimedia project centered on San Francisco's earthquake-damaged Embarcadero freeway. Within this context, we were able to explore the early history of the waterfront area, facts on how earthquakes arise, the October 17, 1989, earthquake itself, the after-effects on various people and groups we interviewed, and the future possibilities for San Francisco's waterfront. By using a central, unifying theme, we were able to explore seemingly disparate subjects without losing our users.

➤ **GUIDELINE**   *Use guides.* [1]

Tourists have tour guides. Museum visitors have docents. Growing boys have parents and teachers. Your teenage daughter has a guy you don't know about who wears a black leather jacket and rides a Harley.

People like guides. A well-informed guide can save us all kinds of time and energy by pointing us in the right direction and telling us what is going on as we walk along. We used two guides in the Embarcadero project, both dedicated to shedding light on the information space. Well, sort of. Actually, one was an expert who could be called upon at any time to explain the True Facts of the situation. The other was a politician who could be summoned to explain how he deeply and profoundly felt that, whatever the issue was, it was an issue that should not be decided through some simple partisan process, but an issue that would require study, an open airing of the facts, and so on and so on. (We were into *cinema verité.*)

The Advanced Technology Group at Apple has produced an experimental project called Guides. It presents an American history curriculum which people are free to explore at will. It also has a series of four guides. The first is the guide to the program itself, who can get you out of trouble no matter where you are. The other three have some rather strong opinions on the subject of American history, being an American Indian, a prairie schoolmarm, and a frontiersman, as shown in Figure 21–1.

---

[1] Guides are a form of agent, the subject of the previous chapter.

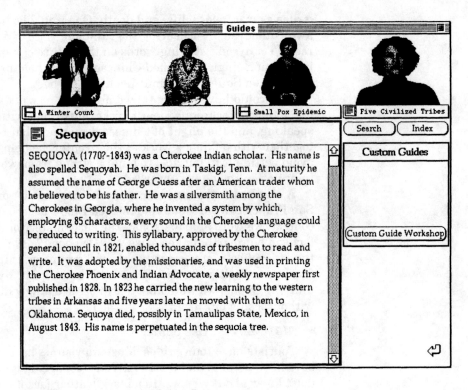

Figure 21–1. *Agents in the Guides Project*

These three guides, like the first, appear as real, animated people anchored at the top of the display. Should they have something to say, they raise their hand to get your attention. Should they be neutral on the subject, they are liable to fall asleep. If they think the subject should be struck from the curriculum, they show their annoyance by carrying out distracting activities, such as whittling. Sometimes they really get into it, as when the subject of Indians stealing horses comes up. The frontiersman and the Indian have quite opposite points of view.

Thus, guides can not only act as pilots as users traverse the system image and information space, they can be subject experts, offer comic relief, set tone, reflect differing viewpoints, and generate a powerful sense of realism.

As the technology for empowering guides improves, we will see guides who will come to know you and your needs and will be able to bring you exactly the right information before you even know you need it.

PART V

More Mail!

"Neither snow, nor rain, nor heat, nor gloom of night stays the mighty TOG from the swift completion of his appointed rounds."

—APPLE EVANGELIST JAMES "HERODOTUS" LANAHAN,
Adapted from the inscription on the main post office, New York City.

CHAPTER 22

The Holy Interface, or Command Keys Revisited

↜ *COLUMN 9: OCTOBER, 1989*

People were not about to let the whole command key thing drop:

❑ ***Dear Tog:*** Consider a typical MS-DOS word processor. It sits there and waits for the user to tell it to do something, and then it gets its next action from a big list something like this:

- If the user pressed a number or letter key, then insert the corresponding character into memory and advance the cursor.
- If the user pressed Alt-W, then write the stuff in memory to a disk file.
- If the user pressed Alt-X, then return to DOS.
- If the user pressed Alt-T, then ask the user what pattern to translate and what to translate it to, and don't let him do anything else until he enters these patterns or presses Escape.
- If the user pressed Alt-F, then ask the user what the new file name should be, and don't let her do anything else until she enters the new file name or presses Escape.

And so forth, unless the user has redefined the command keys, in which case the computer reads the user's list instead of the default list.

This is clearly obsolete, troglodytic, stupid, and all of those other kind things that Apple likes to say about MS-DOS systems and the people who like them.

Now consider a typical Mac word processor, with all of its wonderful new concepts. It sits there and waits for the user to tell it to do something, and then it gets its next action from a big list something like this:

- If the user pressed a number or letter key, then insert the corresponding character into memory and advance the cursor.

- If the user left the keyboard, found the mouse, watched the screen while she moved the cursor to the File menu, pressed the mouse button, watched the screen while she dragged the cursor to the Save item, and released the mouse button, then write the stuff in memory to a disk file.

- If the user left the keyboard, found the mouse, watched the screen while he moved the cursor to the File menu, pressed the mouse button, watched the screen while he dragged the cursor to the Quit item, and released the mouse button, then return to the Finder.

- If the user left the keyboard, found the mouse, watched the screen while she moved the cursor to the Find menu, pressed the mouse button, watched the screen while she moved the cursor to the Translate item, and released the mouse button, then ask her what pattern to translate and what to translate it to, and don't let her do anything else until she enters these patterns or clicks Cancel.

- If the user left the keyboard, found the mouse, watched the screen while he moved the cursor to the File menu, pressed the mouse button, watched the screen while he moved the cursor to the Save As item, and released the mouse button, then ask him what the new file name should be, and don't let him do anything else until he enters the new file name or clicks Cancel.

And so forth, unless the user wants to use the command-key equivalents, in which case she has to remember whether she is in the MPW editor (where Command-S means Save) or the AppleLink editor (where Command-S means Send) or in some other editor, where Command-S means something else. If she wants to use the same editor for C source, Pascal source, letters to Mom, and AppleLink memos, or to redefine the command keys, that's too bad.

It should be obvious that this is orders of magnitude better than the simple-minded MS-DOS interface, and justifies perfectly the choice of an expensive computer with no second source.

Unfortunately, it isn't obvious. Could you explain the difference? Could you explain it in reasonable terms, without sounding like Jimmy Swaggart denouncing Buddhism?

Thanks,

—ANONYMOUS

■ Oh, sure, open up on me with an AK-47 assault rifle and then ask me to fight back with one mouth tied behind my back.

You paint a most rose-colored picture of what I had always thought of as a blue world. Perhaps we have all been misled these years. Perhaps the independent studies that show over and over again that Macintosh users are more productive, can learn quicker, buy more software packages, and so on, and so on, are somehow all flawed. Perhaps...

Let us first examine your ponderous exposition of the tribulations of discovering and using the mouse:

> If the user left the keyboard, found the mouse, watched the screen while she moved the cursor to the File menu, pressed the mouse button, watched the screen while she dragged the cursor to the Save item, and released the mouse button. . . .

Now, that does sound like a lot of work. Particularly since, like most responsible mouse and AK-47 owners, you probably keep your mouse locked up in your bedside chest, with the ball secreted elsewhere, lest the children find it and roll each other to death. I, myself, casting danger to the wind, keep my mouse in the same room as the keyboard! Often actually connected (gasp) to the computer!

Command Keys Aren't Faster As you know from my August column, it takes just as long to decide upon a command key as it does to access the mouse.[1] The difference is that the command-key decision is a high-level cognitive function of which there remains no long-term memory. Therefore, subjectively, keys seem faster when in fact they usually take just as long to use.

Since mouse acquisition is a low-level cognitive function, the user need not abandon cognitive process on the primary task during the acquisition period. Therefore, the mouse acquirer achieves greater productivity. And just to balance the record, here is how you might have phrased the process used by your MS-DOS victim:

> If the user stopped all cognitive processing on the primary task, entered a 2.5-second decision-making process shrouded by amnesia, laterally rotated the forearm at the olecranon joint while simultaneously flexing the fifth metacarpophalangeal joint for purposes of accessing the Alt key, while simultaneously extending the

---

[1] This rather flat statement set off a new round of protest from developers who insisted that command keys were faster, but for all the letters, telephone calls, and assorted anonymous threats, no one offered any evidence of a controlled study showing such an outcome.

second metacarpophalangeal joint in an effort to reach the W, then you should write the stuff in memory to a disk file while the user tries desperately to do a cognitive re-acquisition of her original task.

Let us now move on to the more general questions of a visual versus abstract interface:

There are some really good abstract interfaces. The HASCI system was one. Jef Raskin's[2] Cannon Cat interface is another. At the risk of seeming immodest, I think the Apple II file card interface, as embodied in AppleWorks, is a third. The system you describe might well be a fourth. These systems promote many of the behavioral attributes that are strengths of the Macintosh interface: consistency, freedom from modes and sequences, user-control, feedback and dialog, metaphors from the real world, forgiveness. At the same time, there are bad graphical interfaces, where behaviors are not bound to visual appearance, where consistency is often in short supply.

Still, studies on individual differences indicate that the overwhelming majority of people will never be comfortable with abstract interfaces (see Chapter 23). For example, a remarkable number of people cannot remember 250 different commands.

We programmers are not normal people. We tend to have superior memories, we actually grasp Boolean logic, we have formed priesthoods around the most egregious interfaces, and we have a firm belief that the average citizen is in search of an editor for his daily C and Pascal coding tasks.

We are not firmly rooted in the real world.

I submit that the greatest difference, Brother, between the interface you describe and the Macintosh interface, is that the "lights are on" on the Macintosh. The Macintosh is a visible interface, and people thrive on that visibility.

That is indeed a profound difference.

---

[2] Jef Raskin, before starting his own company, Information Appliance, launched a fairly popular personal computer called the Macintosh. Before he left the project, the Macintosh was far more dependent on the keyboard , and Raskin knew what to do with a keyboard, too. For example, the Find function on the Cannon Cat is some 50 times faster than the same function on the Macintosh. Raskin didn't use "Command-key equivalents": he designed a true keyboard interface from the ground up.

The Cannon Cat did not sell well, but this should be attributed to the hardware on which the system ran, as well as Cannon's decision to target this ideal interface for professional writers almost exclusively to low-level clerical workers, who didn't need its functionality and were confused by its "invisible" interface. The interface was ideal for intuitives in general, and it is sad that so few of its innovations have yet to be picked up by the HI community.

The Macintosh is sweeping away the dying carcasses of the "black cave" interfaces of old. Join with us, Brother, in celebrating the dawning of a new, glorious, single-source day.[3]

---

[3] To those of you who bought the leather-bound edition: If you are feeling queasy from the purple prose, you will find an air-sickness bag in the pocket on the back cover. (OK, OK, so there is no leather-bound edition. There should be.)

CHAPTER *23*

How to Make an Extra Couple Million in the 1990s

➻ *COLUMN 10: DECEMBER, 1989*

(In an early column, (see Chapter 3) I had addressed the experience of first moving to the Macintosh. I did this because I had seen designers and programmers sincerely trying to create a Macintosh application struggling hard because they were holding on to old concepts.

By December of 1989, when this column came out, I had seen another phenomenon: companies making a business decision to bring out a foreign interface on the Macintosh, because it would save them the time and trouble of converting their old application running under a different system. The result was that these products were being panned in reviews and users were dragging them back to the stores as quickly as they discovered the "outlander" interfaces.)

In the spirit of the holidays, I recently looked into buying plastic letter openers emblazoned with a picture of Old Saint Nick. Thought I'd send one out to every developer. Saint Nick's beard changed color depending on the weather. Something quite different would happen to him if you dipped him in water. Eventually, I decided against it. So don't go rummaging through the envelope. The letter opener's not there.

I want to offer a gift much more valuable. Valuable because, as owner of a company, you could pocket an extra few million bucks next year. Valuable because, as an employee of that same company, you could realize an extra $24.78 in profit sharing. Valuable because it ain't gonna cost me anything, and you will undoubtedly have the proper sensibilities to reward me if it works. My kind of present.

For years, people have been porting software directly to the Macintosh. For years, the market has consistently said, "Go away!"

185

Some developers take that message and really do go away. Others try, try again.

Companies don't need to go through this. There is a formula that virtually guarantees success on this platform. That formula is my holiday gift to you. I have seen it improve the bottom line of major corporations. I've seen it turn small companies into major corporations. It is quite simple to do, as long as you suffer from excessive amounts of vision and have an unhealthy absence of fear.

But what happens if you fail to accept my generous offer?

Three Steps to Failure

As the Macintosh has increased in power, more and more developers have attempted to migrate from higher-powered platforms. These developers had, by definition, been supplying "niche" markets: No matter how mainstream the subject matter, most people couldn't afford the $50,000 or $100,000 computers of a decade ago.

These developers, over and over, have initially come up with the same three-step product release scheme:

Step 1. Release a direct port.

Step 2. Release a hybrid, nine months later, that offers some Macintosh "features"

Step 3. Release a true Macintosh interface, to be available nine months after the hybrid.

Hardly a month goes by that I don't hear about this marketing plan from one company or another. I have yet to see it be anything but a disaster.

The problem, simply, is that the second release not only takes two years to get out, it fails miserably in the marketplace. No one will buy it. The original users have no incentive to make the transition, and Macintosh users will have nothing to do with it. This failure not only demoralizes everyone, but the company never realizes the profits they counted on to fund the third release.

Three Steps to Success

You don't ever have to be entrapped by this process. Instead, you can enter the Macintosh marketplace as a success, simply by following Tognazzini's three-step program. (This program is not available through any store. You may only obtain it through this special magazine offer. Read before midnight tonight.)

Evaluate your code

Step 1. Make an honest and complete assessment of your code.

Most companies are absolutely bent on porting over their old code. Sure it took fifty work-years to develop it. But how many of those work-years were expended patching the original code until it became all but unmanageable? And how many work-years would it really take to re-create it from scratch?

These are important questions because it is usually extremely difficult, if not impossible, to convert a port into a true Macintosh application without rewriting most, if not all, of the code: The behaviors of the Macintosh interface go deep into the system. Such user algorithms as select-the-object-then-act (noun-verb) cannot be easily imposed on an application designed with choose-the-act, then select-the-object, then OK-the-action (verb-noun-verb).

For those not familiar with estimating the length of a software effort, let me offer you an amusing, if surprisingly accurate, rule of thumb: Figure how long a project could possibly take, double the number, and move to the next higher time unit. For example, let's say you "guesstimate" it will take one day to add a certain feature. One doubled is two, and the next highest-time unit is a week. So your new feature will take exactly two weeks. This may sound awfully silly, and I'm certainly not offering it as a scientifically proven estimating tool, but it is often chillingly accurate. That one month you decide to spend doing that first direct port can easily end up being two years as you add "just one more" Macintosh feature after another.

If you want to do a direct port, do a direct port. Don't try to make it Mac-like at all. Sell it to your installed base. Then be prepared to abandon large parts of it as you begin your pure Macintosh version.

"But what about the hybrid version?" you may ask. Forget it. There is nothing more antithetical to the Macintosh than a hybrid interface. Nobody ends up happy. I have never seen a company do anything but squander resources trying to make a hybrid version. Get onto the task of making the true Macintosh version.

Trust the Macintosh Market

Step 2: Have courage. Think big. Believe in the Macintosh market.

The niche market of yesterday is the mainstream market of today. How many people were using desktop publishing software ten years ago? How many two-person doctors' offices were computerized ten years ago? How many people were doing tax planning in the privacy of their own homes?

I have seen developers in the perfect position to go from an installed base of one thousand customers to one million customers practically overnight. Instead, they kept focusing on doubling their installed base to two thousand people by getting their old customers to buy some new Macintoshes.

Explore New Market Opportunities   When you enter the Macintosh world, you are in a genuine mass market, populated by people willing to learn, willing to grow. I can think of no product so esoteric that it cannot be slightly refocused to capture a greater population.

A product I particularly like on the Macintosh is ModaCAD. Designed for the fashion industry, it facilitates every step of the design process from conception to fabric selection to pattern creation to fabric cutting. Although it has a true Macintosh interface, it remains a niche market application: The program is divided into a number of segments to be used by specific people within the industry. The designer's interface is quite different from the fabric cutter's. The pattern-maker's interface is based on the method of pattern-making that stretches back over several generations. The application is absolutely locked into the established work flow of the fashion industry.

This is the kind of product that will boost the sales for a company that might have been producing a similar application for a much more expensive machine. Not only does a complete system cost far less, the application has an interface that is far more functional. Still and all, it has not exactly captured the mass market.

The part that fascinates me about the application is its ability to drape fabrics: Slap a piece of cloth on a color scanner or design one into a drawing program and ModaCAD will gently form the cloth into a dress slinkily draped over the image of a model. What-you-see-is-what-you-get. Imagine building upon this idea for a broader market: Put Macintosh IIs with color scanners in fabric stores around the world. People could type in their personal dimensions, then play "what if" with various styles and fabrics. Given accurate measurements, the machine could custom-generate a pattern on the spot, sized to the person and laid out for maximum utilization of the particular width and pattern of the chosen fabric.

Increase Ease of Use   Spreadsheets have been around for fifty or a hundred years. They were done on paper. The recalculations we complain take almost one second on a Macintosh II took two or three days with an adding machine and an eraser. Playing "what if" was out of the question. Very few people did spreadsheets until VisiCalc and the Apple II made it all quite practical.

Many applications sitting in niche markets are simply waiting for the right interface to come along. Every so often one does and, like VisiCalc, it seems like such an obvious idea. When developers have the courage to lay aside for the moment their fifty work-year anchor and re-examine the problem, their applications can simply explode into the Macintosh market.

One such application is Vellum (see Chapter 20, "The Advent of Agents"), a CAD program from Ashlar. By introducing the concept of agents, they increased ease of use and productivity tremendously, while simultaneously reducing the strain of learning even more dramatically. This application is worth seeking out.

Last year I spent more than fifty hours trying to draw my house in a 3-D graphics program. There is not a wall in that drawing that is properly connected to any other wall. The roof kind of floats here and there, depending on the angle. I eventually abandoned the application and built a model of the house out of construction paper. Given a Vellum-like interface, I could have assembled that house with perfectly joined walls in a matter of a couple of hours.[1]

A breakthrough like Vellum's will not only expand a porter's Macintosh market, it will neatly solve any problem with the installed base: Existing users will jump at the chance of learning a new package when it offers such obvious benefits.

Get a Fresh Start

Step 3. Start fresh.

If you are ready to create a true Macintosh application, it is time for an off-site to rethink your market and your product. Explore existing applications. What are they doing right? What's holding them back? Why are some people unwilling/or unable to use them?

Do field studies. Go through formal brainstorming. Create updated scenarios (see Chapter 13). Revisit ten-year-old decisions: If you have 275 individual tools in your existing application, examine that fact. ClarisCAD got rid of hoards of individual tools by creating a few master tools with orthogonal sets of attributes. A few tools times a few attributes times a few attributes times a few attributes equal a whole bunch of tools. These kinds of changes not only simplify the interface, they slash code.

During my career, I have gone through this kind of exercise perhaps fifty times. I have never seen it do anything but streamline and improve a design. Try it. You'll like it.

And don't forget to send me my ten percent.

---

[1] In fact, as this book goes to press, I am doing just that using the new Vellum 3D, and it is a dream.

CHAPTER 24

The Troof about Moof

➡ COLUMN 14: APRIL, 1990

On January 24, 1984, Apple introduced the now-famous dogcow, shown in Figure 24–1, packaged in a light beige carrying case with a screen on the front. The screen, when the case was plugged in, would light up, displaying the dogcow within. The carrying case became known, affectionately, as Macintosh; the dogcow became known as . . . well, she would prefer I not say. This much, however, I shall disclose: When placed near a can of Mountain Dew, she utters a sound. The sound is "moof."

Figure 24–1. The dogcow

Many of you have written to me over the years, wondering about the origins of the beast. Speculation as to the cause of her bizarre appearance has run wild, from rumors of a canine skin disorder to tales of high-finance and corporate intrigue. We have published much about the origins of this beast, but still people write, link, and even call.

Could it be that you have all detected a certain lack of candor in our various explanations? Could it be that you somehow suspect a cover-up? This month, having received yet another link on the subject, I have decided to finally reveal the complete truth, even at the risk of betraying a confidence.

My deepest apologies for any pain this may bring to my dear friend.

❏ *Venerable Tog:* In my contemplations I have come to realize that "moof" is the mantra of the dogcow (or is that cowdog?). Could you, oh, Mac Master, tell me what a cowdog (or a dogcow) is and why she is so honored by those who call themselves MacDTS?[1]

We have considered the Tao of the birdmouse with the mantra "CheapSqueak." Is this the path to Truth & Enlightenment?

Zenfully,

—TOM STAMM, *Boise, Idaho*

■ Yes, Tom, this is the path to truth, the truth about a poor, forlorn life form who reached an enlightenment beyond her years, an enlightenment I will share with you and my readers, in hopes that none of you need suffer as she did.

The dogcow played a pivotal role during the development of the Macintosh interface. Her first public appearance was in 1984, as the character "z" in the Cairo font. She soon became an icon in the Page Setup Options dialog, helping legions of LocalTalk LaserWriter owners to print critical documents in strange orientations. And she has helped us fill countless empty programming hours (or was it countless hours of empty programming?) with engaging speculations as to her origins, hours that would have otherwise been spent staring at computer displays or comic books, waiting impatiently for yet another compilation to be completed.

For years, rumors spread through the industry concerning an early collaboration between the biotech wonder company, Genentech, and the microtech wonder company, Apple. As the story went, this pilot project ended in disaster when a software bug threw off the genetic engineering code of a new cross-breed of canine and bovine. But instead of a sleek, highly motivated superdog, capable of taking out the garbage, buttering toast, and designing MS-DOS applications, the result was the now famous dogcow.

This story is patently untrue. Indeed, the dogcow we know and love today was not a product of careful scientific exploration but rather a victim of veterinary malpractice.

---

[1] MacDTS is Macintosh Developer Technical Services, the group at Apple dedicated to supporting Apple's third-party developer community.

It all began on the Ides of March, 1980, when a certain Dr. Mortimer Starzynski, of the Washington Starzynskis, decided to take a one-day seminar in veterinary plastic surgery conducted in the Empire Room of the local Howard Johnson's.

The good doctor had graduated at the bottom of his class several years before at the Grenada University of Podiatric Sciences. Having been run out of town in East McKeesport for leaving the mayor a foot short, he responded to a TV ad's late-night clarion call to "break into the profitable field of elective plastic surgery for critters. Doughnuts served."

Armed with a mimeographed diploma, a beat-up canister vacuum cleaner, and a turkey baster, Starzynski emerged after eight hours a fully qualified Plastic Veterinarian. Sixteen days later—April 1, 1980—he hung up his shingle and was in business.

The dogcow checked in that fateful day, having tried every fad diet known to animal. Our veterinarian hero was desperate, and the dogcow was flush with cash. Just the sort of patient our doctor was waiting for.

Starzynski separated the critter from her money, and then he separated her from her butterfat. All 1,500 pounds of it. Yes, our friend is a cow, not a dog. Contrast these actual photographs of the two-dimensional beast—shown in Figure 24–2—taken just before and immediately after the botched procedure.

Before:

After:

Figure 24–2. *Surgical Results*

Since then, the folks in DTS have helped her put on some weight and had her tail bobbed, and her horns shortened,[2] but she remains a mere shadow of her former, glorious self. (Her milk ain't so hot anymore, either—said to be the result of emotional distress.)

---

[2] They have also broadened her horizons: A plywood likeness of the dogcow, approximately two feet long, has been carried literally around the world. Her pen on the seventh floor of Apple's City Center IV building, the home of the dogcow, is festooned with photographs taken of her standing (leaning?) before many of the great landmarks of the world.

Yes, my beloved friend is a cow, not a dog, a cow permanently disfigured exactly ten years ago this April 1, by an incompetent liposucker.

Don't *you* be a sucker: Stay away from vets with vacuums.

CHAPTER 25

The "3-D" Look
in the Interface

❧ *COLUMN 14: APRIL, 1990*

❑ ***Dear Tog:*** If you look at the programs coming out these days, many of them are beginning to have "3-D" controls, sometimes similar to those NeXT uses. Each and every developer seems to be using his or her own best judgment as to what these controls should look like.

Apple needs to review what the Macintosh interface should look like and ask itself whether it wants to start including the 3-D look. One of the things that makes the Mac great is the consistency of the interface: If you follow the guidelines, an up-arrow looks like an up-arrow looks like an up-arrow. If everything else were equal, I wouldn't know whether you should design for two interfaces; it would certainly reduce the consistency. But everything else is *not* equal and the question of whether Apple should start including the 3-D look is quickly becoming moot: There are numerous programs written these days that run only on the Mac II family of computers, and many of these are developing rather different versions of the 3-D look.

I think Apple should jump into the fray and decide on 3-D guidelines. Develop two different interfaces, and special-case for the one-bit machines. Why? The main reason is that some of these 3-D effects look cool (emphasis on "some" here; NeXT overdoes it), and people are going to start using them. It is imperative that some sort of guidelines be followed, or Mac interface consistency will deteriorate. Also, the number of machines in the Mac lineup that have more than one bit is certain to increase. That is, I hope that in the near future even the low-end machines will have four (or best, eight) bits.

It's a tough call. No, Apple should definitely not abandon the 1-bit users. But Apple must keep the interface consistent, and developers are already changing it by implementing the 3-D look in many different ways. And they're going to continue to do so, whatever Apple says. I've heard there's substantial resistance at some levels of upper management to changing the interface. If that's the case, Apple should at least offer an alternate set of guidelines.

The time to start planning for a new, consistent, more interesting interface that will run on the Macintosh of the '90s is now.

—ROBERT ANTHONY, *Macintosh Programmer/Consultant, Evanston, Illinois*

■ I am reminded of a time a few years back, when an Apple person was getting married. One of her co-workers had been given the task of rounding up a gift to be offered as a group present. After long thought, he decided that one of those pieces of art where there are three frames instead of one, with the art carved up among them, would be really neat. (His knowledge of art was somewhat limited.) Since he knew me to be a self-proclaimed authority on all subjects, he naturally sought me out and asked where he might secure such a masterpiece. I advised him that one does not search out art on the basis of the number of picture frames involved. As this answer left him with nothing left to go on, he settled for a Cuisinart.

One does not design a human interface based on the fact that 3-D interfaces look "real cool." One only has to sit in virtually any of the "real cool" chairs built in the last fifty years by leading Bauhaus designers to understand why: What looks "real cool" can often be acutely painful to use. First, the interface should communicate; only then should it look "real cool."

Nevertheless, I have always firmly held that guidelines should not only be formulated through "visionary" intuitive leaps, but also by running around to the front of the parade. Of the two, the latter will often add more to the pursuit of consistency. However, the parade is long, and the runners are few, winded, and interested in long-term solutions. Of necessity, should Apple Computer respond to this current fad, it will be a slow process.

Here, then, are my recommendations, for those of you bent on immediately implementing such a look.

➤ *GUIDELINE* Do not attempt a 3-D look in 1-bit graphics.

I have been astounded at the number of really awful-looking "3-D" interfaces that have suddenly invaded the Macintosh, all implemented in graphics one bit deep. The original Macintosh graphics can arguably be accused of making an application appear somewhat "old-fashioned." A grainy, dithered-gray interface, in my humble opinion, serves only to make the Macintosh look just plain bad.

➤ *GUIDELINE* Be wary of interface elements that detract from or overwhelm the content regions of your application.

The interface is there to support, not replace, the task the user is attempting to accomplish. Some applications I have seen, with their Star Trek-style "control panels," make the user's creative content look flimsy and unimportant by contrast. Others are grabbing up so much bandwidth that little is left for real communication between user and machine. Interface elements should tend toward neutral gray, so they don't overwhelm the content region. Using several shades of gray with small differences in value (brightness) among them can produce beautiful results.

➤ **GUIDELINE** *The design of visual elements should be left to people schooled in their creation: graphic designers.*

As with all other visual interface endeavors, 3-D looks are best left to trained graphic designers who are able to communicate ideas and are endowed with a sense of elegance. (See Chapter 11, "Three Key Players.") We can all do a pretty fair drawing using an Etch-A-Sketch, but not too many of us are particularly good at oil painting. The greater the human-computer communications bandwidth, the more trouble we amateurs can get into. Eight-bit-deep graphics are way beyond the scope of us non-artists, no matter how clever we are at bit-twiddling. A few hours of an independent graphic designer's time could make your product beautiful, and beautiful sells.

➤ **GUIDELINE** *Do not invent new objects that behave just like—or, worse, almost like—the original, but that are composed of new and different symbols.*

For example, perhaps you really must make a scroll bar appear 3-D, due, presumably, to some early childhood trauma suffered while wearing green- and red-lensed glasses. If you must, spiff up the arrows by making them leap out of the screen, but do not replace them with the hand, a ferret, or tiny images of Superman. You may want a 3-D modal dialog box, but your users will expect the familiar double-outline to surround it, even if the lines now have a tendency to jump out at them.

As for Apple changing the interface, I know of no resistance among upper management. I think it can be safely said, however, that many people up there in that stratosphere are blissfully unaware of the pressure under which our original interface now finds itself, not only in this area, but in others. I also believe that you, in the development community, could do a lot more toward educating them as to your needs and desires.

We have no intentions of taking this company into the twenty-first century with the 1984 Macintosh interface, but we also cannot leap around every time someone comes up with some new "look." Just as the law often moves ponderously slow for the sake of continuity and consistency, so must we. For one thing, lots of new ideas just don't hold up; we must have thrown out twenty ideas for every one we eventually incorporated into the original Macintosh. We also avoided cluttering the interface by not adding every proposed "feature" and by avoiding visual gewgaws. As Coco Chanel (either the inventor of hot chocolate or a numbered French perfume—I forget which) once said, "Elegance is refusal."

I would love to see us create a fresh, new look. I would love to make better use of our new hardware capabilities. I would also like to see us make it far easier for you developers to make use of our new hardware capabilities, without your having to put such demands on your programmers that their suicide rate climbs alarmingly. There are others within Apple who feel the same as I do. With luck, it just may happen. If other readers feel as you do, Robert, and are as free in expressing their opinion, it just may happen soon.[1]

---

[1] In February, 1990, when I wrote these words, it was not at all clear that System 7 would adopt either color or a 3-D look in the interface. Even as Robert's letter arrived, many of us in the human interface community at Apple were pushing hard for these changes, which were eventually adopted late in the summer of 1990. Letters like the one from Robert, sent to the proper people in Apple management, had a direct impact on that decision.

CHAPTER 26

The Cure for Trash Can Madness

The following letter is a response to Kim Hunter's letter, published in the January 1990 column (see Chapter 10), in which Kim attacked several silly aspects of the trash can's behavior. Kim failed, however, to discuss one magic (and highly inconsistent) aspect of the trash can: the way it slings disks out of the drive, rather than slinging their contents out of the universe:

❑ **Dear Tog:** My suggestion for the worst user interface prize: Dragging a disk to the trash doesn't initialize it!
  —MICHAEL MURIE, *Multimedia Workshop, Somerville, MA*

■ I find one of the more interesting things about the trash-can disk-slinger is not that the original mistake was made, but that it has been perpetuated. Even System 7, which will offer a genuine menu equivalent to trashing the disk will continue to offer the trash shortcut. Two reasons for this stand out: First, people have developed the habit of dragging disks to the trash, and it would be most unnatural to just suddenly have nothing happen. (Far worse would be to actually erase their disks, as the user's action rather literally suggests.)

A second reason none of we interface zealots care to admit is that this method of ejection works really well ergonomically. The user is able to use gross motor movement to propel a large object to a large target. Fitts's law (see Chapter 27) confirms such a scheme to be most efficient. Engineers, such as the one who thought up the scheme, are in all ways pleased.

Unfortunately, the premise that trash cans eject disks is fundamentally wrong, as any four-year-old child can and will tell you. Loudly. So will grown-ups who tend to lose their concentration. (I can't tell you how many times, in the heat of "floppyizing" one of these columns while rushing off to work, I have dragged the original document to the trash, instead of dragging the floppy.)

So what happened that led to this insanity? Is this the only efficient solution possible? No. Even faster and cleaner would be a gesture, such as flinging the disk up and to the right or left. One could even return to ancient times and install a button beside the slot in the drive. We eliminated a mechanical eject on drives so the system would have control over its data, but a switch installed on the drive could act only to tell the system the user wanted the disk, so the system could then do whatever cleaning up it chose.

The trash can "shortcut' was thought up by someone who was less than fully informed on the theory and practice of human interface design. He was "into" the engineering model, and the engineering model holds that the most ergonomically efficient way that can be easily implemented is the right way. Engineers are not bothered by the solution because they often don't even recognize the metaphorical world of the interface. That's for the tourists. The engineers are down below, where the trash can is just another large-scale target that the operating system will see has having been hit (see Chapter 32).

Engineers are not the only ones lacking in full knowledge of the ways of human-computer interaction. Far from it. In fact, all of us who have wandered into this field in the last 25 years or so have started out woefully ignorant, and the smart ones among us have realized we are likely to stay that way, given the explosive growth of knowledge in the field. Fortunately, a forum exists for pursuing further growth and learning: the annual SIGCHI conference. SIGCHI is the Special Interest Group for the study of Computer-Human Interaction within the Association for Computing Machinery (ACM). The members tend to come from three different backgrounds: computer science, psychology, and graphic design.

In addition to demonstrations, exhibits, interactive experiences, and technical secessions, the conference offers dozens of tutorial sessions of four to eight hours duration. If you are new to design, you will find a wealth of relevant, well-presented information. The conferences are thoroughly enjoyable, and, after a few years, you will have formed a strong group of friends you can depend on to tear apart your most precious designs.

You may contact SIGCHI at: The Association for Computing Machinery, 11 West 42nd Street, New York, NY 10036.

The conferences take place in late April of each year. See you there.

CHAPTER 27

Fitts's Law: Why Pull-Down Menus Work Best

❑ ***Dear Tog:*** I've started seeing applications with menu bars in their windows, like those sported by MS-Windows and X. Examples include Kaleidagraph 2.1, StuffIt Deluxe, WordPerfect 2.0, and MacDraw Pro. Is there an official Apple position on window menu bars and what their relationship should be to the global menu bar?

—STEVE HERSKOVITZ, *The MathWorks, Inc.*

■ Human interface is a field rife with uncertainty, being one of those "soft sciences" that harder types find difficult to deal with. Fortunately, in this sea of psychology and artistic aesthetics, one law stands absolute: **Fitts's law.** And Fitts's law proves, beyond a shadow of a doubt, that menu bars have no place in windows.

Fitts's law states that the time required to move from a starting point to within the confines of a target area is dependent on a logarithmic relationship between the distance (D) from the point to the target area and the size (S) of the target.[1] (According to S.K. Card, et al. [1983] the proper formula for reaching the target in a single-level pull-down is Time = $1.08 + .096 \log_2 (D/S + .5)$. There. Now I'm glad we've gotten that out of the way.)

Translated into English, Fitts's law states that the further away the target and the smaller its size, the longer it will take to hit it.

---

[1] The width of the target affects access time, as a narrow target requires the user's trajectory to be quite accurate, for fear of going around it rather than through it. However, the bulk of Card's work in this area, has focused on depth. In his experiments, he will typically have the target stretch the full height of the screen, so as to negate the possibility of going around it.

"Yeah, so what?" you say.

People for years have been explaining to me very patiently that in this era of giant screen monitors, we just have to do something about those menu bars way up there at the top of the screen; that menu bars should be attached to windows, or pop up beneath the cursor, or something. Anything, just so they aren't up at the top of the screen anymore. Fitts's law can help us sort through this mess rather easily.

At the CHI'89 conference, Neff Walker and John Smelcer delivered a paper which set on its ear a lot of our conventional wisdom about pull-downs at screen top versus pull-downs within windows versus pop-ups. (Walker, et al., 1990)

They performed an experiment almost identical to one I carried out three years ago, with identical results. The difference was, that they figured out why it came out the way it did. The answer is one of those marvelous little "of course" sorts of reasons—the kind you might not tumble to in a million years, but once you hear it, seems piteously obvious (see Chapter 15, "Carl Jung and the Macintosh").

First, the Objects Both of us used standard, Apple-like pull-down menus. We both used similar pop-up, hierarchical menus (which they refer to as "walking" menus) containing all the menu items found in a pull-down menu. The pull-down menus, as always, displayed a horizontal line of **menu titles**. Clicking on a title made the menu open to reveal its **menu items**. Opening a pop-up displayed the menu titles in a column. Sliding to the right side of the desired title caused a column of menu items to appear. This behavior is similar (identical, in my experiment) to the way hierarchical menus work within the Macintosh menu bar: Slide down to the sub-title and the sub-menu will appear.

Their Experiment They created a pop-up menu (the "walking" menu) which contained all the menu items in their pull-down menu. This menu would pop up immediately beneath the mouse pointer, displaying the menu titles. Then the subject would move across the needed title, popping the sub-menu open, then slide to the desired item.

For the pull-down, the subject would need to move the mouse pointer as much as 15 cm from the original location, then locate the item in the same way as done on the Macintosh.

The subjects (who were paid $8.00 each) used a Sperry PW 500, with a 12-inch diagonal EGA screen to run through the two types of menus, accessing various menu items as directed. (The details are all there in the original paper. The subjects definitely earned the $8.00.)

My Experiment (An Exercise in Extremes)   My pop-up menu was one of the public domain INITs that use Apple's menu code to pop up a hierarchical menu version of the pull-downs directly beneath the mouse pointer wherever the user Command-clicks.

The pull-down menu was standard, but located on a 21-inch B&W display to the left of the 13-inch color display used for the actual task. The bottom of the shorter color display was located even with the bottom of the B&W display, making the menu bar more than 15 *inches* and a slight dog-leg to the left away from the area of activity on the color screen.

My task was diabolical: I had ten folders in a Finder window on the color display, each in brilliant blue. The subjects (paid nothing, but allowed to touch a real Macintosh) had to change each of the blue folders to magenta, one at a time.

In the case of the pop-up, they had merely to select a folder, Command-click, drop down to the Color menu, and glide smoothly to the magenta swatch. (You can tell where this is leading, can't you?) For the pull-downs, they had to traverse the first screen, go all the way up, up, up to the top of the 21-inch B&W screen, access the Color menu, and select the particular shade of gray representing magenta. (I did let them know it was third from the top.)

Pull-Downs, Hands Down   Both of us found that accessing the pull-downs was significantly faster than popping up the menu beneath the cursor.

Of course, it's easy enough to explain *my* results away: I was using the very hierarchical menus that I helped design and bring into the world, and everybody knows they're awful![2]

That was my conclusion, too. But Messrs. Walker and Smelcer had already spent several years designing various kinds of pop-ups, and they had really good ones (actually, only about 8% faster than ours).

Walker and Smelcer's results showed the fastest access of a menu item using pop-ups (opening the pop-up with the cursor already on desired menu title) was more than 10% slower than accessing the first item in the pull-down. Accessing the most difficult menu item in the pop-up was more than 75% slower than accessing the most difficult pull-down menu item.

How can this be? After all, I started off by telling you Fitts's law predicted that the farther away a target area, the longer it is going to

---

[2] The Apple human interface community has committed to fixing our current hierarchical menus, something that very well may have been done by the time you read this book.

take to access it. True enough, but only if the target areas are the same size. As Walker and Smelcer figured out, they are not even close.

Kids, Do Try This At Home   Here's an experiment you can try as long as you have a Macintosh with two monitors. (If not, we would be happy to sell you one.)

First, set up the experiment I used in the Finder: Create ten empty blue folders, in two neat rows, but place them on the same screen as the menu bar. (You are not using the second monitor at all at this point. However, you have paid for it.) Then, change each of them, in turn, to magenta, while timing yourself, of course. There is no room for subjectivity here.

Next, go into the Control Panel and move your second monitor directly above the left end of the menu bar. You don't have to move the monitor itself; just lie to the system about where it really is. (In fact, you don't even need the monitor, except to convince the Control Panel you have one. The Control Panel works for us.)

Restart the machine so the change will register, and perform your experiment again.

Notice anything?

The Seventy-Three Mile High Menu Bar   With the monitor supposedly above the menu bar, the mouse pointer does not stop faithfully at the top of the screen. Instead, it passes right through, at high speed, heading for the top of the second monitor. The distance you find yourself overshooting is a measure of just how much your personal strategy depends on your mouse pointer pinning at the top of the menu bar.

People can access the menu bar so quickly because they can be really sloppy about it: The pointer always stops at the right altitude, regardless of how wild the attack. The speed advantage of a large target arises directly from this slop factor: Trying to hit a small target requires people to slow down and be careful; with a large target, people can accelerate up the screen without caring how much they would have overshot.

In effect, a bordered target has an infinite height, making it a large target indeed. (In real life, I compute the target as being a mere seventy-three miles in height, as upon passing the seventy-three mile mark, the mouse ball will run out of tread.)

Walker and Smelcer, having deduced this wonderful effect, went on to design various objects that contain impenetrable borders, to offer the same effect away from the menu bar. These included pull-downs with a border on the bottom, speeding up the process of accessing menu items near the bottom; pop-ups with borders top and bottom; and menu bars connected to windows with borders above them, so the user doesn't go flying through the bar. (The researchers' 8% improvement in pop-up menus is a result of top and bottom borders.)

Adding the border at the bottom of pull-downs and top and bottom of pop-ups offers an increased productivity with little downside: Users can still cancel by sliding left or right a short distance, then releasing. Once the object collapses, the border is no longer hanging around the display, ready to snag someone trying to pass by.

However, I do find major problems with adding a long, horizontal, permanent border to menu bars in windows or dialogs: The program cannot predict whether the user is attempting to access the menu bar, or is flying upward to grab the drag region or head for another window. Yes, this problem could be overcome by some scheme whereby the user holds down the option key to grab the border, or holds down the option key to avoid the border, but why? It takes me less than ¼ of a second from mouse acquisition to move from the bottom of the screen to the menu bar on my 19" screen (using a mouse accelerator CDEV). In fact, when I was running subjects through my experiments, the subjects appeared to do no traveling with the mouse at all: One instant they were clicking on a folder, and the next instant the menu was falling open. Our studies during the Lisa project found it takes in excess of two seconds to decide whether to push a key or decide what key to press.

There are problems with the current state of menu bar affairs: People don't have a clue which application they are in much of the time, the menu bar on multi monitor systems is always located on the wrong monitor at any given moment, and modal dialogs lock up the menu bar and throw away the key.

All these problems can be addressed by Apple within the current environment: We can begin to color-code the menu bars to tie in with an application's unique window border colors, we can provide the menu bar, at the user's discretion, on all monitors simultaneously, and we can open up the menu bar to modal dialogs, disabling items not active as we do in every other situation. If you want these kinds of changes, let us know.[3]

➤ **GUIDELINE**   *Big targets are faster to acquire than small ones.*

Summary of Findings   A Cancel button is faster to hit than a close box, a long menu title such as "Spellcheck this Document," can be hit much faster than the small Edit menu title (to say nothing of the Apple menu); and an 8 x 8 icon in a tools palette may save a little space, but it will take almost eight times longer to access than a 32 x 32 icon. (The differential will drop to four times if the icons are against the side wall of a monitor.)

---

[3] The developers responded, and System 7 enabled modal dialogs access to the menu bar.

> ➤ **GUIDELINE**   *Close targets are faster to acquire than far ones: Keeping everything but menu bars and other edge-hugging items close to the area of interest saves the user time.*

> ➤ **GUIDELINE**   *The menu bar needs to be improved by enabling menus from within modal dialogs, placing the menu bar on the same display as the mouse, and giving users better feedback about what application they are in.*

> ➤ **GUIDELINE**   *Pop-ups and other temporarily opened objects could be improved by adding borders.*

So What's a Designer To Do?   Begin thinking about how you can apply Fitts's Law in your own designs: Are you making targets large enough to hit? Do you tend to make normally far-away targets larger than nearby ones? Are you careful to make often-used menu titles longer than rarely used ones? (Our language tends to fight this particular effort.) Where can you make use of impenetrable borders in the open state of your new objects, while making sure the user's escape path remains wide open? For example, in an object such as a pop-up menu, borders that stop the cursor at the top and bottom of the pop-up will enable users to swiftly access first and last items without danger of overshooting. At the same time, leaving the sides fully open enables a user to escape the object, should panic set in.

Six months ago I saw the first draft of the Walker paper. As time has passed, I've found it has substantially changed my model of the interface universe. Read it, let it sink in for a while, and see what you come up with. And do try that experiment with the two monitors. It is positively eerie.

Since this column appeared, I have been quoted as saying that no screen designer should be allowed near a computer without first having read and understood this paper. I stand by that quote. In fact, Fitts's law is so fundamental to what we do that I often use knowledge of Fitts's law as a quick, effective test of whether a designer has ever studied computer design. Here's how several readers reacted.

Is It a Mouse, or a Turtle?

❑ *Hey, Tog:* I liked your latest column. I've often wondered about the menu-bar versus pop-up-menu wars, particularly since I often use a certain CAE program (not on a Mac) that uses pop-up hierarchical menus extensively. I find that I really don't like eight-level-deep hierarchical menus that pop up under the mouse, but I'm always at a loss to say exactly why. I took your article and forwarded it to the programmers involved with the CAE program. Nothing good will come of it, of course, but I feel better.

Your article gave me an idea, and I want to pass it on to you. It seems one of the problems with pop-up menus is that they can be hard to hit—the mouse goes right by them. But suppose the mouse suddenly slowed down the instant it entered the menu. Then it would be a lot harder to miss the menu. Maybe the mouse should only go slower in the vertical direction but still go fast horizontally. Of course, if you move the mouse out of the menu it would go fast again. And if you press the mouse button it would go fast again as well.

What the hell, I'm shooting from the hip here. You can ignore me if you want. I just like to get my two cents in. You guys are the ones with a Cray to play user interface games on. So go play. I'll stick with my poor IIfx, for now.

—DAN PLEASANT, *Lower Falls Software*

■ Great idea, Dan. Your method effectively increases the size of the target. It reminds me of the story about the shallow, dish-shaped Utopian world around 50 miles in diameter where people were six feet high when standing in the middle of the world, but grew progressively smaller, as did everything else in their world, as they moved toward the edges. An infinite world within a finite space.

Those Nasty Flashers

❑ *Dear Tog:* I just read your article about menus and access time. I think it would be a great idea to add borders to pop-up and hierarchical menus. I bet right borders on hierarchical menus would make a terrific difference. The border could be placed on the right edge of the deepest hierarchical menu. I think that would make hierarchical menus not only useable, but desirable. Have you tried it?

. . . As long as you're taking suggestions for changes in menu behavior here is one gripe I have about pop-ups. When you choose a pop-up and release it without selecting a new item, the default item flashes as if it were a new selection. I think that behavior is not only ugly and distracting, but confusing as well. If I didn't really select something, why is it flashing? Could pop-ups be changed to not flash when the current item is selected?

Thanks,

—SETH TAGER

■ We haven't touched our hierarchicals since they were first released, but we've promised ourselves to put such a project on the front burner once System 7 is released.

You have caught an instance of inconsistency with user expectations (see Chapter 33): Pop-ups should not flash when a new item is not selected.

❑ *Tog:* I am developing a product that can have a variable number of menus across the top. The user can define new ones and so the menu bar is theoretically unbounded. I can see that on a Macintosh with a 9" screen you could run out of room.

Is there an "accepted practice" for dealing with this? I can imagine scrolling the menu bar, double bar, and so on, but none seems "Mac-like." Any ideas?

—JOHN PAGE

■ Here are two:

➤ **GUIDELINE**   *Use a single menu bar and do not allow more menu titles in the menu bar than visible space permits.*

We did a great deal of research in this area back in the Lisa days. The only acceptable practice is to not enable hidden menu titles except within hierarchicals.

The penalty for any of the solutions you mentioned is extremely high: One single menu title off to the left or right causes an extreme drop-off in access time for all menu titles, since their position is no longer predictable because the menu bar moves. A second bar takes as much as ten times longer to access as a single bar and only offers another seven or eight options.

Hierarchicals also take a great deal longer, but at least the scheme offers hundreds of extra options. Nonetheless—

➤ **GUIDELINE**   *Use hierarchicals only when necessary and only for less-often-used items.*

The real solution is to redesign the software: I have worked with developers creating software to publish documents exceeding six million pages in length, conditionally assembled, and using graphics, text, and page-layout tools, and we were never even threatened with running out of menu bar space.

Pop-up palettes, hierarchical menus, menus that change with context all offer alternatives.

—TOG

CHAPTER 28

More Short Subjects

➡ *COLUMN 12: FEBRUARY, 1990*

Grappling with Scroll Speed

❑ ***Dear Tog:*** As the Mac product line gets faster and faster, so do the scroll bar arrows in most programs. Back on the 128K you could click the down arrow and move a single line's worth of scrolling. Now you would have to be a video game pro to control the arrows on a IIci. If I'm having trouble, then those with motor control handicaps are really frustrated.

I have a suggestion: Scrolling speed should be related to either key repeat speed or double-click speed. Put it in the Guidelines: Thou shalt not auto-repeat the scroll arrows (or page up/down) action any faster than key-repeat-speed or double-click-time. Hey, do some research! How fast can people release the mouse after a stimulus. There may be a Nobel prize in it for you.

I use code like this:

```
ScrollProc(blah, blah)
{
    scrollTicks = doubleTime * (ratio should be supplied by TOG!!);
    EndTick = TickCount () + scrollTicks;
    Do_The_Scroll();
    while (TickCount() < EndTick) ; /* waste time */
}
```

I do this with a guilt-free conscience so my users will feel loved. The inhuman interface police can't catch me out here.

—ALAN MCNEIL, *Dragon Software*

■ I confess, Alan, that I have no more room on my mantel, so yet another Nobel prize is of little interest to me. While the above ratio, as all other interface decisions, should be supplied by Tog, I'm afraid, alas, that it shall not. Simply a lack of time, I assure you.

I have forwarded your links (as I do most links) into the very heart of Macintosh Engineering Land, and rest assured we will eventually do something official.

In the meantime, let me point out that I have it on good authority that we told y'all in one of the early volumes of *Inside Macintosh* to never, ever make scrolling speed a function of the system clock, that it should be tied to the real-time clock (tick count) instead. (I tried to find the reference in *Inside Macintosh* but ran out of time after spending two hours staring at what seemed to be a bunch of nonsense words and numbers. It was only then I realized I had accidentally picked up the Milpitas, Calif., telephone directory. They look alike.)

The overall rule is easy:

➤ **GUIDELINE** *Human-computer interactivity should not be tied to the speed of the system clock.*

It may be bound by the system clock, since some systems may be slower than ideal, but it should not be tied to it. As for the Human Interface Police ("We are HIP!"), we are entirely in favor of Alan McNeil's desire to make people feel loved, and we hope other developers will emulate this fine attitude. However, make no mistake about it, Alan: We know exactly where you are, and we can catch you any time we want.

And a Response ❏ *Dear Tog:* Wow, all at once, the Tog column responding to a letter that thousands of users might have written about Control Panel scroll speed, and now, finally, the fix in 6.0.5b9! Thank you!

In the change history file, the System software people mention that the scroll speed may still need some tuning, and may be too slow. Did the implementers read Alan McNeil's letter? He makes the perfect suggestion: Empower the user to do the tuning! Make the speed settable. (If anything, I think it might be just a tad too fast on the Control Panel.)

This brings up a general human interface point: When there is a numeric value the user might want to change, give access to both extremes and to the full granularity. It's nice and everything to give a few presets to choose from, but let the user tweak the underlying value itself, if he or she doesn't like the presets. (Of course, it might be nice to translate the real numbers in the implementation into something more meaningful to the user.) A few examples: font size, key repeat rate, key repeat delay, icon field scroll speed, text vertical scroll speed, sound volume, and sound playback speed.

—DAVE YOST

Never Mind the Speed! How About the Size!

❏ *Dear Tog:* I always enjoy reading your human interface columns in *Apple Direct* and have been meaning to drop you a line regarding your May, 1990 column, "Why Pull-Down Menus Work Best," in which you conclude that "big targets are faster to acquire than small ones."

I agree. I agree. I agree. Why, then, doesn't Apple follow its own research? I am speaking in particular about the tiny scroll boxes on the Mac.

If you are looking at one page of a ten-page word processing document on a full-page display, the vertical scroll box is a tiny one-quarter-inch tall and its position in the scroll bar represents your approximate location within the document.

I propose that the size of the scroll box should vary to represent the approximate proportion of the entire document that is currently displayed. In other words, in the example given above, the box should be one-tenth the size of the vertical scroll bar. Likewise, with a two-page document, the scroll box should be half the size of the scroll bar (after all, the FPD is showing you half of the document).

This solution makes the scroll box a much bigger target that should be easier to "acquire" than the current implementation. Also, it elegantly incorporates additional information (proportion of document displayed) into an existing user-interface metaphor that already reveals position.

The thing that really baffles me is that this is exactly how the Apple IIGS already works. Why, then, if Apple has bothered to make this part and parcel of the IIGS, hasn't the Mac interface been improved likewise?

I'd love to hear any inside info you might have on this subject. In the meantime, I look forward to your next column.

—OWEN W. LINZMAYER, *Freelance Writer, San Francisco, CA*

■ Proportional scroll bars first appeared in Small Talk. They have the advantage of letting the user know how big a document is. They may or may not have a size advantage: If the document is small, they appear like giant, white worms, all but filling the scroll bar area. As the document grows, however, they shrink up to the point where they are no longer than the Macintosh scroll bars.

Our research during the Lisa project found that proportional scroll bars were very confusing to new users. Since they were almost always working with one- or two-page documents when first starting out, they were baffled by the appearance and strange behavior of the "worm." We elected to use the tiny scroll boxes to ease the learning process.

The Apple II team recognized that the Lisa and Macintosh teams had simply traded ease of learning for ease of use in shrinking the scroll boxes, so they went back to proportional scroll boxes. I don't think you will see that happen on the Macintosh. However, we are aware that such small targets are less than ideal from the point of view of Fitts's law (see Chapter 27, "Fitts's Law") and have been playing with some new ideas that don't have us revert to worms, but do enlarge the effective target area of the scroll box.

Stay tuned.

Ballooning Balloon Help

❑ **Dear Tog:** I have been adding support for System 7.0 (including balloon help, due to its relative ease and immediate feedback) to my new and yet unreleased application.

I could not help (no pun intended) but notice that when the Show Balloon Help option was on, there was a significant amount of noise introduced to the Macintosh user interface. I found it extremely irritating to watch the balloons pop up over every inch of my monitor. It seems to me that users should have some degree of control over the amount of help that they desire (for example, active application only, no finder level help, and so on). By allowing the user control over the depth of help that they desire, the amount of noise introduced by balloon help could be reduced significantly. I am interested in hearing your comments on this topic.

—JIM MCCARTHY

Jim kind of beat around the bush; David Smith was a bit more direct:

❑ **Dear Tog:** . . . What's with this bubble help *mode* crap. This is one of the most distinctly un-Mac-like things I have seen in quite a while. Are we really expected to clutter up our programs with this? I am sure that there are better ways of doing this (for example, using a key combination and clicking the item of interest—this has the advantage of speed, and doesn't interfere with normal use). I am sure that many years of user testing went into this paradigm, but why does it feel so wrong to me when I use it?

So, thanks for taking the time to read this, I really enjoy your column in *Apple Direct*, it's the only one I read.

Sincerely,

—DAVID A. SMITH, *Virtus Corporation*

■ When balloon help was proposed four years ago, I urged the team to put a spring-loaded key (or series of keys) on the keyboard, so that help could be available without having to enter a hard and fast mode. If they could not get the hardware modified, I suggested that the user should be able to configure a key set, such as Control-Shift or Command-Option that could act as a spring-loaded switch.

User-testing bore me out, but neither of these options were implemented, due to the sheer inertia of Apple. However, this is Macintosh, and if we don't do the right thing, someone else will: Less than two weeks after the release of System 7 and balloon help, I received in my electronic mailbox a copy of a freeware application from Robert L. Mathews. Called "Helium," it enables users to configure a key set, such as Control-Shift or Command-Option, to act as a spring-loaded switch.

Way to go, Robert!

Looking for a Way Out

❏ *Hi Tog:* Here's an interface question that we've had trouble with:

In a modal dialog box, hitting Return will normally have the same effect as clicking in the highlighted button (normally OK). However, what should be done for those dialog boxes where the user may have to enter a Return as part of the text (for example, entering a U.S. mail address)? The options we've looked at are:

(a) No keyboard equivalent to clicking OK. Our customers don't like this; they insist upon a non-mouse way to make the dialog box go away.

(b) Use Command-O, Command-Return, or something else bizarre as a keyboard shortcut. Nonstandard as hell. Tech support threatened us with large knives over this one.

(c) Allow Enter to make the dialog box go away, but don't show it on the screen. Users didn't realize this feature, and so we got complaints as in (a).

(d) Allow Enter to make the dialog box go away, and highlight the OK button. Users complained that the outline around the button means that Return makes it go away, so why were we doing something odd?

After experimenting, we've settled on (d). It doesn't take users long to get used to it, and seems to generate less complaints than the other options. Still, it's not perfect. Do you have a perfect solution?

—DONALD BROWN, *CE Software*

■ Hi, Donald, Fortunately, I do have a perfect solution. Well, almost perfect.

Combine the best features of your items (b) and (d). Specifically, enable users to close the box with either a simple Enter or Command-

Return. (Tech support threatens me with large knives all the time. Don't worry about it. You learn to live with big cuts all over your body.)

These two keystrokes are the most likely ones for users to attempt. By making either one work, you are significantly increasing the user's chances of striking the right combination. Also, the Enter key is a little tiny, seldom-used vestige on some Macintosh keyboards.

If anybody complains, you may either say I told you to do it, or point out existing applications that in fact enable both these keys, such as Quicken from Intuit.

—TOG

A Small Case Study

❏ *Oh Great Tog:* Please help us in our time of strife! We have a semantics question unanswerable by our ranks of wise men! We turn to you, your boundless knowledge, and your boundless enthusiasm for direction and guidance...

(Maybe that'll get ya to bear with me, huh?)

It goes like this:

We make a piece of hardware that sits at the center of a network and informs you of the status of the network, errors, and so on. It has sixteen ports that the network connects to.

The software that allows you to view the network from the box's location allows you to set each port's name, and to turn them on or off. The box also has some intelligence in it that will shut off a port if it senses a problem with the data on that port.

So. Our software has two radio buttons that allow you to turn a port on or off. If the box has shut off a port for one reason or another, it will put the word "Error" to the right of the radio buttons. Figure 28–1 shows what it looks like, sorta . . .

Port#	Port Name	Port Status On | Off
1	My Place	• OK
2	Engineering	• Off
3	LW IINT	• Error

Figure 28–1. *Port Dialog B.T. (Before Tog)*

The confusion is this: One side says that the text to the right of the port name is reporting the status of the port, OK, Error, or Off. The other side says that the Error condition is so rare that it is unlikely most users will ever see the word "Error." So, they say, it should be Off and On, not Off and OK. On is the opposite of Off, not OK.

So what is thine divine word? How shalt we confuse our users least? (Did this make any sense at all?)

—CHRISTIAN JACOBSEN, *Nuvotech*

■ Hi, Christian, Here are the problems I see:

1. Two people are controlling the same buttons: the user and the programmer. The effect is that the radio button is both a status indicator and a control. Very confusing to the user.

2. On and Off have two ambiguous sets of meanings: On and OK, Off and Screwed-up.

➤ **GUIDELINE**   *Avoid piling too many or ambiguous meanings, user behaviors, and resulting behaviors on individual objects.*

To avoid the current confusion, I would use a standard check box beside each port name, as shown in Figure 28–2.

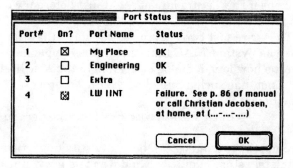

Figure 28–2.   *Port Dialog A.T. (After Tog)*

The fourth item's check box would be grayed out. Note that the word, "error," which users assume means they have done something wrong, has been replaced with a proper alert message, letting users know there is a problem and leading them toward a solution.

Note also that On? and Status are completely separated from each other: Device four has been turned on by the user, but is not OK; device three has not been turned on, but is OK.

—TOG

❏ *Dear Tog:*

Sub: Macs held hostage by dialogs

I always enjoy reading your column in *Apple Direct*. I thought you might be able share your thoughts on the following subject.

A number of the programs I work with sometimes present an alert/dialog box that must be acknowledged (by pressing a button or entering some info) before anything else can happen on the computer. Usually this is not a problem.

However, there are a number of cases where presenting such dialog boxes really screws me up. For instance, some INITs present a dialog box if they detect a problem during startup. This effectively hangs the machine until I come along and click OK. But what if I'm trying to access my Mac remotely via Timbuktu or some such? I'm out of luck, that's what.

Another example is when my fax modem presents an alert box notifying me that it has received or sent a fax successfully. What happens if this occurs late at night just before my automated backup is supposed to take place? Again, I'm out of luck.

These are just two examples. I imagine that the problem will get worse as System 7 IAC takes hold. Does Apple have a guideline that governs how long a dialog box can hold the Mac hostage before letting go? If not, has such a guideline ever been proposed? What are your thoughts on the matter?

—OWEN W. LINZMAYER, *Freelance Writer, San Francisco, CA*

■ Sometimes a dialog can be really stupid, particularly when it completely stops operations and won't go away until the user returns. Even through the user would have instantly cleared it if she'd only been around.

You've come up with some good examples. Here's my favorite: You select Print, so you can print out a 75-page document, with lots of pretty (slooowwwww) pictures, grab your coat, confirm that enough paper is in the printer, and leave for the night. When you return in the morning, the friendly dialog you forgot to wait for is sitting on the display, asking you how many copies of this 75-page document you would like it to print.

When people are still around to answer dialogs that have well-designed, usual-case defaults, the two possible mental responses to the dialog's arrival are "Gee, I'm glad you asked me that" or "Yeah, yeah, yeah, let's get on with it."

In the first case, the person is actively waiting around for the print dialog, for he wants to make a change, such as printing two copies, or printing only pages 3 through 13; he has no illusions that such variations will occur without his explicit instructions.

In the second case, the person has previously made the decision to print a single copy of the whole document, according to the standard defaults of the print dialog. There are no further decisions to be made, and his wife is waiting for him to get home and cook dinner. He forgets he is supposed to wait around to tell the computer that he wants to make no decision.

In a very real sense, in the second case, the computer is asking an inappropriate question. But currently the system goes beyond asking an inappropriate question, it demands a response from a user who isn't even there! If a live employee asked such a question and just stood there, rock-still, for fourteen hours waiting patiently for a response instead of getting the work done, he or she would be fired. Particularly if he or she was asking how many copies of a 75-page document should be printed when 100 pages was the most the paper tray would hold.

Your examples present an even worse case: The user has not forgotten about the dialogs, the user is not even expecting the dialogs, but the dialogs are still there to lock up the system.

Enter the timed-closure dialog.

➤ **GUIDELINE**   *Use timed-closure dialogs to avoid displaying obsolete information, locking up the system, and failing to carry out reasonable instructions.*

The timed-closure dialog waits an appropriate time, such as sixty seconds, and then, in effect, presses its own default button—in this case, OK. The dialog then clears, and, in our example, in the morning, all 75 pages would be waiting.

Timed closure is appropriate in all cases where these three conditions exist:

- The user may not be aware or remember that the dialog will appear.

- The dialog may be the last step performed on the computer or a given screen before turning attention away, or the dialog may be displayed while the user is away.

- Not clearing the dialog will cause potentially more harm than clearing the dialog and accepting a reasonable default, or the dialog simply ceases to be valid and the user has no need to know it existed.

If you make your dialogs temporarily dynamic like this, be sure to use an indicator to let your user know it's a timed closure dialog and how much time he or she has left.

Dialogs should not show up unless needed; if they do show up, they should time out and go away. Why I need to know on a Tuesday that at 3:58 A.M. the previous Friday a file server "will be shutting down in ten minutes" is beyond me.

—TOG

An Attitude Adjustment

❏ *Dear Tog:* . . . The biggest problem we have is one of attitude—the arrogance of we programmers who make arbitrary decisions about how the user shall use our products.

One portion of the attitude problem may dwell in the statistical tendency for active programmers to be relatively young (20s to early 30s), and frequently without mate or children. There are lessons to be learned in the pursuit of a lasting relationship with another adult, and in the conversion of small humanoids into full-fledged human beings. These lessons can be extrapolated into user-interface philosophy, but they seem to be lost on most of the younger programmers, who find more interest in implementing the latest geegaw than in giving serious thought to the plight of the user. They tend to see the world as composed of

(a) people who are like them, and
(b) people who really can't cope, and can't be taken seriously.

They fail to truly understand that the marketplace consists of the latter, although most magazine reviewers (and project managers) tend to be the former.

Fortunately, advances such as OOPs and TCL make it possible for old 40+ codgers like myself to be competitively productive, even after we have abandoned the wee hours and Jolt Cola programmer lifestyle for saner habits. A large part of my human interface testing consists of watching my happily computer-illiterate wife and eight-year-old son wade into programs without reference to documentation. I watch what they do, and more importantly, what they are intimidated into not doing.

—KIRK KEREKES, *Paper Clip Products*

CHAPTER 29

OOP Is All Greek to Me

➡ *COLUMN 16: JUNE, 1990*

❑ ***Dear Tog:*** I feel as if I am under attack by forces clamoring for me to use object-oriented programming. Their exhortations are frighteningly similar to sermons that offer only vague promises of the rewards of the afterlife, but provide exquisitely detailed descriptions of the suffering of the wicked, to wit:

"See this full text editing program? Well, it took me only one and a half lines of code to write it. Besides, if you don't use this new system, in mere months you'll be totally unemployable and will find yourself lying in a gutter somewhere. The New Breed of Magnificent Young Programmers will make sport of your total incompetence as they spit in your face."

Does this sound appealing to you? It doesn't to me, either. I think my problem is the incredible zeal with which the OOPSers are pushing their product. Granted that it's great to have the system's default objects and methods take care of ordinary windows for you. What, however, do you do with a window such as (the one shown in Figure 29–1,) with the vertical scroll bar controlling both panels?

In the system I'm using, it took me more than half a day to figure out exactly where to override one of its default methods to tell it, "It's OK to have a scroll bar that doesn't go all the way across the window."

I think my biggest problem was that I started believing the hype that "Object-oriented programming is Where It's at," and was unpleasantly surprised to find that I still had to do a lot of dirty work myself.

I've been through this before. I've been told I was a stick-in-the-mud if I didn't learn FORTH. I was told I'd go bald if I didn't use PROLOG. (I am going bald, but suspect that heredity and age have more to do with it than predicate logic.)

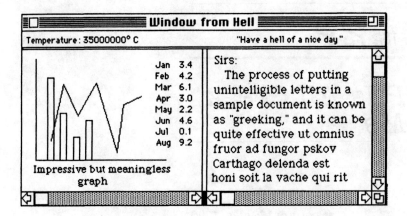

Figure 29–1. *Beware of gifts bearing Greek*

Is this new object-oriented programming a religion or a fashion statement? Or will I indeed turn green, scream, and die if I don't jump on the bandwagon?

Awaiting your advice on the matter, I remain sincerely yours,

— STUPEFIED IN SAN JOSE

■ I read an article some years back written by a programmer decrying the arrival of the first high-level language. He spoke in anguished tones of young Turks proclaiming the righteousness of the new approach with a fervor bordering on fanaticism. He was not against "progress"; he was against barriers that would separate him from communicating with his machine on the most intimate level. The new language, by generating a purely artificial construct through which he had to communicate, isolated him from the kind of deep understanding he had maintained with his computer. Sound familiar?

This article was written in the 1950s, and he was speaking of the transition from machine language (raw, binary numbers) to assembly language (three-character mnemonic substitutes for the same numbers). Don't laugh; that programmer had a valid point: The pattern of each number had corresponded to the structure of the processor. He had learned what effect each binary digit had on the processor, so he could build commands at will without having to memorize any of them. If he wanted to load something rather than store it, he had only to turn the second binary digit on. To do the load indirectly, he had merely to leave the third binary digit off. With the advent of letters unrelated to that structure, he had to memorize each and every command, mnemonic though they might have been, and he lost the relationship of one command to another, communicated formerly through their binary representation.

Formerly, he had known where every bit of code existed in memory. Suddenly, he had to depend on the system to allocate memory for him. He could no longer so easily prevent collisions caused by inadvertently using the same memory location for two different purposes, now that he was "protected" from knowing where things were.

It is difficult to imagine that one could create, let alone maintain, a system as complex as the Macintosh using machine language. Nonetheless, I share "Stupefied in San Jose's" concerns: Every step up in power seems to bring with it ever more restrictions on how languages could be applied. Some languages, such as Pascal, were even created for the express purpose of blocking people from programming as they wished. A supposed student language with built-in "discipline," it was forced on those of us in the real world who like to play around as we code, trying different ideas. (Playing "what if?"—what a novel idea!)

Pascal's rigid structure was there to force students to write lock-step, top-down, structured code, rather than the kind of loose, wandering spaghetti code they might otherwise have produced during their early months of programming. I could argue the merits of such an approach to teaching, but I will sidestep that discussion. (I learned quite quickly on my own not to write spaghetti code after I wrapped myself up in it until I looked like a mummy.) But I would argue that programming environments with heavily restricted structures invariably stifle innovation and creativity. I remember the struggle I had in order to "trick" Pascal into letting me create the kind of live interaction I have always employed in my programs. I was able to create state machines and live, interactive animations, but only by swimming upstream against the tide of the natural structure of the language. When one is spending most of one's time attempting to "go around" a language to get one's work done, that language in my opinion, has failed.

Unlike Pascal, OOP environments are limited today not because of any deliberate attempt to discipline us but by the magnitude of the problem. OOP environments are both new and difficult to create, but we should see their structural limitations fall away as time goes on. Yes, developers often quickly reach the limits of OOP systems, as has Stupefied in San Jose, but not because the developers of OOP languages sat around a table and decided that people who want multiple scroll bars are bad people. OOP developers just haven't gotten to the seventh release, into which they will undoubtedly put resizable scroll bars.

Object-oriented programming has the potential to be different— eventually. One of the beauties of the Macintosh is that developers are free to go around any single feature of the interface, if need be, by simply not using that particular black box. I have seen nothing inherent in OOP environments that precludes this same approach; OOP designers, I trust, will eventually structure their systems to be less restrictive, perhaps by building OOP systems out of ever-smaller objects, so that we can easily take a larger object apart and put it back together in a slightly different form to fill our special needs.

Fire, Brimstone, and Object-Oriented Programming Several years ago, I visited the hydrothermal area in Rotorua, New Zealand, a country where sheep actually outnumber lawyers. A few well-placed signs in a park filled with boiling mud pots and sulfur geysers explained that falling into a mud pot or geyser would not only prove painful but also cause friends to shun you because of the sulfur smell you would take on by so bathing. Armed with that information, visitors were then perfectly free to walk anywhere they wanted, including into the depths of a boiling mud pot. Strangely enough, the day I visited, people stayed out of the mud pots in droves.

A few months later, I visited a similar area, Bumpass Hell in Lassen National Park in California. Due to the sheep/lawyer ratio maintained in the state of California, the Feds were taking no chances: People were being herded onto a wooden platform edged with high steel fencing, located somewhat near the area where the neat stuff was going on. From a distance, I saw the mud pots and fumaroles, but I did not, in any sense of the word, experience them.

I had experienced them before, however, when I was a kid. Then America also had more sheep than lawyers, and I was free to fully experience Bumpass Hell, which I did by stepping into a foot of sulfurous mud. I wasn't burned, but my friends did shun me for some time. And I wouldn't trade that experience for anything.

Object-oriented programming has the potential to take the form of a wood-and-steel barrier or of a few signs and some sulfur-proof boots (uh, I mean "sulfur-resistant"—no warranty expressed or implied). I will gladly trade the occasional high-top full of sulfurous muck for the ability to create a no-compromise application.

We all want an easier, more natural way to interact with our systems. We want a development environment that encourages, rather than fights, the kinds of structures we need to create within our own application. We don't want to be talked down to, we don't want someone else's vision of the one right way to do things woven into the fabric of the environment, and we don't want protective pathways with steel fences keeping us from getting down to where we need to be to accomplish our work.

As for the rest of Stupified's question, as to whether the dervishes seen whirling in the brilliant glow of each new language are swept up in a fashion statement or a religion, I think "cult" would be closer to the truth.

—TOG

Postscript This particular column had a surprise ending—for me. A couple months after it ran, I was talking to my old friend and partner David Eisenberg when he suddenly asked, "So what were people's reactions to my letter?" "What letter?" I asked. "I'm Stupified," he replied. "I know you're stupified. What letter?"

When David and I were writing Apple Presents . . . Apple, the program I used as an example in the chapter on user testing (see chapter 14), he and I became known as the Sunshine Boys, named after two vaudevillian characters in the movie of the same name who were constantly fighting with each other. We were the best of friends, but would scream at each other over the simplest design issue.

In my answer to Stupified, I recalled my struggle in writing a state machine in UCSD Pascal.[1] What I didn't recount was what happened when Dave got hold of the code I had written. He became absolutely livid:

"You (person of dubious derivation)! You (offspring of canine parentage)! You wrote this stuff as a state machine! And you did it just to infuriate me!"

"Why do you think so?" I replied calmly. (I was always the moderate one in these encounters.)

"There is no more difficult way you could have written this code, and you did it just to infuriate me!" (Actually, he didn't say "infuriate me," but that was the gist of his message.)

I just smirked and went on about my work while he continued ranting and raving in the background. I never did admit to him that writing it as a state machine was the only way I could figure out to get it to work. I suppose he's going to read this, so now I'll never hear the end of it.

---

[1] For those of you who are neither practicing nor recovering programmers, the Macintosh Event Loop, that keeps checking for key presses, mouse movements and clicks, is a state machine (see Chapter 3). It enables the user the freedom to carry out any action in any order.

CHAPTER 30

Freedom, Rules, and the Illusion of Control

➤ *GUIDELINE* *The user's sense of control arises from neither tyranny nor anarchy but from the freedom of a supportive environment constructed of reasonable and consistent rules.*

Programmers, historically, have restricted the movement of their users to narrowly defined paths, while simultaneously giving them unrestricted access to every conceivable program option. The result has been that the user has been left in a state of high anxiety.

The goal of today's software designer is also to restrict the freedom of the user, but in such a way that the user feels empowered over the computer environment.

If the designers of yesterday sought to restrict the user's freedom, with a deleterious outcome, why should the designers of today expect a different and opposite result? The answer lies in the nature of freedom, and the nature of the rules being used.

When it comes to freedom, people don't want it. At least, they don't want it absolutely:

> Ordinarily we think of freedom as an unequivocally positive concept. Throughout recorded history has not the human being yearned and striven for freedom? Yet freedom viewed from the perspective of ultimate ground is riveted to dread. In its existential sense, "freedom" refers to the absence of external structure. . . . "Freedom," in this sense, has a terrifying implication: It means that beneath us there is no ground— nothing, a void, an abyss. A key existential dynamic, then, is the clash between our confrontation with groundlessness and our wish for ground and structure. (I.D. Yallum, 1980)

It is a careful modulation of freedom versus rules that results in people feeling a sense of control. One can see this in children: Young children test their parents to see how far they can push them. If the parents restrict the child too harshly, the child becomes angry and rebellious. If the parents fail to offer any restrictions at all, the child may feign happiness, but inside will feel terror at the lack of boundaries. Eventually the child will withdraw into idiosyncratic and inconsistent boundaries of its own making. The truly happy child is the child who discovers reasonable and consistent boundaries—rules. (No child worth his salt will admit this, of course.)

Grown-ups are not immune from this phenomenon either. Several years ago, a study was done on stress in the work place. The highest stress job? Day-laborer. These people have all the freedom in the world—don't even have to show up for work—and no control over their lives. Many of us can remember some time in our lives wishing fervently for a long, relaxing vacation, only to have one suddenly thrust upon us with the loss of a job. Remember how stress-free that experience was?

The rules of the Macintosh are cool: Users are given boundaries that restrict their ability to hurt themselves, like initializing their hard disks without prompts via some magic undocumented shortcut key. What they experience as a result is the sense of control that results from knowing they can explore without risk. With the addition of rules that say that all Macintosh objects shall be visible, and all operations possible will be carried out through direct manipulation, people begin to feel downright comfortable.

People want the redundancy of primary rules. They want to be able to count on simple scrolling to be accomplished with a standard scroll bar. They want to find the zoom box in the same location every time. They are willing to put up with the limitations of a single kind of cursor, if it results in their being able to predict how their software will respond to various control keys.

They also want the comfort of working in an environment based on secondary rules, so when developers change the way the interface looks or feels, the user will be able to predict how the new interface will behave.

Throwing Off the Yoke of Tyranny

We have a tendency to hold on to restrictive rules long after they have ceased to work, then to let go with great fury. A case in point: AppleLink inside Apple assigned every employee a "name" based on their last name, with the number of employees with the same last name who were hired earlier + 1 tacked onto the end, for example, Smith28. People yelled and screamed long and loudly, and when the AppleLink folk gave in, they gave in completely: Instead of creating a series of acceptable forms, they now allow people to use anything they want. So John Smith may be J.Smith, Smith.J, Smith28, or Blunderhead. Had they set a formula for last-name-plus-initial to be, for example J.Smith, the new, less-machiney names would have been predictable. As it is, each and every one must be looked up. Such a scheme needn't have eliminated the lunatic fringe from choosing Blunderhead, Cream Puff, or Tog. It would simply have offered a standard syntax for those who wanted to use the most popular option: last name plus initial.

For years, people have asked for colors in their window borders. For years, we have refused them that right. (Not that it mattered much; plenty of folks out there developed colorizing programs.) With System 7, we enabled colorization of window borders without rules. Was this the right thing to do? I don't think so. If one could actually see the colors, I suspect they would be generating a fair amount of noise in the interface. As it is, fearing that noise, we made the colors so subtle as to be virtually invisible. (Undoubtedly someone will soon correct that with a system extension.)

I think the window border colors should be tied to the color of the document icon. Or to a color chosen for the application's menu bar. Or to a combination, where the menu bar always reflects the color of the icon, and a new document reflects the color of the application until the user changes it. Any of these would give people the freedom to have colored window borders, but would also give them a redundant cue about the window and its content's relationship to the rest of the world.

Before System 7, ordinary folk were stuck with the standard icon representing their application, document, or container (folder or volume). With the advent of System 7, anybody can change almost any icon to look like anything: Folders can look like applications, documents can look like folders, applications can look like the trash can. From no freedom to absolute freedom.

When my son, Joshua, found out he could change the icon representing his personal folder, he immediately turned his folder into a piranha. This destabilized the social structure of our household, and little time passed before daughter Rebecca was a cat, Mom was a bunny rabbit, and I was an irritated-looking duck. (Typecasting?)

We now have four file folders that bear utterly no resemblance to file folders, nor any other container known to man. (I suppose one could argue that the piranha is a container of sorts, containing anything that might have been swimming in the neighborhood fifteen minutes earlier, but this would be stretching the metaphor.) What could have been done for System 7 would have been to provide a number of outlines representing containers—file folders, bookcases, file cabinets[1]—along with a facility for adding decoration to those outlines. Freedom would have been extended, but chaos would have been avoided.

As it is, in our small household, little damage has been done, and little confusion will result; we as end users affected our own destiny—the very spirit of the Macintosh. What I fear is that new people will come into work places and be saddled with computer systems steeped in office tradition, sporting containers that look like corporate logos and baseball caps. Or worse, containers that look like documents or applications. Try building an accurate mental model of the system under those conditions!

From rigidity to chaos. Neither one is much good at filling people's needs. Any time you are prepared to loosen a restriction, think about what the best use of that new-found freedom really is. Should you let go absolutely, or should you generate new rules that are less restrictive but stop short of being chaotic.

---

[1] Even here, I would have wanted the designers to be true to the object: If I had a four-drawer file cabinet, I would have wanted to label each drawer and be able to "pull out" each one independently.

CHAPTER *31*

Three Corners for Reform

➡ COLUMN 25: MARCH, 1991

❑ ***Dear Tog:*** In light of the fact that I haven't hassled you in a long time, prepare yourself.

The Human Interface in the November, 1990 *Apple Direct* (see Chapter 18, "Natural Law") hit a chord or two that caused my mind and interest to react. I, too, have spent time in and around the Lassen area. I remember waking up one night in December or January about 3:00 A.M. while trying to stay asleep/alive in a light sleeping bag laid on branches in the snow. (I had no idea the bag was going to be so ineffective in the snow.) After I realized that the shivering wasn't going to stop but was continuing to increase in severity I got up and beat on this stump that we built a fire in, hoping to rekindle the fire. It rekindled. Seems the fire had started down the roots. It is 22 years later and for all I know that sucker is still burning. OK, I was young and not particularly woods-oriented, having grown up in Arizona. Besides, my camp mate was carrying a pistol, had the keys to the car, and *hated* to be awakened before he was ready. He also outweighed me by about sixty to eighty pounds, looking not unlike a brown bear and acting like one because of the cold. So, one way or the other I was looking death in the face . . .

But that wasn't the point; your missive left me with one question. Say what? Granted it was fun and interesting reading, but somehow I think the developers want and need more precise information on user interface. I agree that Macintosh applications are fairly easy to use, but each new application or rev to an existing application seems to add complexity. Certainly, giving the developer specific examples of different problems and ways to resolve them might be a *great* way to get them to start *thinking* when they are doing their own designs.

Later,

—JOE SHELTON, *Paris*

■ Joe, your link has changed the course of my life. From now on, it's strictly specifics. I don't know what I was thinking of! I can't thank you enough for leading me back to the straight and narrow.

As the first step toward my reform, I want to discuss three little corners of the world which harbor some of the worst examples of human interface design. (Official Tog disclaimer: They also harbor some of the best.)

Vertical Markets   Vertical markets include both the narrower slices of the general marketplace, as well as in-house applications. My current favorite applications, MacMapp, Point of View, and Vellum, are all vertical market applications, thus proving that vertical market applications can be done not only right, but superlatively. Buyers of other vertical market applications are not so fortunate:

Last week, in the mail, my wife received a vertical market application with the attractive price of just $200 per year, or $2000 per decade. Cheap at half the price. It sported a massive data base of over one full megabyte, and opened with the dazzling screen shown in Figure 31–1. (The words and non-essential elements of the appearance have been changed to protect legal departments various from having to work weekends.)

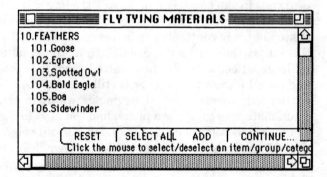

Figure 31–1.   *My, how ties fly*

Note the delicacy of the pleasing design. Note the 2½-D effect achieved by overlapping the buttons—saving valuable real estate on my 19" display. Note the convenience of the Reset button, presumably so we can avoid having to reach for that dratted programmer's switch.

Beyond appearance lay function: When I did a full keyword search of the data base, attempting to discover information on fluorescent fishing line, it took a blinding 3 minutes and 41 seconds. On Location performed the same search on the same data in somewhere under 1.75 seconds.

I am quite convinced this company did not set out to create a poorly constructed application. Nor were they being cheap: They could have built a great-looking application in less time, for less money, and with even less knowledge of the computer they were designing for. For many collateral reasons, this application is an ideal candidate for HyperCard. Armed with only a decent search engine extension (which I'm sure one of you readers would have been happy to license to them), the entire application could have been assembled by one of the fly fishermen that started the company, without even having to hire a programmer.

What went wrong here? Apparently, no one in the company had ever used a Macintosh before building their program. Apple failed in its efforts to market its developer support programs. Sports magazine reviewers, schooled in fly fishing, not computing, failed to inform the public that the application was poorly designed, and the fly-tyers out there have been so unsophisticated that they actually kept the software! Now they have learned that computers stink, have put away their shiny new Macintoshes, and won't be buying any of your software, either.

The Apple developer community is a family, folks. We all sink or swim together. If you see an application like the above, pick up the phone, give them a call, and offer them some help.

Fourth Party Environments   These homes-away-from-home, such as big-scale data bases, forms generators, graphics environments, and Hyperesque applications, have special problems requiring intensive, special solutions. The only application that is exactly like the Macintosh is called Finder. Every other application has used a slightly different approach, a slightly different set of human interface conventions. Sometimes the end result is carefully planned; sometimes, as in the Fly-Tying example, it is what was there when the smoke cleared. Smoke-cleared interfaces are not acceptable in fourth party environments.

Since fourth party solutions are typically sharp, vertical-market applications, they tend to attract the kind of computer-illiteratti that are forced to use whatever has been set before them. Developers of the underlying environments have the moral responsibility (not applicable in some states, nor to anyone holding an MBA) to provide end users with a decent, consistent home. Satellite developers have the responsibility to decorate well within these homes, showing care for those who must use them. All fourth party environments should have member associations for the express purpose of developing human interface and other guidelines for use by the parent company, as well as all developers within the community.

Communications Applications and Mainframes   Mainframes are steeped in tradition dating back more than 100 years. (102 to be exact). From the beginning, the guiding principle has always been, "All power resides with The Computer." The priests of ancient religions garnered their power and control by claiming to be seated at the hand of their gods. Early mainframers pulled off the same scam by enshrining their behemoths. (We went so far as to build an awe-inspiring, cathedral-like setting for our Cray.) As a result, communications applications have historically been weak, dumb-terminal emulators, enslaved beyond all reason to their mainframe masters. Thus, we have the bizarre situation of mainframes, at 1200 baud, shipping the same few menus, unaltered, hundreds of thousands of times per day to myriads of powerful computers dumbed down to the point where they can't remember a single character, let alone a whole big menu. Communication ends up being a slow, frustrating, and ugly experience.

Communications products will not be embraced by the masses (and, most certainly, not by me) until the mainframes give up control and start acting purely as servers.

Mainframers see the movement to the micro as a revolution that will leave them behind. Nothing could be farther from the truth. The problem here is viewpoint: The mainframers are so thoroughly entwined with their machines, they see the world through the eyes of their machines. When they finally let go, they will find that not only will control pass to the micro, they will too!

Never Forget Your Roots   A few months ago, I received a letter from a reader. It said in part:

❑ *Dear Tog:* Your Human Interface column in *Apple Direct* has been very informative and useful in elucidating the concepts behind Apple's desktop interface. Recently, however, you have begun to describe this interface as "the Macintosh interface" in your columns. . . .

This term excludes the Apple IIGS which also uses the Desktop interface. All of your columns and the Human Interface notes provide information that is useful to Apple IIGS developers as well as Macintosh developers. . . .

I think it would be useful to return to the term "Apple desktop interface" to include the largest number of Apple developers as possible and provide for future Apple computers.

—CHIP WELCH, *Chipmunk Software*

■ Chip was right. I should have been using the term "Apple desktop interface." How quickly I had forgotten my roots: I was the leader on the original project to put the Macintosh interface on the Apple II, a task carried out under gloom of night, as there was quite a feud going on between the two groups at the time. I also fought hard for the last published edition of the Guidelines to be subtitled "The Apple Desktop Interface," since it covered both lines.

When I finally slipped over to the Macintosh camp for good and forever, I felt like a disloyal rat. I had devoted my life to the Apple II from early 1978, and that computer had been very, very good to me. Now I was abandoning it, just when it most needed help. (The Apple II never gained renown for the consistency of its interface.)

With time, however, the Apple II became the machine I used to use, and Macintosh became the "real" computer. My loyalty to the Macintosh became as strong as it had been to the Apple II before it. And my point of view changed: It was as though, even as I transferred my old files across an RS-232 line strung between the two machines, my soul and my mind went with them, for I quickly saw the world through the eyes of the Macintosh and soon forgot about the poor, lonely Apple II.

I have talked to many former mainframe people who report the same slow shifting of loyalty and viewpoint. Moving to the Macintosh—or any other new system—is difficult, but it is not the end; it is just a new beginning.

Many mainframe people out there today want to do the Right Thing, but they are fighting against their sense of loyalty, fear of loss of control, and 102 years of tradition. Work with them. Support them. People in the communications area tend to become demoralized to the point where they give up. Don't give up. The old ways will fall, and the promise of personal computer communication will come to pass.

CHAPTER *32*

Watch Out for Those Loose Floorboards

➡ *COLUMN 27: MAY, 1991*

❑ ***Dear Tog:*** . . . The AppleLink 6.0 installation seemed to go fine at first, and when I connected, it worked. I updated my files from 5.0.

When I started AppleLink 6.0 for the second time, it informed me that it couldn't find the APPLEModem CCL. It didn't protest the first time, and I don't know where the CCL, whatever that is, went. I changed to the USA CCL; who knows if that is right?

. . . After restarting AppleLink, it said it couldn't find AppleLink Resources 6.0. A monkey could have found it—it was right where it was supposed to be—but AppleLink could not find it. I threw AppleLink away and got a new copy. Now all of my account information was lost. I had to look it up, and if not for luck, this would have taken another half hour. The problem seems to be fixed for now, and I am back on AppleLink. Lucky me.

I have heard that the Macintosh is the computer for novices. Please tell me how a novice could have got this far and fixed this problem?

. . . There are about four million Macintoshes in the world, I've been told. A work-year is about 7.5 million seconds. That means that . . . if you waste a half hour of each Mac user's time each year, you will have destroyed about 900 work-years of effort.

I lost a half hour of time today, and I lost a work-year of confidence. This happens all the time. This is why computers are a mixed blessing, the Mac included. This is also why it is worth work-years of Apple effort to get marginal improvements in reliability and speed.

—BRAD SCHRICK, *ESC*

■ 900 work-years works out to around twelve complete lives. Wasting a half hour of every user's life is equivalent to killing off twelve people a year. Sort of. This is serious business, although the carnage is not even

235

close to the perhaps 4000 American lifetimes snuffed out every year waiting at modern 17-way stoplights and desperately trying to escape 235-acre parking lots with exactly two one-lane exits that are moved while you are in the stores (this is figuring two minutes per day per U.S. citizen).

While we computer types may not be as wicked as traffic safety engineers, we do need to consider the multiplied effects of our actions and inactions. Brad's point is well-taken.

Brad suffered a very common problem seen today on microcomputers. Something went wrong, and he didn't have a clue how to fix it. These kinds of experiences soon teach people not to update, not to buy new software—in short, to leave well enough alone. They quietly slip out of the reach of our cash registers, and we all suffer the consequences.

Paradoxically, the seriousness of this problem is far greater within an environment like the Macintosh than it is in traditional environments like MS-DOS: MS-DOS users know the operating system of their computers. They have to. They spend half their time wandering around in it.

➤ **GUIDELINE**   *If we are to isolate and insulate our users from the reality of the system software, we must take great pains to ensure that isolation is complete.*

Macintosh users don't know the operating system. They know a fanciful illusion called the desktop.

A couple years ago, I shot a tape on the principles of the Macintosh human interface called "World Builder" (Tognazzini, 1989b). To dramatize the difference between the operating system and the illusion that surmounts it, I took our cameras to the Hyatt Regency Hotel in San Francisco. I began with a tour of the basement,[1] pointing out its remarkable resemblance to traditional operating systems, with its steam pipes belching and noisy motors rattling. (The following is excerpted from the official script, written up, in grand software tradition, shortly after the video had shipped[2]):

---

[1] Actually, to be completely accurate, the basement belonged to the ophthalmology building at University of California at San Francisco Medical Center. The PR people at the Hyatt Regency invited us to film their lobby, but refused to let us into their basement, stating that they did not allow people to see "the back of the house." They are keenly aware of the delicacy of their visual illusion and do not take lightly shattering it. Fortunately for us, the people at the ophthalmology building could have cared less about their visual illusion. Strange, when you think about it.

[2] Riley McLaughlin, the producer, and I "winged" the whole tape. It made the result very fresh and alive, but it left the crew half-dead.

Scene 1

We see Tog in a baffling, highly technical looking environment. He's in the basement of a modern highrise hotel. We watch him walk through the pipes and wiring that let the hotel operate.

TOG: We're in the subterranean world of a hotel complex. Nothing very natural here. This is a lot like the interfaces we used to present our users: dangerous, confusing, confining.

This is the operating system of the hotel, supplying power, water, communication. All necessary, of course, but not the sort of place the user should ever have to deal with.

Like many computer programs of the past, there's plenty of functionality here, but no way for normal users to be able to access it. It's a world only an engineer could love.

Figure 32–1. *Storyboard of Basement*

Scene 2

Tog enters an elevator.

As programmers and designers, we're condemned forever to wander the twisty passages of the operating system. But like the hotel, we've created for Macintosh users a separate virtual world upstairs. A world where they can operate comfortably.

Scene 3

He walks out into the magnificent, eighteen-story hotel lobby area.

Now this is a world a user could love. No maze of twisty little passages here. Instead there is a carefully constructed reality three stories above the street, above the operating system, in which the user can feel very comfortable. And it's not just beauty, it's functionality. I'm surrounded here by every service I can possibly imagine, seemingly within arm's length. Just as on a Macintosh we surround the user with every service the user needs within arm's length, using the mouse.

The user need not navigate. The services are brought to him or her. It's "user-centered" design.

Figure 32–2. *Storyboard of Wide-shot of Lobby*

Scene 4

Tog walks up to a metal pipe intruding rudely into the lobby. It is similar to the ones we've seen down in the basement.

This is a user's world, created from the viewpoint of the user, not the hardware engineer. As designers, we need to gain an understanding of how to have simultaneous viewpoints, looking down from above as the user, while still looking up from underneath, like the programmer, in order to create the most efficient designs. And whatever else, let us not have the operating system suddenly come popping up into the user's world.

He pulls the pipe up and tosses it out of the frame.

Figure 32–3. *Storyboard of Pipe in Lobby Scene*

Scene 5

We see Tog at a table in one of the hotel restaurants. He is having a cup of coffee.

> This restaurant and the entire Hyatt Regency Hotel in San Francisco are here to guide me in ways that will make me successful, not dictate to me.
>
> They didn't determine that I must register before I'm allowed to eat. I was able to do it in whatever order I wanted, although there's a greater range of options open to me if I register first.

Tog goes on, as he absentmindedly sprinkles salt into his coffee.

Figure 32–4. *Storyboard of Tog Sprinkling his Coffee with Salt*

I've only been in this hotel lobby for a short time and yet I find it difficult not to believe that I'm on the street level and outside, as they wished me to believe. Similarly, when I look at a file folder on a Macintosh screen, I find it impossible to believe that it's just an arrangement of light. When we set about to fool the senses through a carefully constructed reality, it becomes very important that we have no hidden rules that violates the user's sense of trust.

As he sprinkles the salt, a sudden dialog box appears in the air.

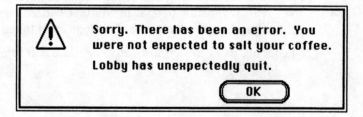

Figure 32–5. *The Fatal Alert*

The screen breaks up and he finds himself, with the salt shaker and coffee, in the basement again.

Tog holding the coffee and salt shaker, back in the operating system.

When the illusion is shattered, when the safe feeling is suddenly jerked out from under the users, they become confused, frustrated, and finally, they take their business elsewhere.

Figure 32–6.   *Storyboard of Tog back in basement*

When we undertake to fool users with an illusion such as the Macintosh desktop, we must accept the responsibility for keeping the users from crashing into the basement. We must ensure we have not left gaping holes in the floor.

There are quite a few things AppleLink could have done to make Brad's job easier and keep him at the lobby level, including eliminating as many auxiliary files as possible so his housekeeping was simplified; offering immediately available, directive help for obscure, infrequent operations; and doing something about those error messages.

➤ **GUIDELINE**   *System-level error messages should state the assumed problem, then offer the alternative possibility that the message-giver has gone berserk.*

Brad might have had a chance of correcting the problem without starting over, but not in the presence of misleading error messages. Nails 'em every time. "Cannot find AppleModem CCL" merely threw him off the track; "Cannot find AppleLink Resources 6.0." finished him off. I just had this same problem myself with another popular communications application that kept claiming it couldn't find one of its auxiliary files, even though I had slid the file so close to the application that they were actually overlapping on the screen. (Sometimes I resort to superstition.)

When systems go wrong, they go really wrong, and system-level error messages need to acknowledge the unexpected. There is nothing that undermines a human's relationship with a computer like a computer found claiming one thing is wrong when what is really wrong is that the computer has lost its mind. Such occurrences completely undermine trust and make people feel like damned fools for "believing" a machine. As in Figure 32–7, error messages must acknowledge this common tendency toward insanity.

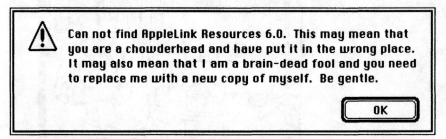

Figure 32–7. *The All-eventualities Alert*

➤ *GUIDELINE* *Use the release name as part of all file names.*

One thing AppleLink has done ever-so-right in release 6.0 is to display the release names. I once spent an entire evening with AppleLink 5.1.1, or some such, desperately trying to get it to recognize "AppleLink Resources." It couldn't. It was the wrong Resources file. The title gave no indication of release. Get Info would say any 5-series resource was AppleLink Resources 5.0, but only release 5.1.1 would work. Nightmare on Link Street.

Reader Jay Kaplan responded:

"Guideline: Use the release name as part of all file names.—TOG."
I beg to differ. One should never rely on your release number being part
of the file name. It should not even be included in the file name. Please,
no more MacDoItAll3.5.1v3 on my disks. The first thing all of my users
do (and I have a lot) when they copy new files to their Macintosh
computers is to remove any pesky 2.3.5 or 3.5.1 extensions. I thought we
got rid of things like extensions when we dumped our IBMs.

The *real* place a version number should go is next to the word
Version in the Get Info window. It should be there on *all* files and
should be the complete version number, all the way down to the 7.0.1c
and beyond.

I truly hope you agree and will take back that horrible statement
you made.

Ever watching your interface,

—JAY KAPLAN, *National Geographic Society*

■ Hi, Jay, I find the Get Info window to be laborious to use in the
extreme, in that it is not even smart enough to change contents
depending on what file I select. I agree adding version suffixes is ugly,
but when people are wasting enormous amounts of time trying to figure
out why software won't work because old and new applications have the
identical name but are incompatible with their supporting files, which
also have identical names, that's ugly too. It is equally ugly when I
accidentally "downdate" a piece of software when I assume I'm updating
it by dragging what I thought was the new version over the old, when it
was really the other way around.

➤ *GUIDELINE   When the users cannot be completely isolated from a
reality of the operating system, we must fully expose the users to
that reality, no matter how painful a prospect that may appear.*

I have found that the only way I can control my system, as ugly as it
may seem, is to have those horrible version numbers there. I would like
to see the Get Info box replaced with a far more dynamic object, but in
the meantime, if developers require very specific version-numbered files
to work together, they need to stop hiding the version numbers. And
even when compatibility is not a problem, major version numbers are
often an important part of a product's name. For example, Excel 2 and
Excel 3 are quite different products, and users need to know which one
they are about to open.

We live in a society awash with euphemism: If something unpleasant is going on, rename it and no one will notice. I'm reminded of a recent scandal involving the then-dean of Boston University's College of Communication, who had allegedly appropriated without attribution fifteen paragraphs (as well as the central theme) from an article written by a PBS film critic, which he delivered virtually word-for-word during a particularly stirring commencement address. The *Boston Globe* broke the story, and the *New York Times* followed up the next day with an article on the "alleged plagiarism" (the *Times'* words).

A week later, Jon Carroll, columnist for the San Francisco *Chronicle*, noticed that the *Times* was back with a follow-up piece: It seems their original article had appropriated without attribution five paragraphs (as well as all the quotations from the speech) from the *Boston Globe* article. This action, however, apparently did not fall under the category of plagiarism. Rather, according to the *Times*, their article had been "improperly dependent on the *Globe* account." Jon Carroll, remarked, "Hmmm. 'Improperly dependent'—you have to wonder how long they labored over that phrase."

Users have enough trouble figuring out how to use our computers. We should not add to their burden by hiding or disguising information they need to be successful. So, I'll stick by my guns, Jay: If users need to know that this is MacDoItAll3.5.1v3 to be able to use the application, that's what it should be called.

In deference to your arguments, however, I would add a corollary:

➤ **COROLLARY** *Never display more of a version number than the user needs.*

If users need no version number, hide the number in Get Info. If they only need to know this is version 2, just tell them that. If they need to know this is version 3.5.1v3, tell them. With such an elaborate number, there is obviously something seriously wrong with the developer's approach to design, which is something users *really* need to know.

—TOG

CHAPTER 33

Making an Interface Articulate

➥ *COLUMN 17: JULY, 1990*

❑ ***Dear Tog:*** I recently started working for a Macintosh programming firm. My previous programming experience was with minicomputers, but I had always been attracted to the Macintosh, with its snappy-looking displays, quick interaction, and consistent user interface. Even some mainframe programmers, often derisive toward personal computers because of their small MIPS ratings and "toy" operating systems, were impressed by the Macintosh's versatile user environment and interapplication cut and paste. No career programmer, in my experience, cared too much about its being "intuitive" or "consistent." This is fortunate, because after using a Macintosh for more than two years, I have found it to be neither intuitive nor consistent.

For example, examine the Macintosh use of icons. I agree that they are more versatile and interactive than typed filenames or device names, and a lot harder to misspell. But I don't believe they are somehow more "intuitive," especially when the icon bears no resemblance to the visual appearance of the device or document it represents. Noting that applications have a little hand in their icon is no more obvious than noting that their names end in "EXE" and is harder to enforce. More often, icons are used to demonstrate their creator's artistic whimsy or as free advertising space in which to display the company logo as prominently as possible.

And what of "consistent"? You say clicking an icon selects it? Not if it's in the menu bar; in a program in which it activates a command; or in a dialog box where it may be selected, activate a command, create a menu, switch you to a different task, or do nothing—with or without being highlighted first to warn you that something may or may not happen. In fact, creative new icon subspecies (such as the highlighting nonselectable option-toggle menubar icon) are appearing on my desktop constantly.

245

My example was of icons, but there are many other examples. I have used applications in which the horizontal scroll bar changes grouping in a data base and menus disappear or change contents, and I've also run across word processors in which Command-P prints the document (Command-T changes the font style to Plain). There are cases where interapplication cut and paste, the most envied Mac feature in the minicomputer world, is not supported by high-end programs.

So what can anyone do about it? I can try to be conscientious, and you can carry the gospel to Mac developers, but in the end it's the users who say what interface gets accepted.

—RICHARD HOUGH, *Software Developer, Vancouver, B. C.*

■ The Macintosh computer sports the most jumbled-up, inconsistent, confusing interface ever made, with the exception of those of all the other computers.

I spend a lot of time in this column and elsewhere (Tognazzini, 1989a, 1989b, and 1990) talking about consistency, just because it's so hard to achieve and maintain. The kinds of degradation of the original interface that Richard is addressing are quite natural: Unless we constantly work to counterbalance the effects of this sort of "noise" creeping into the interface, it will continue to arise. (see Chapter 16, "Information Theory.")

I don't spend a lot of time in this column talking about intuitive interfaces, because there ain't no such animal. Just what does intuitive interface mean? Quite literally, for an interface to be intuitive, it must be able to intuit: to perceive the patterns of the user's behavior and draw inferences. No commercially available interface with which I am familiar is capable of this rather daunting task, although some might lay claim to the most rudimentary capabilities.

The engineer who first adopted the term certainly meant "intuitable" that users could intuit the workings of an application by seeing it and using it. But even that is a less than useful goal since only 25 percent of the population depends on intuition to perceive anything. (See Chapter 15, "Carl Jung and the Macintosh.")

The Articulate Interface[1]   I propose that we replace **intuitive** with **articulate.** First of all, articulate fits rather well with what I see as a job of the interface: speaking clearly to users through words meaningfully arranged. In the case of the Macintosh, those words are

---

[1] I wrote this column before adopting the concept of the visible interface. (See "Introduction.") Because both theories are useful ways to view the interface, I have left them both in place. It's a similar situation to the two theories that light is a particle and light is a wave, except not nearly so important.

often objects—icons and control structures such as close boxes, scroll bars, and pop-up menus—but they are words nonetheless.

Second of all, this word "articulate" has been dying for work, not having been needed as an adjective applied to people since the passing of Winston Churchill and the arrival of the "sound bite." (You can now make a two-hour campaign speech secure in the knowledge that your media specialists will extract for the TV ads the only fifteen seconds in which you didn't sound like a total boob.)

Human-Interface Objects   As I wrote before in the article on HyperCard (see Chapter 8): The Apple human interface is made up of standard, defined objects. For example, there is the file-folder object, which consists of not only a standard visual appearance but standard behaviors. Together they require opening with a double, not a single click, they display contents in the user-selected view, and so on. The appearance and the behaviors are permanently bound together. Neither the programmer nor the user can (easily) create a file folder that acts like a trash can, an application, a scroll bar, or any other standard object in the interface. This binding together was intended to ensure a predictable environment for end users.

We within Apple and you developers out there have been letting a lot of noise get into the system: For System 5, we developed a more complex Control Panel with what appeared to be standard icons running down the left side. Did we require double-clicking? No. Were people confused? Yes.

We popped a small icon of the current application into the upper right corner of the menu bar. Did pressing on it cause a menu to fall down? No. Instead, people were switched to the application they were least likely to desire. Were people confused? Yes.

Developers have invented weird objects such as movable modal dialog boxes that look like modeless dialog boxes, document icons that look like application icons, and the Undo menu item that intuits when the user might really need it and instantly turns inactive-gray. (Maybe there *is* such a thing as an intuitive interface.)

Guidelines for Maintaining Consistency   It's up to each of us to keep this interface together. Here are a few things we can do that will help alleviate the problems Richard has found:

➤ **GUIDELINE**   *Use icons in the menu bar only as menu titles.*

System 7.0 will remove our own violations of this canon. We are hoping that our developers will do their part too.

➤ **GUIDELINE** *Make all icons require double-clicking.*

We at Apple have been particularly remiss about this one. Beginning with the iconic buttons in Find File, we have moved on to such violations as the column of icons in the Control Panel for deciding which cdev you want to access. I am happy to report that we are correcting most of our own violations in System 7.0. Most specifically, we will now require a double-click on Control Panel icons.

➤ **GUIDELINE** *Make any iconic-looking object that requires a single-click also accept a double-click.*

For example, in the Control Panel, the user sets a new background scheme by single-clicking on the little image of the screen. Currently, double-clicking on the screen fails to set the new background. This leads people to form very bizarre rules for setting a new background, including the rule of one user I talked to who believed that setting a new background required three clicks. Generally it's a good idea to assume that people will double-click everything, once the mood is upon them, so plan for the least surprising and least destructive result. (I've decided to leave HyperCard out of this discussion. For my feelings about the HyperCard interface, see my November, 1989 *Apple Direct* column. [Chapter 8].)

➤ **GUIDELINE** *Make all document icons look like documents by including the folded-down corner.*

Document icons on the Macintosh have been absolutely consistent in their use of the folded-down corner—except sometimes. The folded-down corner is an important term in the Macintosh vocabulary; people count on it and become confused when it is not there. (We have no interest in limiting developers' creativity, which is why we have reserved only this tiny symbol in the upper right corner, leaving the remaining acreage free.)

➤ **GUIDELINE** *Make all file containers look like containers.*

Currently we have several containers for files: folders, hard disks, soft disks, and trash cans among them. File folders should always have the file-folder look, physical device icons should look as much as possible like the actual physical device, and real-world analogs should look like their real-world counterparts. In the future, I hope, we will have new and interesting file containers such as file cabinets, books, libraries, and vaults. When this will happen I don't know (probably not until more developers demand it), but when it does, these should also resemble their real-world counterparts.

➤ **GUIDELINE** *Make all application icons look different from documents and file folders.*

Given strict adherence to the standards for document icons and file containers, I am in favor of unleashing full creativity in the realm of application icons. As long as we adhere to the rules for documents and containers, the application rule for users is simple: If it doesn't look like either a document or a container, it's an application.

I disagree with you, Richard, in that I think it's important to offer developers a little advertising space in the form of their application's icons. In fact, I look forward to the day when we will give developers some control over their window appearance too, by letting them design their own scroll-bar or title bar appearance. (This will happen if and when enough developers demand it.)

Application icons must never use a folded-over, upper right-hand corner, which would make users confuse the application with a document (nor should document icons incorporate the hand object). I find it a good practice to avoid an upright rectangular appearance as well, as it tends to trigger the "Gee, it must be a document" reflex.

➤ **GUIDELINE** *Invent new objects, with new appearances, for new behaviors.*

If you need to change grouping in a database, create a new machine designed to change the groupings in a database. Don't use the scroll bar! The scroll bar is not a Vegematic designed to slice, dice, shred, and peel. It is a single-purpose tool, designed exclusively to make things scroll.

➤ **GUIDELINE** *Devise menus that change to reflect the current mode of the system.*

The most dramatic mode changes on the Macintosh occur when applications are switched. Few would argue that switching from WordPerfect to Excel should not cause the menu bar to change. If we just kept adding new menu sets, side by side, we would soon have the menu bar extending out 25 feet, requiring extremely wide, if not so high, monitors. But how about within applications? Is it OK to jump things around and shorten or lengthen menus willy-nilly? Of course not. But many applications have become too complex and too powerful to maintain a static menu structure.

So how do you change the menus without confusing your users? The strategy that works is to change the menu layout within an application when—and only when—users change their own mental mode. My favorite example of this occurs in SuperPaint, which maintains both a drawing and a painting layer. When a user has selected the Draw layer, the paint tools on the palette are replaced by drawing tools and the Paint menu gives way to a Draw menu.

When SuperPaint had been out about a year, I began hearing complaints from human interface types that SuperPaint was violating the guideline requiring that menus never change, a guideline I had always supported. Even though this menu switching had never bothered me personally, I decided to discover whether it was bothering any other SuperPaint users. I spent the better part of a day wandering around through Apple's nonengineering buildings doing a survey of experienced nontechnical SuperPaint users. The results were quite startling: More than 85 percent of these experienced users flatly denied that the menus changed at all. Most were quite insistent that I must be using a different version of the software, since on their machine, both the Paint and the Draw menus were always available.

What was happening here? Both menus *were* always available, in the sense that the users never went off in search of either one without finding it, since the users had consciously changed their own mode in the process of changing the application's mode. When the users decided to draw and let the system know, the universe filled with drawing things. When they decided to paint, everything to do with painting was instantly available. This menu switching worked, not only freeing up a precious column in the menu bar but also giving the users additional feedback about the mode by displaying the Draw or the Paint title in the menu bar.

The triggering of utility sorts of windows, such as a Find or Spell Checker window, also indicates a clear change in the mental mode of the user.

The first goal of any application design team should be to avoid menu switching. Only when that precious real estate has run out should such a scheme be considered, and then only when a strong user mode can be identified and subsequent testing shows either positive benefit or at least the absence of deleterious effects.

➤ **GUIDELINE** *The most important consistency of all is consistency with the user's expectations.*

The Xerox Star design team needed to enable people to file, send, and print documents. In each case, the user would drag the document to an icon representing the desired service. During a file or send operation, the document would be eliminated from the desktop. Several people argued that consistency required that the document likewise be eliminated during a print operation. Others pointed out that this would lead to the destruction of the document, since the machine-readable form would neither be saved nor sent. They argued that consistency with the real-world metaphor should take precedence: copy machines do not have built-in paper shredders (Smith, et al., 1987).

The issue was not settled through shouting matches, but through user-testing: It turned out that people expected their document to remain on the desktop.

In this example, one option was clearly hazardous, but often all options are equally safe. For example, on the Macintosh, dragging a document from one folder to another within the same device simply moves the document. But drag that same document to a folder on a different device, and the document will be copied. Why? Because user-testing demonstrated that that was what users *expected* to happen. The proof of its validity is that few people have ever even noticed this lack of self-consistency. It just seems right.

Before any product ships, take time to do user-testing with the target population. Only that way can you make your program consistent with your users' true expectations.

Users Don't Choose Interfaces Finally, Richard, I disagree with your statement, "In the end it's the users who say what interface gets accepted." Users quite often have little to say in making their buying decisions. They arrive to find a computer on their desk at work, or they need a vertical market application that only runs on a certain machine or on top of a certain database, or they need capabilities only available in a certain package. When users do have some say, they quite often don't have the knowledge necessary to discriminate among interfaces. Worst of all, most of us are positively attracted to dangerous-looking interfaces:

A stove company in the late 1950s did extensive market research into what housewives (this was pre-men's lib) wanted in a cook stove. Almost to a woman, they reported that they wanted a simple stove with four burners, each with a control, one oven, with its control, and nothing else. No clock, no oven temperature probe, no "intelligent" burner, no nothin'. The company set to manufacturing such a stove and soon had a warehouse full of them. To the best of my knowledge, that warehouse is still full of them, because that stove company couldn't give those stoves away. The women wanted every one of those bells and whistles they swore up and down they didn't need, didn't like, and couldn't use.

I stood in a computer store and watched a salesperson try to talk someone out of wasting his money on a giant extended keyboard he didn't need and wouldn't use. It didn't do any good. The guy bought it anyway, thereby insuring that his mouse would be forever further from his reach. He didn't understand and didn't care that this was a problem; he wanted this scary-looking keyboard to impress the hell out of his friends.

This salesperson was not exactly typical, either: I've stood in a lot more stores and seen a lot more salespeople shoving giant keyboards down customers' throats, fully aware that their store would make more money on them.

These are the kinds of issues that drive individual software buying decisions, often pushing interface well into the background. But interface does count, in the end. Because each user has a certain threshold of pain, a certain limit to how much confusion, noise, and torture he or she can withstand. And once that limit has been passed, the purchases cease. Macintosh developers have benefited from an interface with a high threshold of pain: Historically, Macintosh users have bought far more applications per user than have users of other systems. But even Macintosh users have limits, and we are pushing those limits now.

I talk a lot about the Macintosh community and the responsibilities of belonging to that community. You may have the finest interface in history, but if I bought my last application from one of your competitors and found it so bad that I got fed up, I will never see your application. We are all in this together. When any of us is sloppy with our interface, when any of us feels compelled to place the stamp of our own ego on an application instead of following the guidelines, when any of us fails to test and iterate our designs, we are not just hurting ourselves, we are hurting every member of this community. Users don't "accept" interfaces, they veto them. By closing their checkbooks. Permanently.

PART VI

Overcoming
Barriers to Success

"I love honeybees and those bees are all my friends." I spoke with quiet intensity from a lifetime of experience.

"And I hate bees," a husky young man in his late teens retorted as he and his two companions gathered closer around me....We were standing within fifty feet of an old pepper tree, hollow at the stump, which was the home of a large swarm of wild bees. As a few bees flew around in circles near us, I looked steadily up at the young man who had spoken....

"I want you to put out that burning torch you've lighted and leave those bees in that tree alone. They are my friends, and I don't go for this burning business."

"Well, we do, and we're going to burn out those bees—see?" He and his friends took another threatening step toward me.

"I told you those bees are my friends...." And I turned and walked into the circle of excited bees....

"Are you crazy?...They'll sting you to death!"

"No they won't," I replied. "I told you these bees are my friends—and they are."

The poor persecuted bees were indeed glad to see me come. They flew all around my head and shoulders and some landed on my arms and hands, at the same time emitting their joyous hum of welcome.

—ORMOND AEBI (1982)

The difference between Ormond Aebi and those three teenagers in their perception of that swarm of bees lay not in what they saw with their eyes, but in what they saw with their minds: Ormond Aebi saw the little friends he had held so dear all his life. The teenagers saw a great swirling cloud of crazed insects bent on destruction.[1]

We perceive the world through the filter of our mental models, and when they are inaccurate, it can lead to misunderstanding and destruction. Donald Norman states:

> Mental models are often constructed from fragmentary evidence, with but a poor understanding of what is happening, and with a kind of naive psychology that postulates causes, mechanisms, and relationships even where there are none. Some faulty models lead to the frustrations of everyday life....Far more serious are faulty models of such complex systems as an industrial plant or passenger airplane. Misunderstandings there can lead to devastating accidents. (Norman, 1988)

I've studied tennis under two masters in my time: John Gardiner and Tim Gallway. John Gardiner took a crack at me in 1958 and gave up in disgust after three weeks. I couldn't volley to save my soul. In fact, there seemed to be only two places to which I could hit the ball: my side of the net and the outside of the court. "It's a high fly ball to left center! Going, going, gone!"

I didn't touch a racket from that day until Tim Gallway took me on as a patient in 1988. Tim had me volleying, accurately and consistently, within ten minutes. John Gardiner had me concentrate on my stance, the way I was holding the racket, and the movement of my feet during the swing. Tim had me count the number of times the little lines of the tennis ball flashed by as it tumbled in flight towards me. John wanted my conscious mind to work on the problem. Tim realized my conscious mind *was* the problem.

I held in my conscious mind a false model of the physics of tennis ball flight. I also held a false model of the dangers of being hit by such a high-speed projectile. Tim knows the way around these problems is to get the conscious mind out of the way, since the subconscious mind is quite competent at tennis ball trajectory tracking, thank you very much. He has his students count the lines on the tennis ball, so that they can't

---

[1] Ormond's model is more accurate; he captured the world's record for most honey from a single hive of bees: 404 lbs. (See Chapter 15, "Carl Jung and the Macintosh.")

concentrate the conscious mind on screwing up the game. It works. (Gallway, 1976)

Betty Edwards, author of *Drawing on the Right Side of the Brain* (1989) was beginning yet another class for college students who would end up learning almost nothing after a required semester of drawing. Out of frustration and desperation, as she was handing out a reproduction of a master drawing for them to copy, she, on impulse, told the students to turn the image upside down and draw it that way. She was pleasantly surprised to see how accurate the resultant copies were. She went on to discover that students who could not possibly draw a chair planted on the floor had no trouble doing so if she hung it upside down from the ceiling. She attributes this to the student's conscious minds not "knowing" what an upside-down chair looks like, and therefore not getting in the way of the subconscious mind drawing what was actually there.

The models that developers sometimes have of the way human-computer interaction should work are as inaccurate and damaging as some of these examples. For years, when I would talk one-on-one with developers, I would attack dated, defective models head-on. After two years of dancing around the issue in my column, I decided it was time to do the same thing. The result was the following series.

I have presented many of the concepts in these chapters from the standpoint of the developer who has an existing Macintosh product and has decided to bring out a new release, or has a product on a different platform and has decided to port it to the Macintosh. The concepts, however, are just as valid and just as important if you are embarking on a new project or have no current project at all. The viewpoint I took was necessary to break some old models, before replacing them with the new. Should you not be saddled with the old models, you will find the going just that much smoother.

CHAPTER 34

Rationalization, Assumption, and Denial

➥ *COLUMN 28: JULY, 1991*

Have you ever watched a company bring out release after release of a product, every one with the same tragic flaw? Have you ever talked to the people involved, only to discover that they think what you see as a flaw is really, really cool? I once asked the designer of an editor-compiler if he realized he had failed to fix a fatal existing bug: If you selected Compile before saving your source file to disk, it would instantly, without notice or recourse, erase all your new work from memory and go compile some version you saved last Tuesday. Rather than the look of horror I expected, he threw back his head, laughed heartily, and said, "If you think that's funny, in the new release, if you hit Control-X during the first part of the compile, it will clean everything off the disk, too!" Most amusing.

Have you ever called a company to complain about some really heinous design screw-up, only to be told that you are the first person in the history of the company ever to complain? Have you had a friend call two days later, only to be told that *she* was the first to have ever complained? If these things have never happened to you, you probably have more constructive hobbies than I. Nevertheless, these are symptoms of rationalization, assumption, and denial—traits necessary for human survival, but threatening to the survival of our jobs and our companies.

Rationalization

If people were unable to rationalize, they could not hurl themselves out of airplanes with nothing to save them but a parachute packed by an unseen stranger making minimum wage. If they were unable to rationalize, they would regret buying on impulse that truly ugly pair of brown shoes. If people were unable to rationalize, they would not insist they just won $235 in Atlantic City, when it cost them $14,372 over the last two years to do it.

257

Rationalization enters the software design cycle any time we decide to cut some corner: "Yeah, we're not going to support the *Q* key until second release, but how many words have a *Q* in them, anyway?" It is most prominent, however, at the end—you know, just after shipment and right before user-testing? It then takes the form of a healing process called "overcoming cognitive dissonance": We have made certain decisions we must now live with. Our mind goes through the process of thinking up as many reasons as possible for how we were infinitely clever in making the decisions we did, while suppressing all the counter-arguments we raised during the decision-making process.

Let us examine those ugly brown shoes: In the store, we found two pairs of shoes we thought we could live with, both marked down 75%. (I wonder why?) The black pair would go great with that mauve and magenta suede suit. Besides, it had augmented heels and soles and would make us look really tall. On the other hand, the brown ones would do well with that nylon jumpsuit we wore when we parachuted out of that airplane: The shoe color just matched that faded bloodstain where we tore into the tree.

We might spend twenty minutes hemming and hawing in that store before buying the brown shoes, but by the next day we would have fully overcome our cognitive dissonance: The shoes we didn't buy were the ugliest things ever made. That mauve and magenta outfit is too small anyway, and even if it weren't, platform shoes have been out of style since 1972. Meanwhile, the brown shoes have taken on an almost magical quality to them.

Rationalizations help us put the past in order, but they can also block our vision of the future.

Assumption In the summer of 1943, as war tore across the face of the earth, Reinhold Niebuhr, the most famous resident of Stockbridge, Massachusetts, penned a short prayer for a Sunday morning church service.

> God, grant me the serenity
> To accept the things I cannot change,
> The courage to change the things I can,
> And the wisdom to know the difference.

Niebuhr's fame in Stockbridge was to be eclipsed some 25 years later by the proprietress of Alice's Restaurant, but not before his prayer had spread around the world, adopted not only by many religions, but the millions of members of Alcoholics Anonymous and other 12-step groups.

Once we have accepted something, it becomes one of many assumptions upon which we base our lives. This is necessary to our survival, for if we had to wonder every time we saw a great tree whether or not it was going to run after us and eat us up, or ask every cooked chicken that crosses our path whether it would be willing to do our laundry, we would have no time left to watch television. (Do you remember those magic years before age five when racing trees and laundering chickens seemed like real possibilities? Assumptions do make life a bit dull, don't they?)

Assumptions can be formed of True Facts, guesses, and rationalizations. True Facts go out of date. Guesses are just guesses. Rationalizations are fantasy. The more comfortable the assumption, the more it cries out for periodic review.

Denial Denial arises when we can neither accept a situation nor do a damned thing about it. Little children deny breaking the window their parent just watched them break because they can't unbreak the window and are terrified of being punished or, worse, shunned.

Denial, like rationalization and assumption, is a normal, healthy aspect of human mental functioning. Were it not for denial, few women would sign up for a second child-birthing experience, thereby threatening our very existence. (It used to be that women could take a numbing drug and go through childbirth in relative comfort. Now they're required to gaze adoringly at their husband, breathe deeply, push-push-push, and smile for the camcorder, all with nothing more powerful than oat bran to dull their pain.)

Unfortunately, the downside of denial is very real and very dangerous. Family therapists call it "the elephant-in-the-living-room syndrome." A classic example is the outrage of a recovering alcoholic's family when the counselor suggests that booze is why Mommy has been so tired she has passed out in her dinner plate every night for the last ten years. Neither Dad nor the kids ever connected her need for sudden naps with the whiskey bottles hidden all over the house. Then there are the battered wives and children who struggle year after year to figure out why they are such bad people, never once seeing that they are living with an abusive man, who in turn is often in denial about the abuse he received while growing up.

We have our own denials in our industry, denials as amazing and sometimes as tragic as the family examples above. Tragic, because sometimes entire businesses cease to exist.

Let's look at one universal denial. Since we're all in denial about it, let me attack it laterally, with a fable.

You've got the opportunity of a lifetime to get a brand-new, super-automated, family sports sedan. You are positively salivating. This baby is a dream: room for all three kids and the dog, and still hits 250 miles per hour (in a 55 mph zone). After you sign the papers, they mention that you should never let yourself run out of gas. No problem.

You take delivery, pack up the family, and head for Florida. Forty miles outside of Atlanta, you hear the faintest little cough as a bubble of air gets into the gas line. You realize you forgot to buy gas and figure you're about to be stuck on the side of the road in southern Georgia, right? Wrong. You're suddenly back in your own garage in Newton, Massachusetts, with the door closed. When this car runs out of gas, it instantly and irrevocably returns to its point of origin. ("Oh, didn't we mention that?") You're dead-tired from driving fourteen hours, the kids are screaming bloody murder, your spouse is asking exactly how much you paid for this car, and you haven't left the garage.

Would you give someone two cents for a car like that? No. But you'll pay thousands for a computer like that, won't you? You'll spend eight hours typing in the ultimate secrets of life, and when the power goes out for a ten-thousandth of a second, guess what? If you didn't save like a good little boy or girl, you're hosed. Now that's what I call user-friendly. And yet we designers spend all our time trying to get that dialog box laid out just right, when our users are constantly one ten-thousandth of a second away from sheer disaster. That's denial.[2]

Fortunately, our users are in denial, too: When the power goes out, they blame themselves! Weird! How long would it take from the time users got fed up for every new PC to have a two-minute battery backup and automatic put-away-and-shut-down? Maybe three months?

Given that the entire industry, from volatile-memory manufacturers on up, are in denial about the fundamental undependability of their hardware products, it is little wonder that software designers grab themselves a piece of the action. I've talked here before about the sorry fate of developers who have insisted on porting a product with a foreign interface to the Macintosh. Some have gone out of business. Others have hung on for years, figuring if they just add a scroll bar or two, then it

---

[2] Of course, we don't have to wait for power failures to destroy our customer's work. We can jump right in there ourselves. Take this example, supplied by Kim Hunter:

> . . . I leave you with what I think is a most classic example of an interface miscommunication. Queried by a friend to recommend a computer, I said "Get a Mac II with a hard disk". He bought a single drive Mac Plus. Tough way to go. He put ten hours into a proposal using Microsoft Word. Then, when he wanted to quit, a dialog asked if he wanted to "Save the changes?". After thinking about the changes he had just made, he answered "No." Later he complained to me that everything he had done "just disappeared." He hasn't used the computer since then.
>
> From now on I will have TWO flags in my software: Dirty & Virgin! And two different dialogs to go with them.

While Kim's variable-name vocabulary might be a bit puritanical, his methodology is sound. Only two things happen after a loss of data of this magnitude: Users join the priesthood of the power-user, or they retire the field. Far too many retire the field.

will be all right. These people are not bad designers, bad engineers, or bad business people: They are in denial about a very real market situation. Even as their products are shredded by reviewers and their customer base dwindles away, they cannot see the real reason for their troubles. It's always something to do with business plans, distribution channels, or something.

Denial kills software, and it kills companies. Next month: What to do about it.

Up from Denial...   ❑ *Hi* . . . I read your piece on "Rationalization, Assumption and Denial" with much interest. I agree with you that denial is a killer, and it's not *just* in software companies. Any company that is not willing to admit when the Emperor is naked has the same problem.

I am a member of an online service with a Mac interface. This service is about to release the next version of their Mac software, and I have been one of those folks beta testing the new versions. Another of the testers and I joke that the programmers must be using the "Martian Interface Guidelines." But it's really pretty sad.

The buttons aren't "real." Instead of using modeless dialogs, they use windows dressed to look like modal dialogs. The software handles basic functions strangely, like the way it handles the mail files (it makes them in two places . . . go figure). There are plenty of other things which need to be changed or improved and plenty of people asking for them, but instead of fixing them, the programmers are concentrating on sexy, fluffy, feature-rich stuff which will never fly if people can't *use* the software. All we beta testers hear are defenses of the way things are being done and "It's too hard to do it that way." How does the customer get through to a company that's in denial?

Well, in the world of 12-step programs, one way is called "Intervention." In an intervention, the coworkers, friends, and family of an addict (of whatever ilk) get together with the addict. Each person takes a turn telling the addict how the addiction affects him or her. For instance, "Mom, when you drink, I feel like I don't have a mother."

I think that software customers ought to have the same sort of honesty with people they buy products from (especially something so intimately interactive as software). It requires honesty on the part of the customer, and the customer also needs to realize nothing may change and to be willing to have the software company continue in its denial. (God, grant me the serenity, and so on.)

The companies who listen do well, and the people who use the products thrive, even if there are problems. Consider CE Software, for instance. They do not ship absolutely perfect products, but they listen to their customers and have tech support people who know what they are doing.

I think I am starting to ramble here, but I wanted you to know that your article has made an impact. I have been thinking about the companies I work with (as a customer) in the terms you propose, and it's a very compelling idea.

How do we help the companies who make the software we love, or *could* love, to abandon their denial and get on with the business of making good software? And what about the companies who won't listen? Well, we'll just have to let them go, I guess.

—CAREY ALICE TEWS,
Applications Developer, Catalog Media Corporation

■ Hi, Carey, The problem with customers complaining is that they rarely speak with one voice. It's like the alcoholic who hears from his wife on Monday that he drinks too much, his boss on Tuesday that he drinks too much, and his daughter on Wednesday that he drinks too much. Intervention works because they all nail him at the same time.

I don't really know what the answer is in all cases—or even most cases. I think sometimes we have to let these companies go. Other times, we have to let them bottom out, or get near the bottom, so that they are at least prepared to listen.

I have been a beta tester on projects like the one you describe. In fact, one Apple hardware project team whose hardware I was testing received three human interface bug reports from me in the first week and thereupon dispatched someone to pick up the hardware so "we can give it to someone who will appreciate it." The hardware never was released, thank God.

—TOG

I Want That Car! ❑ *Dear Tog:* Just finished reading your latest article, "Rationalization, Assumption, etc."

"Would you give someone two cents for a car like that?"

Damn straight I would, I'll even give you a couple hundred for the patent. This thing is teleportation! Beam me up, Toggie!

Denially yours,

—AARON REIZES, *Stanford University*

CHAPTER 35

Second-Release Software

➻ COLUMN *29: AUGUST, 1991*

> ➤ **GUIDELINE** *Be wary of rationalization, assumption, and denial creeping into the design process.*

New releases don't need new software teams. They don't need "fresh blood." But they do need a fresh look and a fresh approach. Last month, we talked about the three great demons of second-release software: rationalization, assumption and denial. They are colorless, odorless, and tasteless—very tasteless. They well up slowly and steadily over time, until they envelop you in their swirling midst. You can't see them or feel them. The only way to escape them is give yourself and your team members what Roger von Oech calls "a whack on the side of the head." (von Oech, 1990)

The most effective "whack" I've found is the brainstorming session I described in Chapter 13, "Brainstorming and Scenarios." In addition to providing lots of fresh mental air, it provides a forum for attacking the three great demons of second-release software.

I work with the team to reopen every original issue in light of the advances of time and technology. It's no great trick, it's a matter of listening to what is being said and questioning every assumption you hear. Once you begin this questioning process with others—and it is so much easier with others—you will soon find yourself examining your own rationalizations, assumptions, and denials.

Forget for the moment all that sacrosanct code you have piled up. Think about what you could do if you were free to start over completely. (You may have to gag the programmers for a short time during this discussion.) You'll get fanciful for a while, but in the end, you will come back toward a new and better center. You will then be in a position to think about how you can use your existing body of code. You will discover you can eliminate reams of that old code that seemed so vital, while still being able to use other code you never thought you could.

Second releases suffer from two sources of inertia: Existing code and tradition. All subsequent releases suffer from the errors and limitations of what came before. Is your company prepared to carve out twenty percent of its code just because it's so lousy it's laughable? Is it prepared to abandon one hundred percent of what came before, even though it "works perfectly," just because nobody except the original engineer can figure out how to use the program? It takes guts to make those kinds of decisions, but they can be and are being made. Far harder is the task of abandoning tradition. Members of a team may be unaware that they are trapped in tradition, or they may be working with others, perhaps in management, who are tied to tradition. Some tradition may also arise from the environment: People working with mainframe and mini systems are particularly controlled by the inertia of that world and must fight constant uphill battles in the name of progress.

Regardless of how difficult the quest appears, we must commit to the struggle, for when we abandon our efforts at fixing glaring problems in the human interface, we are also abandoning the vast majority of users who can barely cope with the current application. We are offering even less hope for the thousands or millions of users who will be faced with having to comprehend our new release without ever having experienced a computer before, let alone our previous application.

A design team attacking a new release of a product should question every decision about that product ever made. Questioning does not mean attacking: Quite often an original assumption remains valid; questioning the assumption will prove its validity. The important thing is to go back over every piece of evidence and shed light on any anachronous facts, any guesses, and any rationalizations that led to that assumption. More often than not, something has changed.

Denials can be more intractable. They have usually arisen from a condition that was not acceptable but seemed immutable. A team lacking a graphic designer displays a form of denial: The applications often look uniformly awful, but nobody on the team sees a problem. If you point out that their paintbrush icon looks far more like a penguin than a paintbrush, they'll have the programmer whip up a new icon by tomorrow, and this one will look like a muskrat with an overbite. The way to overcome such a denial is to remove its need: Bring in a freelance graphic designer and the denial will take care of itself.

The most entrenched denial I've seen among software teams surrounds sacrosanct code. Over and over again, I have watched developers spend hundreds of thousands of dollars trying desperately to protect their investment in fifty thousand dollars worth of code—and end up with a mediocre product for all their trouble.

Resist the efforts of those who arrive at preliminary meetings with nonnegotiable pronouncements about what must remain sacrosanct for reasons of economy, history, or time. As with a completely new product, the floor must be opened absolutely for new and fresh thoughts. What are the problems out there? What have users told you they want? What do they really need? (Users are good at offering suggestions about finite, small-scale improvements; they are notoriously bad at offering new approaches that result in real breakthroughs.)

➤ **GUIDELINE** *Brainstorming is vital to the task of casting off old ideas and embracing new ones.*

Brainstorm. (See Chapter 13, "Brainstorming and Scenarios.") Kick ideas around. Consider the product you would build if history could be completely erased, if not a line of code currently existed, if you had all the time and money in the world. Only after this stage can you pull back into the present and see what you can make of the carcass of the last release. Only then will you have developed the basis to decide what you can and cannot change.

People will leave such a session ready to face the long battle ahead, armed with a new approach, a new attitude, and a new determination.

I had a consumer electronics store before I fell in love with computers, and every few weeks a couple of people would come in with a television set that their Uncle Charlie had given them for free. The story was always the same: Uncle Charlie had told them the TV just needed a tube and it would be in great shape. I would tell them it wasn't worth even checking the tubes, let alone really repairing it, and they would go away. Three days later, they would be back, having checked and replaced every tube in the set. (The do-it-yourself tube tester guys had this great little trick: Never clean or replace any of the tube sockets in the tester and after a year or so your tube sales will skyrocket, since every tube will test bad. Running this scam requires a more insidious form of denial.) They now had invested $173.12 in a ten-year-old, 17" black-and-white TV. By just adding a new picture tube, two capacitors, and a resistor, they could fix that baby up for only $423.19. When finished, they would have a working ten-year-old TV worth an easy $35.00. Gee, I wonder why good old Uncle Charlie was willing to give it away?

There is a lot of ten-year-old code and a lot of twenty-year-old design concepts out there that are just as valuable as Uncle Charlie's TV, and it costs developers money, years, and sometimes their very existence to cling to them.

The Payoff In December of 1989, I devoted my column to the subject of direct ports coming to the Macintosh from other machines. I did so because I had had two recent experiences with companies moving previously successful applications to the Macintosh. One of the companies went against the advice of myself and others at Apple and tried to do a direct port. The reviewers killed them, and users refused to buy. The company foundered. It was so sad to watch it happen.

The other company listened, in shock at first, but then with growing enthusiasm. They had wanted to have a really hot product for the Macintosh, and they were committed to doing it right, no matter the cost. They had ambition, creativity, and the technical wherewithal to back it up.

That second company is Time Arts, a well-established, high-end graphics company. When I first met with them, they had set out to port their product to the Macintosh, but were not sure that the existing interface would be successful. They were looking for minor changes that would get them up and running. I told them that their existing interface was fine for the platforms on which it ran, but it was not going to fly on the Macintosh. I told them to start over. And they listened. It took them time, money, and, most of all, guts, but today they have a wonderful new product out on the Macintosh called Oasis.

Oasis users can perform graphic operations that have never existed on the Macintosh before, and do them easily: Operations that used to require hours of training and development of complex mental models can be performed instantly by the youngest child. They can also be performed at lightning speed with a fine sense of control by members of their target audience, the graphic arts industry. Oasis's new features and capabilities are part of a carefully constructed overall design. They were not shoved and glued into place over an existing design. Time Arts has a product of which they can be proud, and an architecture in place that will serve them for many years to come.

A new release provides a new beginning, a new opportunity to deploy our resources in the most effective way possible. Last month, I quoted Reinhold Niebuhr's famous prayer:

God, grant me the serenity
To accept the things I cannot change,
The courage to change the things I can,
And the wisdom to know the difference.

When facing a new release, only by stripping aside every rationalization, questioning every assumption, and breaking through every denial can we accept the things we cannot change and change the things we can. For only then can we have the wisdom to know the difference. Oasis found that difference. So can you.

CHAPTER *36*

Case Study: One-Or-More Buttons

➥ *COLUMN 30: SEPTEMBER, 1991*

❑ ***Dear Tog:*** Have you ever come across a good control which gives the user a "one or more, but not none" selection? What I need would be something like a cross between radio buttons and check boxes, allowing users to select as many options as they want, but always keeping at least one selected.

And if such a control does not exist, how should it look? I would have no problem writing the control definition(s), but I need a good visual way of conveying to the user how the control behaves.

—NEIL STEINER, *DesignSoft*

■ Right after I got his letter, I contacted Neil and told him I had accepted his challenge. Not only is this just the sort of thing I like to do, but I thought I could use the project to demonstrate many of the design principles that I've been propagating these many months. What I hadn't expected was that I would have to fight every inch of the way against the big three enemies of successful software design: Rationalization, assumption, and denial. Since I've been writing so much about them lately, I just assumed I had gained at least temporary immunity. "Assumed..." Yes, I think I see the problem.

Here are the guidelines for expanding the Macintosh interface from my December 1990 column, "The Evolving, Adaptive, Consistent Environment"(see Chapter 19):

- If it ain't broke real bad, don't fix it.

- Build on existing visual/behavioral language.

- Invent new objects, with new appearances, for new behaviors.

- When possible, evolve objects, rather than starting from scratch.

- Make changes clearly visible.

- Interpret users' responses consistently.

- Multiplex meanings.

In addition to these, I also intended to follow one other piece of my own advice:

- Prototype, user test, and iterate.

At Apple, we have million-dollar user-testing labs with one-way mirrors, staffed by serious, white-coated psychologists with more initials after their names than can normally be found in a can of alphabet soup. We have some of the finest graphic artists in the industry. Somehow, using all these resources and talents seemed like cheating. After all, anyone could turn out a decent song if they had Paul McCartney ghostwriting for them. I wanted to see what I could do with the kind of resources available to the average two-, three-, or ten-person shop.

Radio buttons and check boxes have done pretty well for themselves in the eight or so years since they first appeared on the Lisa, and I figured that this new object needed to work at least as well. In fact, this object needed to work better, because it was not going to be appearing in any tutorial: People were going to have to be able to figure out how to use it on their own, first time out.

The behavior of the new object was a hybrid of the behavior of radio buttons and check boxes, so my approach was to create an appearance that would reflect that marriage, by combining visual elements of both. The elements I chose were the $\times$ of the check box and the ● of the radio button. They resulted in early prototypes shown in Figure 36–1.

Figure 36–1. Early Prototypes

I put together a paper test based the dialog box shown in Figure 36–2, changing only the appearance of the middle three objects between tests.

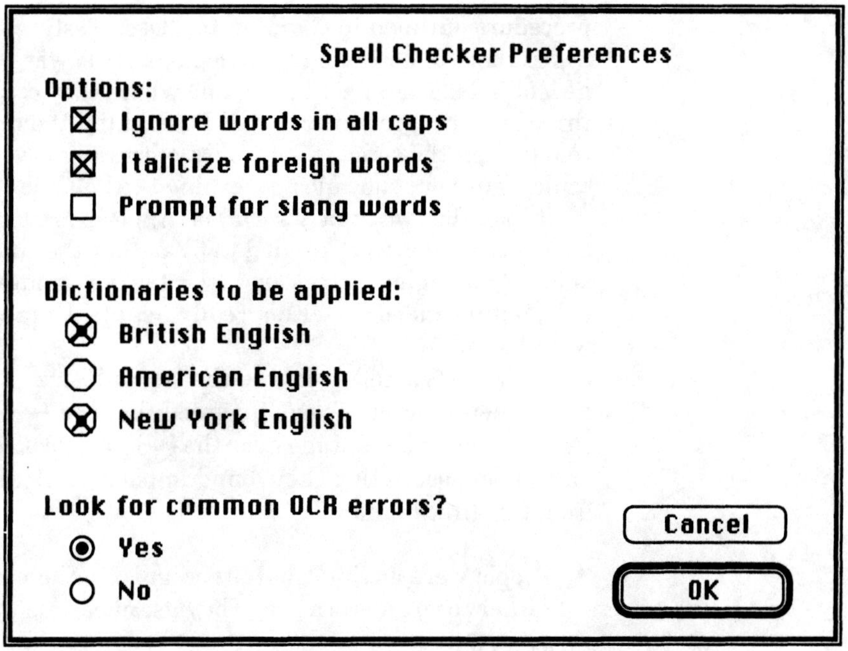

```
┌─────────────────────────────────────────────────────┐
│ ║                                                   │
│ ║          Spell Checker Preferences               │
│ ║   Options:                                        │
│ ║     ☒  Ignore words in all caps                  │
│ ║     ☒  Italicize foreign words                   │
│ ║     ☐  Prompt for slang words                    │
│ ║                                                   │
│ ║                                                   │
│ ║   Dictionaries to be applied:                    │
│ ║     ⊗  British English                           │
│ ║     ○  American English                          │
│ ║     ⊗  New York English                          │
│ ║                                                   │
│ ║                                                   │
│ ║   Look for common OCR errors?      ┌──────────┐  │
│ ║     ◉  Yes                         │  Cancel  │  │
│ ║                                    └──────────┘  │
│ ║     ○  No                         ╔══════════╗   │
│ ║                                   ║    OK    ║   │
│ ║                                   ╚══════════╝   │
└─────────────────────────────────────────────────────┘
```

Figure 36–2.   *An Early Approach to One-or-More Button Design*

In addition to the new cluster of one-or-more objects in the center, please note the third question, "Look for common OCR errors?" I have had a note glued to my monitor for months to discuss OCR (Optical Character Recognition) and spelling checkers with y'all, because most spelling checkers, in their "suggestion" mode, fail to consider errors caused during computer recognition, for example, errors like the letter "m" being interpreted as "ni." I added this question to my dialog so I would be reminded, as I write this, to tell all you spelling-checker guys and gals out there to talk to the OCR guys and gals when you are developing your algorithms.

I left the question in throughout every prototype (since I knew if I took it out, I was going to have to stare at the note on my monitor for another six months), and always got the same question from test subjects, "What's OCR?" I was violating one of Tognazzini's laws:

➤ ***GUIDELINE***   *Never present a power-user option in such a way that normal users must learn all about it in order to know they don't need to use it.*

Back to the subject at hand: I tried the three appearances on three different people in nearby cubicles, using the ten-step User Testing procedure outlined in Chapter 14, "User Testing on the Cheap." I first asked them to describe the dialog box. This was to see if they noticed the new objects. Then I set up a game where they could "click" on any of the three one-or-more buttons, and I would tell them what would happen "in real life" on the screen. The object of the game was to see whether they could figure out the rules governing the behavior of the new buttons.

It took the two area associates (Applespeak for "secretaries") a little over three minutes combined to figure out the rule. The third initial subject, an engineer, took just over twelve minutes to figure out the rule, but he ended up with a really neat truth-table spread across his whiteboard.

After the "game," I showed the test subjects all three objects and asked their opinion. They all agreed that the ⊕ was too busy, and the ⊗ showed no advantage over the ⊕, and looked less like a radio button, an association they found important. I learned several things from this first round:

- People were having trouble recognizing the new object as a control, rather than a decoration. They ascribed this to its unusual size.

- The ⊗ was working best.

- It was working best because it most resembled a radio button.

- Paper prototypes of behavioral models have limited effectiveness.

I slowly reduced the size of the object from ⊗ to ⊛ to ⊛, at which point three additional people I tested (I never repeated any subject) clearly recognized it as a control, but all failed to notice that it wasn't a radio button!

Going back to the elements differentiating a check box from a radio button, I focused on the straight-lineness of a check box, producing the following designs: ▲, ◈, ▣ and ▣ . The first I rejected as just too weird. The second fell to exclamations that it looked like a diamond with a cockroach inside. The third I rejected out of hand because the unselected form of it would be identical to an unchecked check box, thereby violating the guideline against making new objects look identical to old objects. The fourth object seemed to have possibilities: It looked bug like too (kind of like a water-bug), but people didn't seem to have the visceral reaction to this particular bug that they had to the cockroach.

I'm sure it must seem as though I had spent at least twenty or thirty hours on the project so far. Actually, I was at just under two hours.

At home that weekend, I cobbled up a HyperCard version of the prototype, so that I could run some decent behavioral tests. Back at work, I ran three new people through the new ▣ object, asking them, as before, to describe the screen to find out how long it took them to recognize a new object, then asking them to figure out the rules governing the new object by playing with it.

They experienced the following problems:

- Thought it looked like an icky bug.

- Thought the X through a highlighted object meant that it was inactive (cancelled).

- Thought that the rule was that you had to use British English. Or American English. Or New York English.

The "Superstitious" Rule

The way this third problem worked was this: The user would, for example, turn off everything except British English. After discovering he could not then *also* turn off British English, he would make up a rule that British English was sacrosanct and could not be turned off. Then, for the next five minutes, no matter how much I encourage him to turn on and off buttons, he would never, ever again attempt to turn off British English.

At this point, I began to think of this design quest as merely a useful subject for a column on knowing when to abandon design quests. I saw no way out of this dilemma: Once a button got "locked up" and people made up that superstitious rule, I was sunk.

I tried making the button gray out when only one item was selected, so they would know not to push it:

🔲 **British English**

I tried it on one test subject. She reported her belief that the gray meant the selection was not available and therefore, the British dictionary would not be used. She also reported that my graphic looked like a *dead* bug. Normally, I don't put much stock in a single test subject's responses, but this outcome was pretty unequivocal. I abandoned gray.

I further abstracted the appearance, succeeding in removing the buglike appearance or making it look like a badly injured bug, depending on your point of view:

🔳 **British English**

I called it the "train-tunnel" button. I tested it in conjunction with an even further abstraction:

▥ British English

In tests on an additional five people, all were able to figure out the rule without getting locked up. When shown the other design, the majority favored the ▥ .

Was I ready to move ahead with validation testing (discussed in the next section)? No, but until I came to my senses, I thought I was. After all, I had developed an appearance that people found pleasing enough, and I had successfully tested it on five people. What more could anyone want?

Gee, maybe an object that actually worked.

Rationalization
and Denial

I was in denial about the superstitious rule problem: It was still there and not getting any better. So why did everyone pass my last test? Two reasons: I learned early on in my prototypes to always start people out with at least two buttons on, so they wouldn't get locked up on their first attempt. And now, when people did get locked up, I kept after them until they would eventually try clicking on the immutable button. "Gee, are you *sure* you've tried *every* possible combination?" I rationalized that this activity was OK, because I was not telling them directly to click on it. I was only making their lives miserable if they didn't.

Second, I was not listening to my intuition. And it was screaming: Not only had my intuitive observation (see Intuitive Observation, Chapter 15, "Carl Jung and the Macintosh") picked up on the fact that test subjects were having problems, it was clearly (and annoyingly) aware that the observer (me) was very nervous about a supposedly successful object. But I came up with a great rationalization: I was going to do this testing "scientifically" all the way—after all this was a scientific experiment—so I could ignore my intuitions!

These are just some of the reasons we have our white-coated experts do our validity testing: They don't give a damn whether my design works or not, so they do not tend to bias the results. (Actually, I think a few of them actually want my designs to fail, but they have been unwilling to admit to this so far.) But most developers don't have white coats. Fortunately, you can do your own testing if you are willing to face your own denials and rationalizations—in reality, it took me all of a half an hour to "get honest" with myself about the object's failure—and if you can find a group of dear friends who will support you . . .

> ➤ **_GUIDELINE_**   _Use peer design review to infuse fresh ideas and explode false assumptions that may have crept into your design._

Every week at Apple we have a gathering of the human interface people from around the company at a meeting called WHIM, the Working Human Interface Meeting (as opposed to the usual corporate Talking But Doing Nothing Meetings). I brought this marvelously successful new object to one of the meetings, in the hopes of roping one of the graphic designers into either endorsing or fixing up my semifinal, ⬛ object. After all, my design was not bad, but I do know my limitations.

They laughed, they jeered, they derided. (They are not very nice people sometimes.) Where had I learned to draw? What was that funny line underneath the black dot?

I explained to them the funny line was the last vestige of the X in the check box. They responded, "Yeah, right! I would have figured that out right away." I showed them earlier drawings, and when they spotted the cockroach and the water bug, they went wild.

When the clamor died down, John Sullivan, one of the key designers on the System 7 project, said, "If you want a cross between a check box and a radio button, why not make a ▣ ?" (It's amazing the way these designers can actually speak in drawings.)

I offered a scholarly reply: "I thought of that early on, but I rejected it because, in its off state, it would look just like a turned-off check box. And everybody knows you should 'invent new objects, with new appearances, for new behav . . .'"

The whole room answered in unison, "In its off state, it _is_ a turned-off check box!"

- Turned-off check box: Clicking will turn on option, without affecting any other option.

- Turned-off one-or-more: Clicking will turn on option, without affecting any other option.

The two objects did seem kind of similar, now that I thought about it. Somehow, I had just assumed they were different.

Assumption   Assumption. It had really laid me low this time: One of the earliest drawings I had made was that square plus my little insect legs: ▣ . It appeared on my scratch-page of experiments along with all the other objects I'd made, and people had been drawn to it like a magnet from the very beginning. I kept explaining to them about how two different objects, and so on, and so on. I never once revisited my original decision to reject it, even in the light of its overwhelming popularity.

I told the WHIM meeting I'd had some problems with superstitious rules, but that I was going to solve them by telling developers not to actually use the thing. They gave me a series of lectures on the inherent problems of writing a column warning people not to use an object, followed by exacting detail on how to use it.

I installed the ■ and tested again. Now that I was no longer biasing the tests, people got stuck again.

Back to the WHIM meeting. I'd give them a final look at the design; then I could write up this article, and tell you really, really not to use the result.

Now that the WHIMmers saw the ■ object implemented, they recognized that it is used as a radio button in another leading brand of graphic user interface. So much for the ■. I then broke the news that the naive rule problem was worse than I had thought. I was given a new series of lectures.

As the din died down and spitballs ceased flying, I became aware of my friend, Frank Ludolph, repeatedly pressing his thumb down on the table in front of him as though he were attempting to assassinate some offensive bug. "You remember," he said, "when we were kids, playing with a drop of mercury (before we all knew it was poisonous)? Remember how it used to squish out of the way when you tried to press down on it? Why don't you make your buttons do that?"

We were in the presence of genius. Such a simple solution, and no one else had tumbled to it. I certainly was walled off from ever finding it: I'd figured out two weeks earlier that the naive rule problem was unsolvable. Based on that assumption, I'd stopped trying. Yet, on an even deeper level, I knew that radio buttons don't move. A natural law of some sort.

Rationalization, assumption, and denial. I'd suffered from all of them during this project. I had also, fortunately, escaped their worst effects by doing extensive user testing and peer review. Time into the project so far? Seven hours.

I installed the mercury behavior into the prototype, following the simple rules suggested by the WHIM group: Pressing the only button turned on will cause it to turn off and the button below to turn on, unless there is no button below, in which case the button above will turn on.

It seemed wooden and unnatural to chase the ● up from the bottom option, only to have it turn around when the next button is pressed and go back down. I made the middle button conditional: If the ● had been chased from below, turn the button above on, else, turn the button below on. This felt much better.

I decided to extend the metaphor to extremes. (I was brainstorming, and that's what you're supposed to do.) Mercury has a tendency to pop out in an unexpected direction when you press down on it, so I made the middle button pop randomly up or down. It stunk. I tried making it even more like mercury, so if you pressed toward the top, it would squish down. If you pressed toward the bottom, it would squish upwards. It was very disconcerting; it still seemed kind of random. So I returned permanently to the more simple behavior, as specified herein:

- If a currently turned-off one-or-more is pressed, turn it on.

- If more than one one-or-more is turned on and a turned-on one-or-more is pressed, turn it off.

- If a single one-or-more is turned on and that one-or-more is pressed, turn that one-or-more off and turn on an adjacent one-or-more according to the following rules:

  - If the current option is other than the bottommost (or rightmost, for horizontal layouts) and the go-up flag discussed below is not set, turn on the next one-or-more down.

  - If the current option is the bottommost (or rightmost), turn on the next one-or-more up (or to the left) and set the go-up flag so that movement will now occur upwards (or leftwards).

- Turn off the go-up flag when

  - the top is reached

  - a button is selected that is not currently turned on

  - the user clicks somewhere outside the cluster of one-or-mores

I tried the object out on my son, Joshua, age eleven, and soon as he saw the ● move he announced the one-or-more rule. No hesitation, no wondering. Instantaneous. I figured we had a winner.

Now, the only problem remaining was picking a visual appearance. For that, I submitted the prototype to Elizabeth Moller, a human interface designer with a formal graphic design background, who gave me back the designs shown in Figure 36–3, one of which the WHIM group liked best (note the two-pixel white border between the outer and inner diamonds)

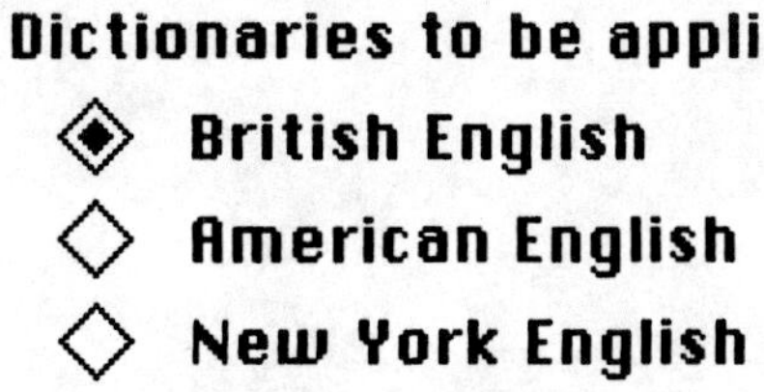

Dictionaries to be applied:

◈ **British English**

◇ **American English**

◇ **New York English**

Figure 36–3   *One-or-More Final Design*

You don't race around the building looking for warm bodies when you are testing for validation. Racing is OK as long as you are using a reasonably representative sample of people and are finding problems to fix, but running out of problems is not a sign you are finished, just a sign that racing is not uncovering any more. Running out of problems merely means you are now ready to do some serious validation testing, which requires a thought-out, carefully chosen, representative population. Why? Because even the first fourteen people you happen to run across may not come even close to representing your real target audience.

The last five people I tested were

- A nine-year-old child with limited Macintosh experience

- A nine-year-old child with no Macintosh experience

- A woman who uses a Macintosh perhaps two hours per week

- A woman who uses a Macintosh two hours per day

- A self-identified power-user

Each of these people were able to ascertain the rules for one-or-more buttons within fifteen seconds without any problems.

The object was finished.

A Solution in Search of a Problem?

"If it ain't broke, don't fix it": That one-or-more buttons work does not make them a candidate for inclusion in every application from here on out. After all, check boxes and radio buttons have held up pretty well. Nonetheless, my experience has been that once I have developed or heard about some new fundamental object, I find that it begins to solve a lot of problems I previously didn't even know I had.

Whether you use it or not, I hope you have received some insight by watching me stumble and bumble my way through this experience. New objects and behaviors do not have to be developed in a vacuum. There is an alternative to guessing at user behavior. Try this method out. It need not take long, and it's a lot easier than putting out release 1.01 a week after you ship.

CHAPTER 37

A Glimpse of the Future

❏ ***Dear Tog:*** I really enjoy hearing about how one should use the existing Mac user interface but I would also be interested in hearing about Apple's ideas for future user interfaces. The Macintosh made a quantum leap forward in user interfaces by moving from a one-channel, one-dimensional tty model to a two-channel two-dimensional model for human-computer interaction. How about the next leap? Any ideas or speculation about multichannel communication (voice, vision, data glovelike spatial manipulation) or three-dimensional user interfaces and graphics?

—JON PITTMAN, *Wavefront Technologies*

■ Jon, let's handle your question in three phases: Immediate, mid-term, and the world of tomorrow. Understand that I cannot reveal details of our actual plans for the next five years; that would be telling. Besides, we don't know what they are yet. (Oops! That *is* telling.) Nevertheless, there are clear trends within the Macintosh community and the world at large that I can discuss.

Immediate Plans

Let's begin by looking at some approaches that designers should be taking right now.

Dynamic Objects

➤ **GUIDELINE** *Use dynamic objects to relieve overcrowding of visible space by making the objects assume a small or subtle form until activated at the user's command.*

In the late seventies, when we began designing the Lisa and the Macintosh, our target audience was largely made up of people who had never touched a computer before and were loath to try. As a result, we designed an interface that was static and serene. Now, more than twelve years later, our audience has changed: Millions of people are familiar with microcomputers, and the ones who aren't at least grudgingly acknowledge their value. They can see where an investment in learning about computers could result in worthwhile benefits.

We are still designing our interfaces for the 70s, with dull, static objects. Of course, there have been a couple of bright lights: The pop-up menu arrived to replace a lot of large, ugly scrolling lists. The pop-up palette is displacing a lot of slow, cumbersome dialog boxes.

We're running out of real estate, and we're running out of time. Dynamic objects offer a way out. Look at Vellum shown in Figure 37–1 with its myriad of little text strips popping up to converse with the user:

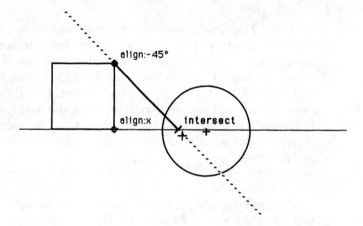

Figure 37–1. *Vellum for the '90s*

Does this follow the guidelines? Of course not! Why, Vellum should be presenting this information in alerts, with proper confirmation as shown in Figure 37–2.

Notice the two-second delay while the alert is drawn. Notice the darling graphic and rich use of language within the alert. Notice how the alert has been carefully placed to obscure the area of interest. Notice that the user has stopped drawing and started searching for the designer's home phone number.

➤ **GUIDELINE** *Dynamic objects can bend the barriers of time and space, but they must not break them; every object must still have a physical representation, however small or subtle.*

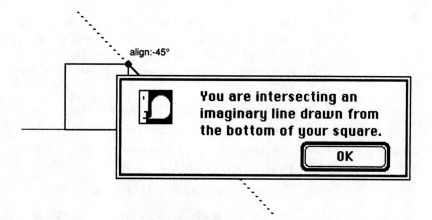

align:-45°

You are intersecting an
imaginary line drawn from
the bottom of your square.

OK

Figure 37–2. *Vellum for the '70s*

The pop-up menu takes up a fraction of the real estate of a scrolling list, but it is still a visible object. The Vellum Drafting Assistant may not converse in modal alerts, but still something appears on the display. People cannot deal with invisible objects and invisible concepts. An example was the Macintosh's pre-System 7 handling of fonts, which were placed inside the System file just as they are now. The problem was that people couldn't see them go in there; it had to be done through an abstraction called Font/DA Mover. Shrink your objects in time and in space, but don't make them disappear.

Relative Color

I came up with a scheme back in 1987 called Relative Color, based on experiments I did with video back in the 1960s.

➤ **GUIDELINE** *Use relative color to enable a user to swiftly change anything—from a single object to the total environment—to an entirely new color scheme without having to change any individual element and without having to rely on any presets.*

Currently, to change environment colors (scroll bar, menu bar, and so on) using one of the many shareware control panel applications, you either change each and every item in the environment, or you select a preset formula for the items.

Let's look at how relative color could be used instead: Perhaps a user has recently invested in a new and improved Mood Crystal down at Tiny's Flea Market and New Age Fashion Mall. On Monday, the crystal is of a definite turquoise (cyan) hue. That day, he sets his desktop colors so that:

- The background color is a deep blue
- The menu bar is a rich turquoise
- The menus are pastel green
- The title bar is medium cyan
- The thumb (elevator) is bright red

Tuesday morning, he discovers the crystal is radiating magenta and realizes to his horror that his desktop is no longer vibrating in rhythm with the universe!

No problem—he simply goes into the Master Color Picker. The Master Color Picker enables the user to manipulate the entire color space whose limits are defined by all his choices made the day previously. The color space is represented by a single point, or color, which lies in the center of that space.

To change every environmental color simultaneously, he moves the current master (center) color from medium cyan over to light magenta. Upon accepting the change, the following will have occurred:

- The background is a medium red
- The menu bar is a medium-saturation magenta
- The menus are of the lightest blue "wash"
- The title bar is pastel magenta
- The thumb is bright green, but with less saturation than previously.

The colors all continue to bear the same *relationship* to each other: Only the overall color has been changed, by virtue of a single decision.

Hue would be considered circular in this model: No matter how wide the range of hues in the objects, the master (center) hue could be set to any available. Any individual object's hue that reached blue would spill over through the "nonexistent" color, magenta, into red and beyond. (This is consistent with the model presented by the current Color Picker.)

Color saturation and brightness would be considered linear: A very bright object would not suddenly "wrap" and become dark. Nor would a heavily saturated color suddenly "wrap" and become pastel. Instead, as the user approached any linear limit, be it full saturation or total darkness, the dynamic range among devices would become compressed.

To understand how this compression would work, think of moving an extended coil spring across a room. As long as you touch neither wall, the spring remains fully extended. This extension, shown in Figure 37–3, represents the dynamic range of, for example, the saturation of the objects.

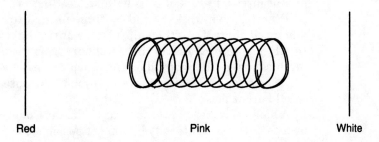

Red   Pink   White

Figure 37–3. *Uncoiled White Spring*

As you touch a wall with one end of the spring (hit white), the spring begins to compress: The other end begins to move toward the end against the wall, with every point along the spring compressing at a rate in exact proportion to its location between the two end points (fully saturated, "rich" blue has become medium-saturated red, but pastel green, having little distance to go, has only become a slightly lighter blue "wash"). See Figure 37–4.

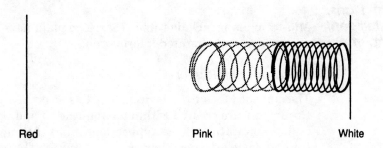

Red   Pink   White

Figure 37–4. *Coiled White Spring*

At any given time, the relationship among the points along the spring is maintained, even though the distances have been compressed.

As the spring is once again moved away from the wall, it uncoils, restoring the dynamic range once again.

The concept of Relative Color would enable those users who want to change colors frequently to do so with great ease. But beyond that, it would open up some interesting background processes. Perhaps the colors would change with the passage of time, with relatively sharp breaks in hue between the hours or half-hours; one would soon develop an unconscious sense of time without needing to glance at a watch.

Presets, meanwhile, would continue to exist to enable users to choose among clusters of relationships: Do I want a slight difference between the thumb and the rest of the scroll bar, or do I want the thumb, as the mythical user did, to stand out in sharp contrast, clear on the other side of the color space? Do I want the thumb to be more saturated than the scroll bar, or less?

A small number of presets plus a Master Color Picker would give the user fast access to literally billions of possible color combinations, rather than the couple of dozen that presets now enable.

Users could potentially declare some object colors to be "non-relative." This would enable the user who always leaves the elevator pink to continue to do so.

I hope to see this scheme eventually cover color icons, too. Developers would be required to have a dominant color in their icons, perhaps in the form of one visual element that took up 35% to 40% of the total area of the icon. Beyond that, they could use as many colors as they wanted. Users could change that predominant color to anything they wanted, and the rest of the colors would rotate about the color wheel with it, maintaining their relationship.

Mid-Term Plans: The Intelligent Document

Mid-term plans include three areas: The plain paper metaphor, active documents, and liberated information.

Plain Paper Metaphor

The current Macintosh environment has at its heart the application. Documents are created within an application and reflect the capabilities of that application. Some applications allow the importation, through cut and paste or some other means, of pieces of other documents created with other applications. Publish and Subscribe allow the importation of data that remains tightly connected to the original source. Nevertheless, creation of complex documents on the Macintosh typically requires the use of several applications and many documents. "The plain paper metaphor" is the metaphorical wrapping that can make the far more advanced technology child's play for the average user.

The context in which a computer user performs his or her work has historically been dictated by the needs of the machine. As we approach the era of widespread multitasking and multiprocessing, we have the luxury of rethinking decisions made in the era of low-power computers. Application-centered design is one such area of decision.

History   Documents were typically created within tools called applications. Applications were able to stand alone. From the early machines' point of view, this was ideal. Since applications didn't need to interact, memory requirements were kept at a minimum and no complex memory management needed to take place—just the sort of scheme you want when you've built your computer out of several thousand vacuum tubes or a microwave oven control processor.

Where We Are Today   We now have the power, with the advent of multitasking and multiprocessing, to really make the document-within-tool system sing. We can have twenty-three different applications open at once and flit among them rapidly, allowing us to assemble amazing documents. In a windowing system like the Macintosh's, clicking on a document window not only calls forth the application, but all the other windows launched from that application, all automatically. What more could we want?

Integration. Efficiency. Context. Our own context, that is—not the computer's.

Applying User-Centered Context to the System Image
Documents-within-tools can be likened to having to place your house inside a giant hammer so you can nail in a picture hook in the living room. Nevertheless, it has survived a surprisingly long time.

The document-within-tool metaphor is for the sake of the computer, not the user. It has led to reports and papers being made up of bits and pieces created in three, four, or even more applications. The final document is assembled by copying "dead" pieces from other applications into a single "master" document as shown in Figure 37–5.

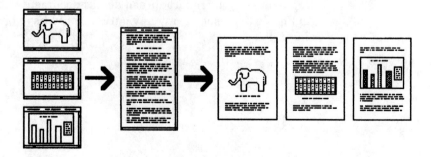

Figure 37–5.   *Creating Documents Out of Fragments*

Observe the efficient Macintosh user, and you will see the user move rapidly from window to window, collecting, pasting, altering, pasting again, and again, and again. It looks efficient, but it can be really labor-intensive. Figure 37–6 represents my navigation during the creation of a set of slides:

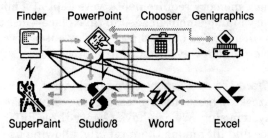

Figure 37–6. *Movement Among Applications*

My movement is represented by the thin, dark gray lines; my data's movement, by the thick, light gray lines. The last set of slides I did, I moved between applications more than 500 times, and my data did the same. I don't know which of us was more worn out.

Compound documents, in the supporting plain paper metaphor, do away with the *application* as the primary object and replace it with the *document*. Users need create only a single document to get their work done. Applications are replaced by (or simply relabeled as) tool kits, and tool kits can be called upon from within any document.

With plain paper, most of the problems of application-centered context disappear: With all tools available within the document, suddenly the user can do his or her project "without ever leaving home." Everything is in one place. Want to put a drawing in your report? Just click on your drawing tool. Want a chart? Click on your chart tool. All of a sudden, you are working within context again. You no longer have fragments of your report spread across documents all over your system. As Figure 37–7 shows, my navigation would have been reduced to a single act:

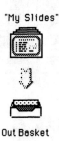

Figure 37–7. *Into the Out Basket*

Multiprocessing and multitasking offer the opportunity for change, but only if we take it. We have the ability to design the overpasses that will lead our users to the superhighways of computing. Let us not get bogged down in designing high-speed traffic lights because we're still thinking in terms of intersections. Nor should you be afraid of the future: The real promise of systemwide support for plain paper will be a flattening of the playing field, increasing competition by making it possible for small developers to gain a hold in the market. Since a new word processor need not have to have every bell and whistle of a ten-year-old word processor—bells and whistles being sold separately—a new player with a great idea can enter the market without a multimillion dollar investment.

Active Documents

Typically, we assign each object in the interface to a given "person": The system owns the Finder windows, the applications own the icons within the windows, and the user owns the titles beneath the icons. Just as a given object can carry several simultaneous communication channels, several *people* or *processors* can be assigned to those communication channels.

As a small example, we now let users have control over a secondary channel tied to the icons: We let people color them.

Future objects can have a far richer series of channels. Consider the example of an object within a document shown in Figure 37–8.

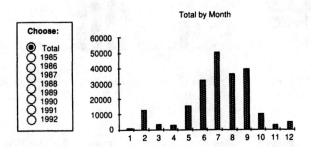

Figure 37–8. *Chart within a "Living Document"*

The following people and processors access this structure:

- Spreadsheet: Beneath the chart is a spreadsheet that drives it. The spreadsheet can update itself through links, thereby affecting the chart.

- Charting application: The charting application continues to update the chart with any changes in the spreadsheet's data.

- "Draw" application: The final layout of the chart can be changed with a drawing application *without affecting the spreadsheet's ability to update the data.*

- The rest of the document: Other portions of the document can affect the chart, in any way from passing data to the spreadsheet to hiding or showing the chart.

- The System: Perhaps this document is only to be seen or manipulated by certain people. The System itself could control access based on who the reader is.

- Author: The creator of the document has control over the Spreadsheet, charting, and drawing applications. Use of any one of these applications does not "do away" with changes made with the others; all remain in control of their attributes of the document.

- Reader: The reader can choose to view the document in an entirely different form, for example, as a pie chart. The reader has also been supplied with a series of radio buttons, enabling him or her to leaf through much more detailed data, such as that shown in Figure 37–9.

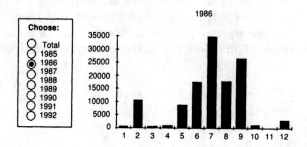

Figure 37–9. *The Same Chart with a Different Radio Button Selected*

With the advent of active documents, for the first time there can be an advantage to getting an electronic copy of a document instead of "the real thing." Couple this technology with hardware advances, such as small, portable "dynabook" computers that will keep themselves informed by grabbing information from your desktop computers when you draw it near, or via phone lines or radio when you don't, and the era of the paperless office could finally begin.

Liberated Information

It's going to be really hard to live in the information age if it continues to be so hard to get our hands on information.

We're coming out of an era when there were two kinds of reference materials available to the common person: Seemingly unstructured collections of random stuff, known as libraries, and tiny, tightly integrated collections of inadequate information bound in fine Corinthian leather, known as encyclopedias. The ideal of information in electronic media is a third form of information, as tightly integrated as that of encyclopedias, but as vast as all the libraries of the world.

Tight integration will be achieved both by application of computer technology—browsers, agents, database structures—and by what I predict will be an increasing emphasis on writing to form, so that information will be more modular and "connectable." Still, it will inevitably fall short: Much of our children's education will need to be directed toward the process of retrieving and interpreting information, replacing today's dying emphasis on memorizing information.

But the process of retrieval, in itself, only solves half the problem. I'm also concerned about the "hoarding" of information I see: People are trying to market videotapes that "self-destruct" after a certain number of playings. Broadcasters buy up "rights" to nationally televise games, then don't do so, but make sure that satellite dish owners and cable subscribers are blacked out from receiving the regional broadcasts. Newspapers put ten years worth of back issues on a $5.00 CD ROM, then sell it for $1000, insuring that no one but a few institutions can afford it.

Information providers are operating under a model of scarcity in a world filled with enormous sums of available information and millions of people who would like to own it. Inexpensive CD ROM systems are just around the corner, but will only be successful if inexpensive information follows.

French photographer Marc Garanger took his lifetime collection of some 50,000 photographs and impressed them on a single video disk, "Regard for the Planet." I don't think I would have spent the thousands upon thousands of dollars it would have taken to bind up these photos in coffee-table books, but I sure was willing to plunk down $80 or $100 to have them all. And I spend hours enjoying them.

I would like to spend $80 or $100 on a lot of other rich information collections, but I can't. Because the providers want to charge me that much for perhaps a hundred images, surrounded by a lot of meaningless fluff designed to fill up the space.

I want the United States Library of Congress on my desktop. I want the collections of every major museum in the world available to project against my wall. I want every issue of every newspaper published in the English-speaking world sitting in my laptop.

Is this really too much to ask?

Long-Term Plans

Long-term plans include changing the way we educate our children and how we experience reality.

The Promise of Education

> I hear and I forget.
> I see and I remember.
> I do and I understand.
>
> —ANCIENT CHINESE PROVERB

I recently visited Open School in Los Angeles. This school, home of Apple's Vivarium Project, has fully integrated computers into the classroom: For every cluster of sixty kids, there are thirty computers. The kids have access to multimedia, advanced simulations, everything. They spend the bulk of their computer time with two applications: MacWrite II and Canvas. The computer is a productivity tool. By the third grade, they all touch type. By the third grade, they are churning out stories worthy of many adults. These are not exceptional kids; they are kids with access to exceptional tools. These tools are the same ones that have reshaped our lives, but these kids are getting hold of them at a much younger age than we did.

Universal access to computers, advanced simulations—these are all very good, but the real promise of computers in education goes one step beyond: Right now, the very best politicians are running our countries, the very best salespeople are running our corporations, the very best gameshow hosts are ruining our airwaves. Everywhere you turn, the best and brightest rise to the top—except in education.

Of course, the very best lecturers rise to prominence. People like James Burke assemble wondrous series for PBS and the BBC, but what of the finest elementary school teacher? He or she is probably teaching a single, grossly overcrowded class somewhere in Kansas City or Birmingham or New Delhi. Where is the leverage there?

Toffler (1980) points out that the school systems of the Western world maintain a covert curriculum, consisting of discipline, repetition, and punctuality. These are the critical lessons that continue to prepare our children for entry into the factories of the industrial revolution.

Under this system, our children are expected to learn to move to the beat of the central school clock, originally provided at no charge by the local factory. Classes do not begin when the kids have finished their farm chores; classes begin at exactly 8:15. They don't end when the subject is taught, but when the bell rings. Bad punctuality is instantly and severely punished; bad grades are often tolerated. When asked whether it should be, "Mary threw the ball to John while Freddy watched," or "Mary throwed the ball to John while Freddy watched," children are required to "write out the whole sentence," instead of just answering the question: That way they learn to handle the boring, mindless repetition of the factory.

Here we have a system with the best teachers reaching only a handful of kids, overcrowded classrooms, and an entrenched educational philosophy designed to bore the students. Gee, this sounds like a job for Mr. Computer!

Teachers today are ready for change: They were bored to death in school, and they have no wish to see their charges repeat the experiment. Schools like Open School are leading the way, by enabling students to become involved in learning, by encouraging them to "do" instead of only read, by giving the children access to important tools, like the computer.

We are not going to solve classroom overcrowding by throwing teachers at the problem; there are not enough of them to go around. But computers will be called into play here, too: We will capture the essence of that finest teacher and put it into a computer, there for all the children to experience. Artificial Intelligence problem? Yes. Twenty years out? At least, but this will be the ultimate answer to the education crisis, because kids need quality time from their teachers and quantity time as well. The spirit of our best, most loving teachers can give it to them.

For a short time when I was growing up, I had the pleasure of going to school in a one-room schoolhouse. One teacher, fewer than ten kids. It was fun; it was engaging. The older kids got to teach the younger. The younger ones might not have remembered that much, but the older ones, having taught, sure did. Those who were smartest could move swiftly ahead, unencumbered by grade level or "emotional maturity." Open School has achieved that kind of ambiance and freedom on a larger scale. Only the inadequacy of time for direct one-on-one engagement remains. Computers will solve that, too.

Virtual Reality

Virtual realities are as old as civilization itself. The ancient temples of the Egyptians, the hanging gardens of Babylon, Mad Ludwig II's Venus Grotto at Linderhof, the Fillmore Auditorium in the '60s—all were designed to carry people away from the realities of the world to another place, another time.

Not long ago, I participated in a study for the National Research Council (Branscomb 1991), speaking to a room full of lawyers on the topic of "look and feel." I told them all about this ethereal "stuff" we weave into the fabric of a virtual reality. They wanted me to produce a balance beam with which they could weigh it. They are still waiting.

I measure the success of a virtual reality by whether I come to believe in it. I believe in Disneyland, with its spotless streets, and it's well-trained "hosts," always in character, always true to the illusion. (Most assuredly, I believe in Star Tours, by far the best virtual reality I have ever experienced.) I don't believe in other "theme parks" I have visited, with their slovenly attention to detail and their absence of costume and character.

I do believe in the Macintosh interface, with its consistency, visibility, and attention to detail. I don't believe in other interfaces with their lack of standard objects and behaviors, invisible operations, and dangerous snake pits waiting at every turn.

The data glove, the Polhemus device (for locating a physical object in 3-D space), stereoscopic heads-up displays, and other such devices enable us to increase the sense of reality our users gain from our machines, but they offer a much more important promise. Until now, computers have been physical devices before which one sits. But project forward twenty years or so, when today's cumbersome 3-D helmets have been replaced with a light-weight, transparent pair of glasses. Move away from your computer screen and look around your office. Notice that in addition to the hard reality of your books, file cabinets, and papers strewn across your desk, there is a glowing electronic reality superimposed, hugging every curve. Announce softly that you are looking for information on kanji, and watch a book on the shelf take on a warmer glow. Touch it, and see its table of contents hanging in the air.

Fanciful? I don't think so. I saw a working prototype of such a system at NASA's Ames Research Center five years ago. And the march of technology won't stop there.

The Spleen Machine

About twenty years ago, I heard an old and apocryphal story about a medical student who arrived late to class, having quite forgotten to study (yet again). The teacher, being a particularly mean sort, immediately began to question him:

"Well, Mr. Johnson. So nice of you to drop by."

"Well, I . . ."

"Perhaps, since you are here, you could inform the class as to the purpose of the spleen in the human body . You have heard of the spleen, Mr. Johnson?"

"Why of course. The spleen is very important. It is used to . . .Um, the spleen . . . Oh, darn it all! I knew what the spleen was for yesterday!"

"Well then, Mr. Johnson, it is indeed unfortunate that you have forgotten, because for the last 4000 years, medical science has been trying to figure that out."

By the time I heard this story, medical science had figured out what the spleen is good for, but, nonetheless, it was an organ we could live without, and therefore certain possibilities intrigued me. I proposed we pull it out and replace it with a fairly good-sized portable computer. With the nerve bundle, we could tie right into the brain and be up in no time.

Computers, as information providers, stink. I don't want to read about the French Revolution, I don't want to hear about the French Revolution, I don't want to experience a simulation of the French Revolution—I want to just simply "remember" the French Revolution. The machines we use today are primitive toys. They are like telegraphs to television, like steam trains to the space shuttle.

The spleen machine idea is obsolete today: We've finally found out the spleen has a significant role in the immune system. Besides, William Gibson, in *Neuromancer* (1984), went the spleen machine one better by shrinking a computer down and sticking it behind the ear. But regardless of how it is achieved, the key to human-computer communication and, perhaps eventually, human-human communication will be direct connection with the mind.

We think of computers as silicon machines, but the devices that eventually become a part of us may be of flesh and blood, the product of biotechnology. Or perhaps a blend of silicon and flesh. (A pleasant thought, no?)

And while we're waiting? We will move from direct manipulation to dialog, to agents, and beyond. Of course, none of this will make us any smarter, but our computers will be getting smarter, and eventually, humanity and computer will meet at the apex of biotechnology and computer science. God only knows which of the two species will survive. And which would be better for the planet.

CHAPTER *38*

A Final Word

"Experimental psychology is not noted for its contributions to life; . . . human interface should be."

—DON NORMAN, 1983a

I remember the riveting image some years back of scores of poor West Indians in a vast island sweatshop, huddled over their computer screens, entering in mountains of data from expended airline tickets. They worked eight, ten, twelve hours per day, day in and day out. They may have been using an interface that made their jobs as easy and as enjoyable as possible, but from everything else associated with the operation, I would suspect they were using one that was slap-dashed together in the belief that it was adequate to the job and good enough for the class of people who would use it.

Until Doug Engelbart began his humanist approach to computers less than thirty years ago, computer science was not noted for its contribution to the human spirit. That has changed. Designers today realize that our software is more than some static collection of dialog boxes and windows. It affects people's lives in powerful and profound ways and we have a solemn responsibility to do everything possible to improve the quality of those lives.

Scott Peck (1978) has defined love as "the will to extend one's self for the purpose of nurturing one's own or another's spiritual growth."

Treat your users with love. Seek to help them grow, thrive, and succeed, and you cannot fail.

References

Aebi, Ormond and Harry (1982). *Mastering the Art of Beekeeping*, Prism Press, Dorchester, Dorset, England. This book, and their earlier work, *The Art and Adventure of Beekeeping* (Rodale Press, Emmaus, Penn. 1975) are the finest books on intuitive observation I have read.

Baecker, Ronald M., and Buxton, William A. S. (1987). *Readings in Human-Computer Interaction, A Multidisciplinary Approach,* Morgan Kaufmann, Los Altos, Calif.

Bennett, William R. Jr. (1976). *Scientific and Engineering Problem Solving with the Computer,* Prentice Hall, Englewood Cliffs, NJ, as reported in Campbell, J. (1982). *Grammatical Man,* Simon & Schuster, New York, N.Y.

Berne, Eric (1949). "The Nature of Intuition," *The Psychiatric Quarterly*, vol. 23, pp. 203–226.

Berne, Eric (1955). "Intuition IV: Primal Images and Primal Judgement," *The Psychiatric Quarterly*, vol. 29, pp. 634–658.

Berne, Eric (1958). "Transactional Analysis: A New and Effective Method of Group Therapy," *The American Journal of Psychotherapy*, vol. 12, pp. 735–743.

Berne, Eric (1962). "The Psychodynamics of Intuition," *The Psychiatric Quarterly*, vol. 36, pp. 294–300.

Blake, Tyler (1985). "Introduction to Principles and Techniques for Interface Design," tutorial notes for *CHI'85* Tutorial.

Branscomb, L. M., (1991). Chairman, *Intellectual Property Issues in Software*, National Academy Press, Washington, D.C.

Brennan, Susan E. (1990). "Conversation as Direct Manipulation: An Iconoclastic View," in Brenda Laurel (ed.), *The Art of Human-Computer Interface Design,* Addison-Wesley, Reading, Mass.

Buxton, William (1986). "There's More to Interaction than Meets the Eye: Some Issues in Manual Input," in D. Norman and F.W. Draper (Eds.), *New Perspectives on Human-Computer Interaction,* Lawrence Erlbaum Associates, Hillsdale, N.J.

Campbell, J. (1982). *Grammatical Man,* Simon & Schuster, New York, N.Y. This is an outstanding book that is accessible to normal people and changes their lives.

Card, S. K., Moran, T. P., & Newell, A. (1983). *The Psychology of Human-Computer Interaction,* Lawrence Erlbaum Associates, Hillsdale, N.J.

Card, S. K., Pavel, M., and Farrell, J. E. (1985). "Window-Based Computer Dialogs," *Human-Computer Interaction—Interact '84,* Amsterdam, Holland, pp. 239–243.

Carolino, Pedro (1883). *The New Guide of the Conversation in Portuguese and English,* currently published as *Fractured English as She is Spoke* with an introduction by Mark Twain by Dover Press, New York, N.Y.; General Publishing Company, Toronto, Canada; and Constable and Company, Ltd., London, England.

De Bono, Edward (1970). *Lateral Thinking: Creativity Step by Step*, Harper and Row, New York, N.Y.

Edwards, Betty (1989). *Drawing on the Right Side of the Brain,* St. Martins Press, New York, N.Y.

Engelbart, Douglas C. (1986). "The Augmented Knowledge Workshop," *History of Personal Workstations,* ACM Press, New York, N.Y.

Fitts, P. M. (1954). "The Information Capacity of the Human Motor System in Controlling Amplitude of Movement." *Journal of Experimental Psychology,* no. 47, pp. 381–391.

Gallway, W. Timothy (1976). *Inner Tennis: Playing the Game.* Random House, New York, N.Y.

Gibson, William (1984). *Neuromancer,* Ace Science Fiction Books, New York, N.Y.

Homer (1942). *The Odyssey,* translated by Alexander Pope, The George Macy Companies, New York, N.Y.

Heckel, Paul (1991). *The Elements of Friendly Software Design.* Sybex, Alameda, Calif.

Jeffries, Robin; Miller, James R.; Warton, Cathleen; and Uyeda, Kathy M. (1991). "User Interface Evaluation in the Real World: A Comparison of Four Techniques," *Proceedings of CHI'91,* Addison-Wesley, Reading, Mass., pp. 119–124.

Jung, C. G. (1921). *Psychological Types*. Princeton University Press, Princeton, N.J., 1974. Originally published in German as *Psychologische Typen*, Rascher Verlag, Zurich.

Kay, Alan (1990). "User Interface: A Personal View," in Brenda Laurel (ed.), *The Art of Human-Computer Interface Design,* Addison-Wesley, Reading, Mass.

Keirsey, D. and Bates, M. (1984). *Please Understand Me: Character & Temperament Types,* Prometheus Nemesis Book Company, Del Mar, Calif.

Kroeger, Otto and Thuesen, Janet M. (1988). *Type Talk, The 16 Personality Types that Determine How We Live, Love, and Work,* Tilden Press, A Delta book Published by Dell Publishing a division of Bantam Doubleday Dell Publishing Group, Inc., New York, N.Y.

Laurel, Brenda (1991). *Computers as Theater,* Addison-Wesley, Reading, Mass.

Mantei, M. M. and Teory, T. J. (1988). "Cost/Benefit Analysis for Incorporating Human Factors in the Software Life Cycle," Communications of the ACM 31, 4, pp. 428–439, April 1988.

Marcus, Aaron (1992). *Graphic Design for Electronic Documents and User Interfaces,* ACM Press, New York, N.Y.

Mehrabian, A., and Ferris, S. R. (1967). "Inference of Attitudes from Nonverbal Communication in Two Channels," *Journal of Consulting Psychology,* 31, 248, 252.

Mulligan, Robert M., Altom, Mark W., and Simkin, David K. (1991). "Interface Design in the Trenches: Some Tips on Shooting From the Hip," *Proceedings of CHI'91,* Addison-Wesley, Reading, Mass., pp. 232–236.

Myers, Isabel Briggs and McCaulley, Mary H. (1985). *A Guide to the Development and Use of the Myers-Briggs Type Indicator*. Consulting Psychologists Press, Palo Alto, Calif.

Nielsen, Jakob (1989). "Usability Engineering at a Discount," *Proceedings of the Third International Conference on Human-Computer Interaction,* Boston, Mass., Sept. 1989.

Norman, D. A. (1983a, December). "Design Principles for Human-Computer Interfaces," in A. Janda (Ed.), *Proceedings of CHI'83 Conference on Human Factors in Computing Systems* (Boston). ACM Press, New York, N.Y. pp. 1-10. Also published as Norman, D. A. (1986). "Design Principles for Human-Computer Interfaces," in D. E. Berger, K. Pezdek, & W. P. Banks (Eds.), *Applications of Cognitive Psychology: Problem Solving, Education, and Computing,* Lawrence Erlbaum Associates, Hillsdale, N.J.

Norman, D. A. (1983b). "Some Observations on Mental Models," in Gentner, Dedre & Stevens, Albert L. (Eds.), *Mental Models,* Lawrence Erlbaum Associates, Hillsdale, N.J.

Norman, D. A. (1986). "Cognitive Engineering," in D. A. Norman & S. W. Draper (Eds.), *User-Centered System Design,* Lawrence Erlbaum Associates, Hillsdale, N.J.

Norman, Donald (1988). *The Psychology of Everyday Things,* Basic Books, New York, N.Y. (Also published in paperback as Norman, D. A. (1990). The Design of Everyday Things. Doubleday, New York, N.Y. (This is a must-read for anyone who wants to become competent at the art of human interface design.)

Peck, M. Scott (1978). *The Road Less Traveled: A New Psychology of Love, Traditional Values, and Spiritual Growth,* Simon & Schuster, A Touchstone Book, New York, N.Y.

Root, A. I., Root, E. R., Root, H. H., Root, J. A., and Goltz, L. R. (1980). *The ABC and XYZ of Bee Culture,* A. I. Root Co., Medina, Ohio.

Rubinstein, Richard and Hersh, Harry M. (1984). "Design Philosophy." Chapter 2 in *The Human Factor: Designing Computer Systems for People,* Digital Press, Burlington, Mass.

Schmandt, Chris (1990). "Illusion in the Interface," in Brenda Laurel (ed.), *The Art of Human-Computer Interface Design,* Addison-Wesley, Reading, Mass.

Shneiderman, B. (1983). "Direct Manipulation: A Step Beyond Programming Languages," *IEEE Computer,* August, 1983.

Shneiderman, B. (1987). *Designing the User Interface: Strategies for Effective Human-Computer Interaction.* Addison-Wesley, Reading, Mass.

Sitton, Sarah and Chmelir, Gerard (1984). "The Intuitive Computer Programmer," *Datamation,* October 15, 1984.

Smith, D. C., Irby, C., Kimball, R., Verplank, W., and Harslem, E. (1987). "Designing the Star User Interface," in Baecker, R. M. and Buxton, W. A. S. *Readings in Human-Computer Interaction: A Multidisciplinary Approach,* Morgan Kaufmann Publishers, Inc., Los Altos, Calif. Originally appeared in *Byte,* 7(4), April 1982, pp. 242–282.

Toffler, Alvin (1980). *The Third Wave,* William Morrow & Co., Inc., New York, N.Y.

Tognazzini, B. (1986). "Usability Testing in the Real World," in Mills, C. B. et al., *Proceedings of CHI'86,* pp. 212–215.

Tognazzini, B. (1989a). "Achieving Consistency for the Macintosh," in Jakob Nielsen (ed.), *Coordinating User Interfaces for Consistency,* Academic Press, Boston, Mass.

Tognazzini, B. (1989b). "World Builder: Macintosh User-Centered Design" (video), Apple Computer, Inc., Cupertino, Calif.

Tognazzini, B. (1990). "Consistency," in Brenda Laurel (ed.), *The Art of Human-Computer Interface Design,* Addison-Wesley, Reading, Mass.

Vertelney, Laurie (1989). Scenario and video prototyping section of "Drama and Personality in User Interface Design (Panel), *Proceedings of CHI'89,* pp. 107–108.

von Oech, Roger (1990). *A Whack on the Side of the Head, How You Can Be More Creative, Revised Edition,* U. S. Games, Inc., under special arrangement with Warner Books, New York, N.Y.

Walker, Neff and Smelcer, John (1990). "A Comparison of Selection Time from Walking and Bar Menus." *Proceedings of CHI'90,* Addison-Wesley, Reading, Mass., pp. 221–225.

Yallum, I. D. (1980). *Existential Psychotherapy,* Basic Books, Inc., New York, N.Y.

Index of Principles and Guidelines

PROCESS

The Design Process

See also "User Testing"

	Page
The most successful designs result from a team approach where people with differing backgrounds and strengths are equally empowered to affect the final design.	57
Understanding your own preferences, talents, and abilities is key to understanding your users'.	102
Intuition is crucial to the task of software design. When we are creating the shape of our software design, we need to think in terms of big concepts, and we need to weave our design into a single fabric users can understand and feel comfortable with.	102
Begin your project with field analysis.	63
Field analysis doesn't end at the beginning. It continues with planning sites, alpha sites, and beta sites. All are vitally important to the design process.	65
Brainstorming is vital to the task of casting off old ideas and embracing new ones.	67
Use scenarios to define and develop a sense of the user space.	74
Prototypes can and should be created in a matter of days, not weeks or months.	82

Inexpensive testing should be done by members of the design team as part of a cooperative effort to produce the best software possible.   81

While you are designing a program, continually remind yourself that you are designing for an audience. Think about them, think about their problems, and concentrate on how you are going to communicate your ideas to them.   98

The work to design and build the keyboard interface should not sap resources that are needed for the creation of the visual interface.   27

Be wary of rationalization, assumption, and denial creeping into the design process.   263

In the earliest stage, design the new software to be the best it can be with little concern for the existing system.   8

Use peer design review to infuse fresh ideas and explode false assumptions that may have crept into your design.   273

Toward the end of the design period, test the new software to find out where current users will become tripped up.   8

Objectively weigh every new feature against any resultant increase in the learning burden. Then either:

- include the feature anyway

- throw it out because it is disruptive and not clearly more productive, or

- modify it to get the same effect without torturing current users.   8

Then redesign and test again.   8

User Testing Inexpensive testing should be done by members of the design team as part of a cooperative effort to produce the best software possible.   81

Horizontal prototypes display most or all of the full range of the application—menus, windows, dialogs—without going into depth on any one part. Use to test the overall design concepts.   81

GENERAL
PRINCIPLES

The design of visual elements should be left to people
schooled in their creation: graphic designers.   61, 137, 197

People don't want the most abstract interface. They want
multiple channels of information. They want neither just
words nor just pictures. They want both. The more visual,
verbal, vocal, tactile the interface is, the more natural it feels,
the more feedback and response it provides, the more confident
the user becomes.   126

The system image is an illusion designed to convey the design
model. Have it communicate the design model clearly and
concisely.   132

Be wary of interface elements that detract from or overwhelm
the content regions of your application.   196

Guidelines that
Affect User
Behavior

Keep the system's behavior consistent. The same class of object
should generate the same type of feedback and resulting
behavior, no matter in what part of the
program or release of the software they appear.   139

Interpret user behavior consistently. Consistent interpretation
of user behavior by the system is even
more important than consistent system behavior   139

Make all icons require double-clicking.   248

Make any iconic-looking object that requires a single-
click also accept a double-click.   248

Invent new objects, with new appearances, for new
user behaviors.   155

Invent new objects, with new appearances, for new behaviors.   48, 249

Susan Brennan provided the next five guidelines:

"Don't continue until an understanding that is
sufficient for current purposes is reached."   162

"Assume that errors will happen and provide ways to negotiate
them."   162

Guidelines that Affect System Behavior

APPENDIX *C*

Index of Letter Writers

Index

319

Hough, Richard, letter from, 245–246
Housekeeping with new releases, 4
Human Interface Police, 209–210
Human interfaces. *See* Design;
　　Interfaces
Hunches, 109
Hunter, Kim, 31, 53, 164, 260n
Hybrid programs, 186–187
HyperCard
　　and response time, 164
　　application for, 231
　　as interface, 39–44
　　for prototypes, 82
　　nonstandard features of, 54–55
　　putting away the cards, 172–173

Icons
　　appearance of, 248–249
　　changing, 227–228
　　color, 282
　　content zoom, 155
　　document, 248
　　guidelines on, 315
　　"home," 157
　　inconsistencies in, 245–246
　　in menu bars, 247
　　magnifying glass, 155
　　multiplexed meanings in, 157
　　multiplexed meanings with,
　　　156–157
　　words for, 49, 116
ID'89, 29, 53, 55
Ideas, brainstorming for, 67–74, 189,
　　263–264
Illusion
　　Command-key speed as an, 27
　　in design, 154
　　in real world, 236–242
　　system image as, 131–132
Improper dependency, 244
Incubation period for intuition,
　　108–109
Inertia, sources of, 264–265
Information
　　gathering, as intuition step,
　　　106–108, 111–112
　　generated by users, brainstorming
　　　considerations for, 72
　　liberated, 287–288

Information space in multimedia, 173,
　　176
Information theory, 115–116
　　and communication, 121–123
　　and human interface, 123–127
　　and redundancy, 118–121
　　rules in, 117–118
Input, two-handed, 27
Insanity, computer, error messages for,
　　241–242
Integrating new features, 18
Intellect vs. intuition, 103–104
Interface Design '89 Conference, 29,
　　53, 55
Interface Design in the Trenches
　　(Mulligan, Altom, and Simkin),
　　78
Interfaces. *See also* Design
　　abstract vs. visual, 182–183
　　agents for, 159–167
　　articulate, 246–247
　　bad examples of, 230–232
　　choices in, 251–252
　　consistency in, 245–246
　　designers of, 59–60
　　entropy sources in, 124–125
　　extending, 93, 151–157
　　guidelines on, 304–305
　　HyperCard, 39–44
　　and information theory, 123–127
　　intuitive, 245–246
　　for multimedia, 169–176
　　and natural law, 145–150
　　sensory, 102
　　smoke-cleared, 231
　　3-D look in, 195–198
Interleaf 5
　　brainstorming for, 68–74
　　scenarios for, 74–78
Internal reality and personality,
　　100–101
Intervention, 261
Intolerance, 95–96
Introverts, 94, 96–101
Intuition
　　applying, 105–106
　　importance of, 272
　　improving, 102–104
　　vs. intellect, 103–104